Congregational Song in the Worship of the Church

Congregational Song in the Worship of the Church

Examining the Roots of American Traditions

William L. Hooper

⌢PICKWICK *Publications* · Eugene, Oregon

CONGREGATIONAL SONG IN THE WORSHIP OF THE CHURCH
Examining the Roots of American Traditions

Copyright © 2020 William L. Hooper. All rights reserved. Except for brief quotations in critical publications or reviews, no part of this book may be reproduced in any manner without prior written permission from the publisher. Write: Permissions, Wipf and Stock Publishers, 199 W. 8th Ave., Suite 3, Eugene, OR 97401.

Pickwick Publications
An Imprint of Wipf and Stock Publishers
199 W. 8th Ave., Suite 3
Eugene, OR 97401

www.wipfandstock.com

PAPERBACK ISBN: 978-1-5326-9072-3
HARDCOVER ISBN: 978-1-5326-9073-0
EBOOK ISBN: 978-1-5326-9074-7

Cataloguing-in-Publication data:

Names: Hooper, William L., author.

Title: Congregational song in the worship of the church : examining the roots of American traditions / by William L. Hooper.

Description: Eugene, OR : Pickwick Publications, 2020 | **Includes bibliographical references and index.**

Identifiers: ISBN 978-1-5326-9072-3 (paperback) | ISBN 978-1-5326-9073-0 (hardcover) | ISBN 978-1-5326-9074-7 (ebook)

Subjects: LCSH: Church music. | Church music—United States. | Hymns—History and criticism.

Classification: ML3000 .H66 2020 (print) | ML3000 .H66 (ebook)

Unless otherwise indicated, all Scriptures are from the Good News Translation in Today's English Version—Second Edition Copyright © 1992 by American Bible Society. Used by Permission.

Scripture quotations marked (CEV) are taken from the Contemporary English Version © 1991, 1992, 1995 by the American Bible Society. Used by Permission.

Scripture quotations marked CSB are been taken from the Christian Standard Bible®, Copyright © 2017 by Holman Bible Publishers. Used by permission. Christian Standard Bible®, and CSB® are federally registered trademarks of Holman Bible Publishers.

Scripture quotations marked (NIV) are taken from the Holy Bible, New International Version®, NIV®. Copyright © 1973, 1978, 1984, 2011 by Biblica, Inc.™ Used by permission of Zondervan. All rights reserved worldwide. www.zondervan.com The "NIV" and "New International Version" are trademarks registered in the United States Patent and Trademark Office by Biblica, Inc.™

Scriptures marked as (NRSV) are taken from the New Revised Standard Version Bible, copyright © 1989 National Council of the Churches of Christ in the United States of America. Used by permission. All rights reserved worldwide.

Manufactured in the U.S.A.   03/05/20

For my wonderful wife,
Katherine Eddy Hooper

Contents

Prelude | ix
Acknowledgments | xiii

1 Congregational Song in the Ancient World | 1
2 Congregational Song in the Old Testament | 31
3 Congregational Song in the New Testament | 66
4 Congregational Song in the Early Church: 100–600 CE | 90
5 Congregational Song in the Western Church | 117
6 Congregational Song in the Reformation | 144
7 Congregational Song in the English Tradition | 163
8 Congregational Song in Eighteenth- and Nineteenth-Century America | 188
9 Congregational Song in America: 1900–2000 | 215
10 Congregational Song in Contemporary America | 246

Postlude: What Have We Learned? | 273
Appendix I: Zwingli's Zurich Liturgy | 275
Appendix II: Presbyterian Church (U.S.A.) Order of Worship | 280
Bibliography | 283

Prelude

THE SEED FOR THIS book was planted when I team-taught a required course in worship at New Orleans Baptist Theological Seminary. Years later, at Southwest Baptist University, I originated and taught a required course for Christian ministry and church music majors titled "Worship and Song in the Church." Since a suitable text was not available, I began to develop my own materials. This book is the result of that endeavor.

Congregational Song in the Worship of the Church is a study of how congregational song developed and has been used in the worship of Western churches in general and specifically in the United States. Beginning with the worship of ancient peoples, the Hebrews, early Christians, and continuing to the present, the author examines historically how song has been and is used as an intentional sacred ritual action, like prayer, or Scripture reading. Written primarily as an introductory text for college and seminary students, the overall goal is to make a historical journey with the people, events, and ideas from which have evolved the various types of song we have in American worship today. To help readers think more deeply about the material, study questions are given at the end of each chapter.

The basic premise of the author, given above, is that people have used song as an intentional sacred ritual action, like prayer, or Scripture reading. This premise generates three primary questions that determine the historical content and organization of both the book and each chapter:

- How and why has song been used as a sacred ritual activity in worship?
- Who and what determines when and how a song is appropriate for worship?
- What are the biblical and theological criteria that inform the discussion?

We need ways to respond to the revelation of God in Christ, and to act out our relationship with God. The term most generally used to describe these actions is "ritual," any corporate symbolic behavior that helps to create shared thoughts and experiences. A ritual is any action in a particular religious setting for a particular religious purpose. In this case, singing is a sacred action within a worship setting.

Ritual actions include words that are read and spoken, gestures, body positions like kneeling, and words that are sung. If corporate worship requires affective ritual activities, how has song been used as a ritual activity in worship? How has the use of congregational song changed, if at all, over the years? What is the intention of the singer when she or he is singing? What songs do the singers think God accepts for the divine-human interchange?

These questions raise a few additional questions to explore: How does singing give structure and meaning to worship? What is the purpose of a specific body of song and what is its function in worship? What variations, if any, are allowed in the order of worship from week to week to accommodate the inclusion of a variety of congregational song? Granted that singing is a part of worship, what is sung and why are words sung and not merely recited? How has this question been answered by churches at various times in history and how do their answers relate to the sacred ritual activities in church worship today? We attempt to answer some of these questions, but any finality in answers is not claimed. Many questions remain.

The roots of worship go deep into the most ancient religious documents, both biblical and non-biblical. No one knows exactly when or why mankind first began to worship. The Hebrew people were not the first to worship, but they were the first to worship Yahweh. We know humans have always worshipped as evidenced by ancient burial mounds found in many places of the world. When these sites were excavated archaeologists inferred people had worshipped because of the artifacts found, the position of bodies, and the remains of what appeared to be an altar of some sort. Of course, we know nothing about the god or gods many of these people worshipped, how they worshipped, or what they believed about an afterlife. The existence of ancient burial customs would seem to indicate that people have an inner awareness of some ultimate power or powers that are unconditioned by human experience.

Worship seems to be a natural response to that awareness of the unconditioned. The apostle Paul acknowledged this when he wrote that "what can be known about God is plain . . . for God himself made it plain. Ever since God created the world, his invisible qualities, both his eternal power and his divine nature, have been clearly seen; they are perceived in the things that God has made" (Rom 1:19–20).

I am defining worship as *the human response to God's revelation of himself*. When we bow down before the Lord and serve him with our lives, we are responding to God's revelation of himself. This definition of worship is more precise than the definitions of action words, because we need to determine when our worship responses are acceptable. Sometimes people in the Bible worship Yahweh and at other times they worship some pagan god and/or idol, but the words for worship are the same: bowing down or serving. Even when directed toward God, worship was not always acceptable, as in Exodus 32 and Isaiah 1. Word definitions leave it open for us to determine what God requires and what responses to God are acceptable in worship. What we think is right and proper worship might be offensive to God though our rituals and liturgies may fit the word definitions.

As we study you will discover that biblical worship is more than some kind of religious ceremony. Sometimes we don't know what the ceremony was; we just know someone worshipped. You will discover that for the Hebrews, and early Christians, worship was a way of life, a life style or life orientation. A person's private life, work life, and corporate religious life were all related to God every day.

You will discover, too, that worship should be a way of life for Christians in the twenty-first century. David Peterson emphasizes that worship is "a comprehensive category describing the Christian's total existence."[1] The ethical requirements of the Bible inform us about the kind of people we should be as God's people.

If we define worship as the human response to God's revelation of himself, it raises at least three questions: How does God enable us to respond to him? What does God require of us so can we worship him acceptably? What kind of human responses are acceptable to God? We will search for answers.

Hopefully, this book will enable worship leaders to connect to the wonderful history of Christian congregational song. By understanding from where we have come, perhaps we can better understand where we are today and where we should go tomorrow. That is our purpose in writing.

May God bless you with his love, his peace, and his presence as you read. To God be the glory, great things he has done!

William Hooper

Bolivar, Missouri
June 24, 2019

---

1. Peterson, *Engaging with God*, 18.

Acknowledgments

I am indebted to several colleagues who have read and commented on portions of the text. Thank you so much. Any errors are mine alone.

Dr. Carol Bevier,
Southwest Baptist University

Dr. Rodney Reeves
Southwest Baptist University

Dr. Zack Manis
Southwest Baptist University

Guy Shaked, friend and independent musicologist

Dr. Mark Porter
London University

Dr. Carol Cooper
Rochester University

A big "Thank You!" to the Wipf and Stock editorial staff who have been most helpful in making the book more readable.

1

Congregational Song in the Ancient World

> His brother's name was Jubal, the ancestor of all
> musicians who play the harp and the flute.
>
> —Genesis 4:21

THIS CHAPTER BEGINS OUR study with a look at the archaeological evidence for ways primitive humans created song and other objects for worship. This background is then connected to the worship and song of ancient Israel and Abraham. The roots of congregational song go deep into the most ancient religious documents, both biblical and nonbiblical. No one knows exactly when or why mankind first began to worship, but music was part of it.

Christian song also began in these deep roots of human prehistory. No discussion of worship history should ignore these roots, for they have contributed to who we are and to the various forms of worship we have today. Those roots reach back both to prehistoric peoples and to the ancient cultures that existed side by side with Jewish culture found in the Hebrew Bible (the Christian Old Testament).

Prehistoric Peoples

The term "prehistoric peoples" may seem strange to some of you. It simply means people who existed before written history and are generally listed as either *Homo neanderthalis*, *Homo erectus*, or *Homo sapiens*. According to Ian Tattersall, *homo sapiens* is the species to which all modern human beings belong and is one of several species grouped under the genus *Homo*, but it is the only one that is not extinct.[1] The name *homo sapiens* means "wise man," and was created by Carolus Linnaeus, the father of modern biological

1. Tattersall, "Homo sapiens."

classification, in 1758 CE. The Latin noun *homo* means "human being," and *sapiens* is the Latin participle that means "discerning, wise, sensible."

There is evidence that perhaps *Homo neanderthalis* and *Homo sapiens* existed at the same time briefly. Skeletons of both populations are found in several adjacent caves in Israel on Mt. Carmel and in Galilee, and Israel is one of the few places in the world where this is so. A wide variety of studies regarding the origins of modern humans (our species) and the demise of the Neanderthals have focused on these remains in Israel. It is also no surprise that the cluster of prehistoric caves on Mt. Carmel was recently declared as a UNESCO World Heritage Site.[2]

How Do We Learn about Prehistoric People?

Obviously, we are limited in our knowledge of prehistoric people because we have no written records to help us. Our information comes primarily through archaeology, but some information also comes from the field of anthropology. Both of these fields use scientific tools in making their discoveries.

Archaeology is basically the study of humanity and its past through the excavation of sites. Archaeologists study things that were created, used, or changed by humans. They do this by studying the material remains, the stuff we leave behind, such as tools, pottery, jewelry, stone walls, dwellings, food remains, toilet remains, and monuments. The goal of archaeology is to understand how and why human behavior has changed over time.

Some archaeologists were interested in the individuals, nations, and geographical places mentioned in the Bible. Consequently, the field of biblical archaeology was developed and the first biblical archaeologists set out to discover if the Bible was a reliable source of information. As a result, biblical archaeologists have verified many of the places, names, and events through archaeological digs. Though archaeology is the primary way to reconstruct a real-life context for the biblical world, archaeology can never prove any of the theological suppositions of the Bible. Archaeologists can often tell you what happened when and where and how, and even why, but no archaeologist will tell anyone what it means.[3] To do so would go beyond the purpose and method of archaeology.

---

2. Szalay, "Neanderthals."
3. Dever, "Archaeology of the Hebrew Bible."

Prehistoric People and the Bible

Some Christians may feel uncomfortable thinking about prehistoric people for whom we have no written records. Where do we find them in the Bible? Since the book of Genesis is the flashpoint, we should approach the book as an ancient document, and use only the assumptions that would be appropriate for the ancient world to gain understanding. God gave his authority to human authors to record his message and share it with the world, writes Walton, "so we must consider what the human author intended to communicate if we want to understand God's message . . . We must understand how the ancients thought and what ideas underlay their communication."[4]

The ancients were concerned with questions about the mysteries of life, such as: Who made the world? How will it end? Where do we come from? Who was the first human? What happens when we die? Why does the sun travel across the sky each day? Why does the moon wax and wane? Why do we have annual agricultural cycles and seasonal changes? What beings control our world, and how can we influence those beings so our lives are easier? The first eleven chapters of Genesis are the answers of ancient people to those questions based upon their understanding of the Creator God and his purposes.

We ask the same questions today, but ancient people answered those questions differently than we do, and we have to interpret Scripture according to the answers that they gave and recorded for us.[5] We do a disservice to Scripture when we impose a twenty-first-century mindset upon these ancient thought forms. Because of God's revelation in Jesus the Christ, Christ followers in the twenty-first century have a knowledge and understanding of God and his purposes and a knowledge of the universe that ancient people did not and could not have.

Christians who take the Bible seriously believe that God inspired the thoughts of the writers when they wrote the Bible, but the words used are tied to the writer's world and his understanding of God and God's purposes. The words were not dictated by God. The Bible was not written to us; but it was written for us. What message did the biblical writers send? What was the message the first readers received? When we understand that, we can discover what the message should be for us today. Since we are far removed from the original sacred writings, it is very possible that we could misunderstand the communication that is intended.

---

4. Walton, *Lost World of Genesis One*, 15.

5. For further information about how ancient people thought, see Armstrong, *Short History of Myth*.

The authority of Scripture comes from what the Bible affirms, and its affirmation is that (1) God has wanted a people to call his own, (2) God took the initiative and continually seeks those who would be his, and (3) there are consequences when humans refuse to be God's people. Some theologians refer to this as "salvation history," and this affirmation of salvation is rooted in the culture and thought patterns of the world in which Old and New Testament writers lived. The Bible is a book of faith, so there should be nothing contrary to Christian belief and the authority of the Bible in studying ancient people and trying to understand how they thought and communicated.

Prehistoric People and Religion

Since Neanderthals are our nearest human cousins, according to geneticists, we shall start our journey with them. One of the hottest topics in scientific research right now involves determining just how intelligent Neanderthals were. For years, the prevailing view was that Neanderthals were primitive, poorly developed brutes when compared to modern humans, only capable of expressing themselves in grunts and groans. Discoveries in the last few years have brought this assumption into question.[6]

Though extinct, the Neanderthal species of human beings is closely related to modern humans. Recent genetic studies show the DNA of Neanderthals differs from that of modern humans by just 0.12 percent. There are some anatomical differences between Neanderthals and modern humans, and changes in climate, diet, and disease control could account for these differences. However, archaeologists have discovered evidence of a Neanderthal culture, and if archaeologists are correct, people were worshipping 50,000 years ago. Archaeologists have unearthed Neanderthal graves containing weapons, tools and the bones of a sacrificed animal. All of these suggest some kind of belief in a future world that would require these tools.

An approach combining a global field recovery and the re-examination of the previously discovered Neanderthal remains has been undertaken in the site of La Chapelle-aux-Saints, France, where the hypothesis of a Neanderthal burial was raised for the first time. This project has concluded that the Neanderthal of La Chapelle-aux-Saints was deposited in a pit dug by other members of his group and protected by a rapid covering from any disturbance. These discoveries attest to the existence of West European Neanderthal burial and of the Neanderthal cognitive capacity to produce it.[7]

6. Worthington, "Neanderthals and Humans."
7. Rendu, "Evidence Supporting," 81–86. See also Than, "Neanderthal Burials."

The Neanderthal graves show that when these early people became conscious of their mortality they created some sort of explanation that enabled them to come to terms with death and dying. The animal bones indicate that the burial was accompanied by a sacrifice. In the Neanderthal graves, the corpse has sometimes been placed in a fetal position, the correct spiritual or psychological posture for right action in this world or the next. Some 50,000 years ago, someone took great care to dig a grave for this unknown persons and to protect his body from scavengers; all of which suggest some kind of belief in a future world that was similar to their own. The Neanderthals might have told each other stories about the life that their dead companion now enjoyed. They were certainly reflecting about death in a way that their fellow creatures did not. Animals watch each other die, but as far as we know, they give the matter no further consideration.

The Neanderthal graves show that when these early people became conscious of their mortality, they created some sort of counter-narrative that enabled them to come to terms with it. The Neanderthals who buried their companions with such care seem to have imagined that the visible, material world was not the only reality. From a very early date, therefore, it appears that human beings were distinguished by their ability to have ideas that went beyond their everyday experience.

Excavations at Raqefet Cave on Mt. Carmel have revealed a number of fascinating insights on prehistoric Israel. Archaeological investigations show that the Natufians—hunter-gatherers living 15,000 to 11,600 years ago in the Levant—held feasts at the burial sites of the deceased and decorated their graves with flowers. Excavations at ancient sites all over prehistoric Israel have yielded, among other things, stone tools, butchered animals, and evidence for the control of fire.[8]

As Barbara J. King has noted, religion is best understood both as practice and belief. In more advanced cultures, practice and belief may also include sacred texts that prescribe a set of beliefs. When texts are involved, what a person believes about a god or sacred forces really matters. In many human societies, past and present, there is no text. Everyday life involves appeasing gods or spirits, honoring the ancestors, and a sense of the sacred and/or the supernatural. "It's within this context," writes King, "that the case for Neanderthal religion—for ritual practices steeped in connecting to the sacred world—is most convincingly made."[9]

---

8. Ghose, "Oldest Grave Flowers"; Nadel, "Archaeological Views," 24–25, 64; Ngo, "Earliest Matches"; Zaidner, "Series of Mousterian Occupations," 1–17.

9. King, "Were the Neanderthals Religious?," para. 29.

To support the possibility of Neanderthal religion, King refers to the Gobekli Tepe, a massive hilltop site in Turkey. After carving limestone pillars with all sorts of animal images, they hauled the sixteen-ton stones into multiple huge rings without the help of wheeled vehicles or domesticated animals. The Gobekli Tepe people carried out symbolic and sacred activities on a hilltop they adorned with massive architecture 5,000 years before Stonehenge.[10] What forms those religious practices took are unknown at this point.

Prehistoric Visual Art

Archaeologists have long supposed only *Homo sapiens* had the ability to develop symbolic behavior, including art. A discovery made in 2012 and reported in Science magazine in 2018 indicate Neanderthals were capable of symbolic thinking. Abstract images made by Neanderthals were found in Spanish caves that date back 65,000 years. "Not only do the dates point to Neanderthals making the art, they indicate Neanderthals came up with these ideas on their own," reported Kate Wong.[11]

Art of various kinds and the ability to think of abstract concepts like God is what distinguishes our species from other animals. It is these same capabilities that also led us to use fire, develop the wheel, and come up with the other technologies that have made our kind so successful. This ability to make and use tools is one of the things that make us truly human.[12]

Prehistoric peoples produced three types of visual art: cave paintings, glyphs, and megaliths. These art objects are not limited to one group of people or geographic location, but are found in many different parts of the world.

Cave Art

Cave art typically depicted animals, but also included humans, weapons, crude maps, and symbols. This art has been found around the world from Europe, Australia, Africa, and China, as well as other places. Many of these paintings have been repainted several times and are deep inside the caves where a light would have been needed for the artists to do their painting. These two facts have led scholars to suggest that the paintings may have had a social or religious significance to these early people.

---

10. King, "World's First Temple." See also Curry, "Gobekli Tepe."
11. Wong, "Ancient Cave Paintings," para. 4.
12. Zilhão, "Symbolic Use of Marine Shells," 1023–28.

Some questions we can ask about cave paintings are: why were they painted in a cave that is dark and almost inaccessible? What is the significance of the animals that were chosen for the subject matter? Were their religious meanings in the paintings? Since some of the animals have spear marks and others have actual spears in their sides, some historians have concluded that the pictures are a form of "magic." The making of an image conferred power over an animal to the painter and perhaps to the tribe.

Some of the early cave paintings were discovered in Spain in 1879. The cave is named Altamira, Spanish for "high views." Additional prehistoric paintings were discovered in a cave in southern France in 1896. This French cave is an example of Paleolithic cave art that developed across Europe, from the Urals to the Iberian Peninsula, from 35,000 to 11,000 BCE. Because of its deep galleries, isolated from external climatic influences, this cave in Altamira is particularly well preserved.[13]

The discovery of 40,000-year-old cave paintings in Indonesia suggests that the ability to think and to create representational art had its origins further back in time, before modern humans spread across the rest of the world. The Indonesian discovery transforms ideas about how humans first developed the ability to produce art. Formerly it was thought that primitive peoples lacked the ability to think abstractly, a necessity for producing art. Therefore, this early art shows the beginnings of human intelligence as we understand it today.[14]

Petroglyphs

Petroglyphs are images carved, pecked, chipped, or abraded into stone. The outer patina covered surface of the parent stone is removed to expose the usually lighter colored stone underneath. Some stone is better suited to petroglyph making than others. Stone that is very hard or contains a lot of quartz does not work well for petroglyph making; however, a nice desert varnished basalt usually works very well.

The word comes from the Greek words *petros* meaning "stone" and *glyphein* meaning "to carve." Petroglyphs have been found in all parts of the globe except Antarctica, with highest concentrations in parts of Africa, Scandinavia, Siberia, southwestern North America, and Australia. Numerous petroglyphs can be seen in the National Parks in the state of Utah as well as in New Mexico, Arizona, Colorado, and Arkansas.

---

13. Minneapolis Institute of Fine Art, "World Myths."
14. Thompson, "Rock (Art) of Ages."

Petroglyphs discovered in the Negev Desert in Israel comprise two groups of nearly 7,000 drawings, shapes and motifs. One group can be dated to the Iron Age (c. 1200–586 BCE) and the other group can be dated back to c. 3300–2000 BCE. By examining this art in ancient Israel, a picture emerges of the contemporary Negev culture, with trading posts oriented around outsiders that were seldom visited by the local Negev nomadic groups.[15]

Archaeologist Yehuda Rotblum has an interesting hypothesis that the Negev Desert was the dwelling place of the proto-Israelites before their wandering to Canaan, though they are not given the name Hebrew or Israelite. This idea is based both upon Egyptian sources and because some of the Negev rock art has engravings of the biblical name of Israel's God. Among the Negev's rock art are scenes of hunting, trapping, combat, and worship. On occasion, one also finds depictions of parents accompanied by their children, and animals with their young.

Numerous examples of Negev rock art have engravings of the early explicit name of God. The prevalent engravings have YAH, which is similar to the Shasu god YAHU. In Egyptian sources, the Shasu were nomadic peoples in the wilderness of the southern region of Canaan. Israel was distinguished from all other cultures emerging from the Iron Age because of the belief that Yahweh was their national god.[16]

Megaliths

Megaliths are large stone structures or groups of standing stones that are located at sites in various parts of the world and believed to have religious significance. The term *megalith* means "great stone" which is derived from the Greek words *megas* ("great") and *lithos* ("stone"). However, the general meaning of megaliths includes any structure composed of large stones that include tombs and circular standing structures. Such structures have been found in Europe, Asia, Africa, Australia, and North and South America.

Their origins and purposes have tantalized experts and ordinary people for centuries. There is a general consensus that many were built in the Neolithic and early Bronze Ages. The megalithic monuments of Britain and Europe predate those of the eastern Mediterranean, Egyptian, Mycenaean and Greek cultures. More than nine hundred stone rings exist in the British Isles. Of these, Stonehenge, built between 3100–1100 BCE, is the most well known.

---

15. Eisenberg-Degen, "Archaeological Views," 5, 61–62.
16. Rotblum, "Exodus and Rock Art."

There are no Jewish structural megaliths evident in the Hebrew Bible, such as an Egyptian pyramid, but we do have examples of stones being erected both as memorials to a special event and altars for sacrifice. Though they are not prehistoric, here are some examples:

> Jacob got up early next morning, took the stone that was under his head, and set it up as a memorial. Then he poured olive oil on it to dedicate it to God (Gen 28:18).

> Jacob and Laban make a covenant and to mark the occasion and Jacob got a stone and set it up as a memorial (Gen 31:45).

In Exodus 24 Moses erects twelve stones to commemorate his covenant with the Hebrew tribes. In Deuteronomy 27:1–10 Moses is reported to have set up twelve stones to commemorate God's covenant with the Hebrew people:

> On the day you cross the Jordan River and enter the land that the Lord your God is giving you, you are to set up some large stones, cover them with plaster, and write on them all these laws and teachings (Deut 27:2–3).

An example that is immortalized in song is 1 Samuel 7:8–12. The Israelites have won a major victory over the Philistines, and the prophet Samuel offers a sacrifice to the Lord. Then, "Samuel took a stone, set it up between Mizpah and Shen, and said, 'The Lord has helped us all the way'—and he named it 'Stone of Help.'" "Stone of help" in Hebrew is *ebenezer*. In 1758 Robert Robinson used that phrase in his hymn "Come, Thou Fount of Every Blessing": "Here I raise mine Ebenezer; hither by thy help I'm come."

An example that can be visited is a series of ten standing stones at the Gezer High Place in Israel, one of the strategic cities of the Canaanites. With a possible dating of 1500 BCE, the stones range from 6 to 11 feet in height and stand in a row. The purpose of these stones is not readily apparent, but probably celebrate a covenant of some kind. Because the stones are so huge they may represent a covenant between ten tribes or ten towns rather than ten persons. Animal bones and teeth were discovered that led archaeologists to suggest the covenant may have been renewed every year through sacrifice. Additional evidence for this is a large basin that could be used either for bloodletting or washing sacrificial animals.[17]

---

17. Shanks, "Commemorating a Covenant," 63–65.

Prehistoric People and Music

We have been aided in our study of ancient music by a fairly new field of study called "music archaeology" or archaeomusicology. The combination of these two words is a way of showing what archaeology can tell us about ancient music. Some very fascinating things have been discovered that help us to understand music in the Bible. For example, archaeologists have found connections between the music and instruments of Israel and its neighboring countries. In addition to music and instruments, connections have also been found between some of the Hebrew psalms and similar writings in neighboring countries. Taking a brief look at music in non-Hebrew cultures will enable us to make some inferences about Hebrew music.

Singing

Apparently, we started to sing well before we actually spoke our thoughts aloud, so singing is a basic characteristic of mankind. The origins date so far back that it is difficult to find them in antiquity, but singing is an important function associated with primitive humans as they invoke their gods with prayers and incantations, celebrating rites of passage with chants and songs, and recounting their history and heroics with ballads and epics.

Based on the available evidence, singing was just a simple form of imitation done in response to the various sounds man had heard in nature. At what point the singing of meaningful, communicative sounds began cannot be established, but it was doubtless an important step in the creation of language. There are no bones in the human larynx, so archaeological remains offer no direct physical evidence of the vocal apparatus of prehistoric man.[18]

Instruments

Though we know much about prehistoric music, there are still gaps in our knowledge. At present we have data about prehistoric instruments found in Slovenia and Germany and a possible relation between singing and cave paintings in France.

---

18. Potter and Sorrell, *History of Singing*, 13–34.

Slovenia

In 1995 researchers excavating a cave in Slovenia found stone implements characteristic of Neanderthals. Amid those artifacts was a piece of a cave bear's thighbone that contains four artificial holes in a straight line and resembles a flute. Neanderthals probably used a pointed animal tooth as a punch to produce the holes, which go through only one side of the shaft (like a modern flute). The ends of the hollow bone artifact, which is between four and five inches long, are broken off, possibly gnawed off by cave bears or other animals.

Archaeologists report that similar flutes, made from the bones of various animals, have been discovered at human sites dating from 35,000 to 22,000 years ago. The cave-bear flute, however, is about 82,000 to 43,000 years old and is clearly a Neanderthal creation. It is the oldest firmly dated musical instrument.[19]

Using a reconstruction of the bone flute, researchers have been able to blow into the end of the instrument, much like playing a modern recorder, and finger the holes in various ways to produce musical tones. The pitches and the intervals between them do not correspond to any modern music system, but they do reflect some thought-out purpose for constructing the instrument.

Interested readers may go to YouTube and search for "Neanderthal flute" and find several pages of sources. The most definitive source has the full title "Playing the Neanderthal flute of Divje Babe" and is authored by Sašo Niskač, music is performed by Ljuben Dimkaroski, and scientific adviser is Dr. Ivan Turk, archaeologist. The film shows the 1995 extraordinary find in Divje Babe cave in western Slovenia.[20] It is described in a paper that was met with great enthusiasm on one side and with great skepticism on the other side of the scientific audience.

The dilemma of whether the holes in the bone were accidental or purposely made was finally resolved in 2009 by the curator of the Slovenian National Museum on the occasion of Ljuben's exhibition "Image in Stone." Trumpeter Ljuben Dimkaroski, a member of the Ljubljana Opera Orchestra for thirty-five years, was given a clay replica of the flute on the occasion of Ljuben's exhibition "Image in Stone." In his dreams, about a year later, he got a clue of how to play this prehistoric instrument. The result you can see and hear for yourself.[21]

---

19. Universität Tübingen, "Paleolithic Bone"; Woods, "Neanderthal Noisemaker," 328; Folger and Menon, ". . . Or Much Like Us?," 33.

20. Turk, *Mousterian Bone Flute*.

21. Turk, *Mousterian Bone Flute*. To see and hear this flute go to https://youtu.be/mvmzJqHJ.

Germany

Researchers have discovered what may be the oldest-known musical instruments in the world. They are flutes, made from bird bone and mammoth ivory. They come from a cave in southern Germany that contains early evidence for the occupation of Europe by modern humans, *Homo sapiens*. Using carbon dating, scientists believe the flutes were made between 42,000 and 43,000 years ago.

The bone-flute pieces were found in 2008 at Hohle Fels, a Stone Age cave in southern Germany, according to the study, led by archaeologist Nicholas Conard of the University of Tübingen in Germany. The almost complete bird-bone flute was made naturally from the hollow wing bone of a griffon vulture. It had five finger holes and a V-shaped mouthpiece.[22]

The research also suggests that not only was music widespread much earlier than previously thought, but so was humanity's creative spirit. The ancient humans had a wide range of symbolic artifacts, figurative art, depictions of mythological creatures, many kinds of personal ornaments and also a well-developed musical tradition. The research team suggests the musical instruments may have been used in recreation and/or for religious ritual.

France

Legor Reznikoff, an acoustics expert at the University of Paris, has conducted research that suggests Stone Age caves may have been concert halls. According to analyses of paleolithic caves in France by Reznikoff, prehistoric peoples chose places of natural resonant sound to draw their famed cave sketches. Drawings of horses, bison, and mammoths seem to match locations that focus, amplify, and transform the sounds of human voices and musical instruments in at least ten locations. If the analysis is correct, this suggests that the sites would also have served as places of supernatural power, supporting the theory that decorated caves were places for religious and magical rituals.

In more than ten paleolithic caves across France, with illustrations ranging from 25,000 to 15,000 years old, Reznikoff has found correlations between painting locations and the resonance of their surroundings. Many illustrations are packed together in parts of the caves where the human voice is amplified and where songs and chants would have lingered in the air as abiding echoes.

---

22. Owen, "Bone Flute is Oldest Instrument."

Reznikoff's theory has found support from researchers at the University of Sheffield and Cambridge University who were not involved in the study. Paul Pettitt, a paleolithic rock art expert at the University of Sheffield in England, noted that in rare instances, cave images include highly stylized females who appear to be dancing or enigmatic, part-animal "sorcerer" figures engaging in what seem to be transformational dances. "This is therefore an artistic connection between dance and art. Perhaps in this case the art is recording specific ritual events," Pettitt wrote. "It is inconceivable that such rituals would have taken place in silence.[23]

Conclusions

From this brief study of prehistoric humans, we do not see them as brutes that barely rise above dumb animals. Though primitive and living thousands of years ago, we see them as human beings with an ability to have ideas that go beyond their everyday experience. They held a belief in an invisible and more powerful reality than visible reality. This is a worldview of gods and spirits, a world that has been diminished by modern scientific views that would claim reality exists only in what is physical. Prehistoric art and music could very well be primitive ways of dealing with the facts and mystery of life and death mentioned earlier. These ideas found artistic expression then just as they find artistic expression today. We shall now see how these religious and artistic ideas began to evolve over time.

Archaeologists suggest that humans have always worshipped as evidenced by ancient burial mounds found in many places of the world. When these sites were excavated archaeologists inferred people had worshipped because of the artifacts found, the position of bodies and the remains of what appeared to be an altar of some sort. Of course, we know nothing about the god or gods these people worshipped, how they worshipped or what they believed about an afterlife.

The existence of ancient burial customs would seem to indicate that people have an inner awareness of some ultimate power or powers that are unconditioned by human experience. Worship seems to be a natural response to that awareness. The apostle Paul acknowledged this when he wrote, "What can be known about God is plain . . . for God himself made it plain. Ever since God created the world, his invisible qualities, both his eternal power and his divine nature, have been clearly seen; they are perceived in the things that God has made" (Rom 1:19–20).

23. Than, "World's Oldest Cave Art Found," para. 25.

The First Civilizations: Mesopotamia

Many ancient civilizations had well-organized religious systems long before Abraham came on the scene. There were many similarities between those religious systems and the later religion of the Hebrews, but there were also some significant differences. Of interest to us are the ancient cultures that influenced the development of Jewish worship and song: Sumer, Egypt and Canaan.

The earliest civilizations for which we have records are those in Mesopotamia. This is the area lying between the Tigris and Euphrates rivers that includes modern Iraq and part of Syria. Mesopotamia is the Greek word for "between the rivers." These most ancient civilizations known to man first developed writing, schools, libraries, written law codes, agriculture, irrigation, farming and moved us from prehistory to history. Mesopotamia has the reputation of being the cradle of civilization, and the word Mesopotamian does not refer to one particular civilization using that name. It includes non-Semitic Sumerians, followed by the Semitic Akkadians, Babylonians, and Assyrians. Mesopotamia is part of what is known as the Fertile Crescent.

The earliest people in Mesopotamia were probably nomads that stayed in one place for a time, eating the plant and animal food in that area. When food was no longer plentiful, the nomads moved in small groups to a new area. In their travels hunter-gatherers discovered the fertile land between the Tigris and Euphrates Rivers of Mesopotamia and planted gardens in this region. By 7000 BCE farming had developed to the point permanent settlement was possible. Around 4500 BCE a people archaeologists call *Ubaidians* lived in settlements along the Persian Gulf where the Tigris and Euphrates rivers emptied into the sea. There is evidence that the Ubaidians drained marshes and irrigated their crops by digging ditches to the river waters. They grew wheat and barley and kept livestock and remains of pottery, weaving, and works of leather and metal have also been found.

Ancient peoples, including the Hebrews, did not separate the supernatural from the natural as we do today. There were no natural laws that governed the universe. God, or the gods, were involved in everything that happened. Events that were later to be called miracles were considered to be the actions of deity. Every baby that was born, every tree that put forth leaves, every event of life was the activity of God or gods.[24]

---

24. Walton, *Lost World of Genesis One*, 20–21.

Sumer

The people called Sumerians, whose language became the prevailing language of the territory, arrived in Sumer about 3300 BCE. Sometime around 3000 BCE Sumer consisted of at least twelve city-states. Each city comprised a walled city and its surrounding villages and land, and each worshipped its own deity whose temple was the central structure of the city. Political power originally belonged to the citizens, but as rivalry between the various city-states increased, each adopted the institution of kingship. An extant document, *The Sumerian King List*, records eight kings that reigned before the great Flood.[25] The list is a mixture both of mythic kings and actual kings who reigned later. The flood story has features that are very similar to the flood story in Genesis.[26]

Sumer is the first civilization that we know of that developed a system of writing. Their writing is called "cuneiform" because a wedge-shaped stylus was used to cut wedge-shaped marks in soft clay used as a writing surface. The Sumerians were also advanced in science and mathematics compared to prehistoric civilizations. Sumerians used numerical calculation to keep records of supplies and goods exchanged. They wrote arithmetic based on units of ten—the number of fingers on both hands. They believed in star-gods and mapped the stars and divided a circle into units of sixty. Archaeological findings indicate the people of Sumer had developed a legal code, a system of weights and measures and were skilled in medicine and metallurgy. From what we know about Abraham and the civilization of Sumer, he was probably a well-educated and wealthy man for his time.

The Sumerians are best known for an epic concerning a legendary king named Gilgamesh. These stories probably influenced later biblical literature since the Gilgamesh epic has the earliest flood story and other stories that resemble biblical stories. The British Museum has numerous examples of other types of literature, including a hymn to one of the gods and a harp.[27]

The Sumerians are also famous for the building of tower-temples called ziggurats. The Tower of Babel recorded in the book of Genesis, chapter 11, could very well be one of the ziggurats that can still be seen

---

25. A translation of this list is available at http://etcsl.orinst.ox.ac.uk/section2/tr211.htm.

26. Elliot, *Message of Genesis*, ch. 1.

27. The British Museum has an extensive collection of Sumerian artifacts and other information about Sumer. Included is a complete room dedicated to Sumerian civilization. Booklets about Sumer are also published by the museum. The following website gives basic information as well as many photographs of the Sumerian collection: http://www.britishmuseum.org/explore/cultures/middleast/sumerias.aspx.

in Iraq. These structures were a terraced or stepped pyramid, each story smaller than the one below it, but this architecture is earlier than the Egyptian pyramids. Since there is little stone in the desert, ziggurats were built with glazed brick, a fairly fragile material.

Ur

Ur was one of the city-states with a population of some 250,000 people. In the Hebrew Bible this is where Abraham was born. Its actual location today is disputed, but some archaeologists place Ur in southern Iraq. The center of daily activity was the ziggurat temple whose remains at Ur can still be seen. The Sumerian religious system was a complex one comprised of hundreds of gods, and worship was primarily the sacrifice of animals and gifts of food. The calendar was broken up into a number of religious festivals, especially a celebration of the New Year.

According to the ancient texts, each Sumerian city was guarded by its own god; and while humans and gods used to live together, the humans were servants to the gods. Many gods were connected to the natural forces governing life and fertility. Other gods were connected to sun, moon and stars. The gods had human bodies, gender, and families. The gods differed from humans only in their being immortal and having greater power. In addition to many gods there was a world of good and bad demons. Each family perhaps had its own god with a chapel in the home dedicated to that god. Archaeologists have found remains of people who were buried under the floor of a home chapel. The Babylonians conquered Sumer in 2003 BCE and eventually Nebuchadnezzar became king, the same king who destroyed the Jerusalem Temple and carried the Jews into captivity.[28]

Ugarit

Ugarit is a Bronze Age city whose ruins lie in a large artificial mound called Ras Shamra, six miles north of Lattakia on the Mediterranean coast of Syria. The ruins, about half a mile from the shore, were first uncovered by the plow of a peasant. Ugarit was at its height from c. 1450 to 1200 BCE, but it was inhabited by 6,000 BCE or even earlier. Ugarit flourished from c. 1450 to

---

28. The Khan Academy has an extensive online tutorial titled *The Sumerians and Mesopotamians*. Included are photographs, essays, videos, and links to other sources. This tutorial is one of several on the early Middle East: https://www.khanacademy.org/humanities/ancient-art-civilizations.

1200 BCE, and then it was completely deserted. Most of what is known about Canaan, its people and religion, is from excavations of the city of Ugarit.[29]

Canaan

The Canaanites were a Semitic-speaking cultural group that lived in Canaan (comprising Lebanon, southern Syria, Israel and Transjordan) beginning in the second millennium BCE and wielded influence throughout the Mediterranean. In the Hebrew Bible, the Canaanites are described as inhabitants of Canaan before the arrival of the Israelites (e.g., Gen 15:18–21, Exod 13:11). Little of the Canaanites' textual records remain, perhaps because they used papyrus instead of the more durable clay for writing. Much of the Canaanites' history is reconstructed through the writings of contemporary peoples in addition to archaeological examinations of the material record.[30]

Canaanite Literature

Evidence of the world's first linear alphabet and information about Canaanite religion was discovered in excavations that began in 1929. Both discoveries are highly significant for Hebrew Bible studies, for the language of the Canaanites may perhaps be best described as an archaic form of Hebrew, standing in much the same relationship to the Hebrew of the Bible as does the language of Chaucer to modern English.[31] The Canaanites were also the first people, as far as is known, to have used an alphabet. Around 1400 BCE scribes in Ugarit appear to have originated the Ugaritic alphabet of thirty cuneiform characters, or letters, and were inscribed on clay tablets. The flexibility of the Ugaritic alphabet opened a horizon of literacy to many more kinds of people.

Tablets found in the libraries include mythological texts written in a narrative poetry, letters, legal documents such as land transfers, a few international treaties, and a number of administrative lists. Fragments of several poetic works have been identified, but perhaps the most important piece of literature recovered from Ugarit are clay tablets engraved with cuneiform script preserving the Ugaritic poem known as the Baal Cycle, a story featuring gods from the Canaanite-Phoenician religion These tablets date to c.

---

29. Coogan, *Old Testament*, 80, 199–202, 219–20.
30. Ngo, "What Happened?"
31. Coogan, *Stories*.

1500 BCE but are thought to have been a written record of a much older poem passed down by oral transmission.[32]

Canaanite Music

Clay tablets relating to music, containing the cuneiform signs of the Hurrian language, were also excavated in the early 1950s at Ugarit. One text contained a complete hymn, both words and music, and is the oldest known preserved music notation in the world. In 1972, after fifteen years of research, Professor Anne Kilmer deciphered and transcribed this four thousand-year-old piece of music into modern music notation.[33]

The tablets date back to approximately 1400 BCE and contain a hymn to the moon god's wife, Nikal. Remarkably, the tablets also contain detailed performance instructions for a singer accompanied by a harpist as well as instructions on how to tune the harp. From this evidence, Prof. Kilmer and other musicologists have created realizations of the hymn. According to Kilmer, the tablets represent fragmentary instructions for performing music and show that the music was composed in harmonies of thirds, and that it was also written using a diatonic scale. The interpretation of the notation system is still controversial, but it is clear that the notation indicates the names of strings on a lyre, the tuning of which is described on other tablets.

Another early record of music and musical instruments is a clay tablet from Sumer dated 2600 BCE and housed in the Schoyen Collection, a private collection of manuscripts owned by Martin Schoyen, in London.[34] Other clay tablets that have been dug up include the texts of hymns to various gods. Singers were used in religious services and music schools for the training of singers were established in various parts of the land. Instruments used in Sumer included clappers, cymbals, bells, rattles, drums, pipes, and some type of trumpet.

Canaanite Religion

The discovery of the Ugaritic archives has been of great significance to biblical scholarship, as these archives for the first time provided a detailed description of Canaanite religious beliefs during the period directly preceding

32. Mbzt, "Baal Cycle Tablets."

33. Kilmer, "Discovery of an Ancient Mesopotamian Theory," 131–49; Kilmer and Civil, "Old Babylonian Musical Instructions," 94–98; Kilmer, "Oldest Song in the World," 98–100.

34. This collection can be viewed at www.schoyencollection.com/.

the Israelite settlement. These texts show significant parallels to biblical Hebrew literature, particularly in the areas of divine imagery and poetic form, such as parallelisms, meters, and rhythms.[35]

The earliest god recognized by the peoples of the ancient Near East was the creator-god El. His mistress, the fertility goddess Asherah, gave birth to many gods, including a powerful god named Baal ("Lord"). Baal was manifested in different forms and at different places and times. El is also a name by which God is called in the Hebrew Bible; El, the God (Elohim) of Israel (Gen 33:20). The word *El* is a generic name for "god" in Northwest Semitic (Hebrew and Ugaritic) and as such it is also used in the Hebrew Bible for heathen deities or idols (Exod 34:14; Ps 81:10; Isa 44:10).

Canaanite worship was centered in the fertility god Baal. Statues of Baal that have been discovered by archaeologists show him portrayed as a man with the head and horns of a bull. His right hand (and sometimes both hands) is raised, and he holds a lightning bolt. This image signifies both destruction and fertility. Baal has also been portrayed seated on a throne, possibly as the king or lord of the gods. These are images similar to those in biblical accounts.[36]

"Worship involved both male and female sacred prostitution," writes Koll. After death there was no rewarding of goodness and punishing of badness. Existence was in the place of the dead located in the darkness beneath the earth. People remaining on earth could alleviate the sufferings of the dead through rituals, but if they forgot to do the rituals or did not bury the dead, then the dead would come back as evil demons to trouble them.[37]

Noll has noted that there were aspects of Canaanite life that we would recognize as religious. Based upon his translation of many stone tablets, the following list of behaviors characterize Near Eastern religion in general, including Hebrew worship:

1. Acknowledgment of a supernatural reality usually defined as a god or gods.

2. Reverence for objects, places, and times considered sacred, that is, separated from ordinary objects, places, and times.

3. Regularly repeated ritual activities for a variety of purposes.

4. Conformance to stipulations alleged to have been revealed by the supernatural reality.

---

35. Steinberg, "Ugarit and the Bible."
36. Vander Laan, "Fertililty Cults."
37. Noll, "Canaanite Religion," 61–92.

5. Communication with the supernatural through prayer and other activity.
6. Experience of feelings described by participants as awe, fear, mystery, etc.
7. Integration of items 1–6 into a holistic, though not necessarily systematic, worldview.
8. Association with, and conformity of one's own life priorities to a group of like-minded people.

A study of the Ugaritic text titled "Birth of the Beautiful and Gracious Gods," Keen identifies eight primary ritual activities in Ugarit worship: bloodless offering, sacrifice, procession, enthronement, vesting, invocation/recitation, atonement, banquet, and divination. Worshippers also offered textiles and clothing. From her own analysis of Ugaritic worship, Keen thinks sacrifice was at the heart of the Ugaritian cult and that no ritual was complete without it.

The overall analysis of "Birth of the Beautiful and Gods" showed themes associated with the Ugaritian ritual also had theological and emotive components. The rituals reflect concern for offspring, marriage, the safe passage of the king into the next world, protection from violence, praise for the gods' greatness, forgiveness of sin, success and strength, healing from illness, and general well-being.[38]

The Ugaritians had faith in the willing intervention of the gods who were both powerful and benevolent. They sought help from forces greater than themselves to intervene on their behalf. A song text discovered in 1998 and published recently, praises the goddess Attartu in language similar to that of Exodus 15:1 where Israel is praising God for deliverance from the Egyptians.

Egypt

The civilization of Egypt is one of the earliest in world history. People were farming in the Nile valley as early as 5000 BCE but an organized nation did not occur until about 3000 BCE with the country unified under the first Pharaoh. Of importance to our study is the religion and the music of ancient Egypt.

---

38. Keen, "Beyond Sacred Marriage."

Egyptian Religion

The religion of Egypt was very complex. There were the usual gods, temples and priests and worship included singing and playing of instruments. Thoughts of the afterlife occupied a central place in Egyptian religion. The future life was not simply a continuation of this life, but included reward and punishment for the deeds of this lifetime. The best example of Egypt's concern with the afterlife is the pyramids and the many treasures and tomb paintings that are found in them.

Religion was very important to the ancient Egyptians and was strongly influenced by tradition, which caused them to resist change. According to David, "Egyptians did not question the beliefs which had been handed down to them; they did not desire change in their society. Their main aim throughout their history was to emulate the conditions which they believed had existed at the dawn of creation."[39] One of the very strong traditions was that of Divine Kingship, the belief that the Pharaoh was not only the king (political ruler) but also a god. The Pharaoh was associated with Horus, son of Re the sun god. Later it was believed that at death he became an Osiris, and would help the Egyptians in their afterlife.

Due to these beliefs, the Pharaoh held an immense amount of power. In addition, the priests in Ancient Egypt were also very powerful. When things were going well, the people believed the priest and pharaoh were doing their jobs well; when things in the country were not going well, the people believed the pharaoh and the priest were to blame. The religion of Ancient Egypt was a polytheistic religion, except for one short period of monotheism. Their religion hosted about 700 different gods and goddesses, and it was not uncommon for deities to be combined to form a new deity.

One of the more famous aspects of the Egyptian religious beliefs was their idea of the afterlife. They believed the physical body had to be preserved to allow a place for their spirit to dwell in the afterlife. Because of this, mummification was performed to preserve the body. In addition, large pyramids were constructed as tombs for the pharaohs in the Old Kingdom. Later, rock cut tombs were used to bury the pharaohs.

In antiquity, even the gods had to eat. Temple officials in ancient Babylon and Egypt were tasked with the daily feeding of their deities. The statues of these deities were more than just depictions for their worshipers; they were themselves divine, and they needed to be fed, bathed, clothed and cared for. An elaborate ritual known as the Opening of the Mouth transformed manmade cult statues into "living" deities. The ritual included

---

39. David, *Ancient Egyptians*, 81.

offering choice meats, honey, fruit and beer for the god's statue to eat and drink, and even water to wash with after the meal.[40]

Egyptian Music

In a culture as full of religious rituals as ancient Egypt, music tends to be a significant part of everyday life. Countless wall murals show musicians playing while dancers danced and others stood off and watched. Instruments have been unearthed as well. But, despite knowing how they played, the ancient Egyptian music itself—the notes, the compositions—is wholly unknown to us.

Ancient Egypt had some of the same instruments as Sumer for pictures on vases and bas-reliefs depict people playing various instruments. Many of these instruments found their way to Egypt by way of booty from battle. Records and reliefs depict conquered kings sending tribute payments to Egypt in the form of dancing girls and their music instruments. One vase shows a group of Semitic nomads offering gifts to the Pharaoh, one gift being a lute. It has been supposed by some scholars that these Semites were Joseph's brothers coming before Pharaoh.[41]

Percussion instruments were the most common instruments used in ancient Egyptian music, with the simplest being the human hands. Clapping was depicted on many walls as being a large part of most musical performances. Drums were also popular, and bells being played were frequently seen. Most percussion instruments have a very limited pitch range, so other types of instruments were used as well. Wind instruments included the flute, the trumpet, the parallel double-pipes and the divergent double-pipes. These were often made using reeds, until later, when bronze work was more common.

String instruments were predominantly harps, lutes, and lyres. Harps had a more complex design than other string instruments, and it was also common to decorate a harp with precious materials such as ebony, silver, gold, lapis lazuli, malachite, or anything valuable both monetarily and aesthetically.

There is very little evidence of music notation prior to the Greek invasion (332 BCE). It is believed that some of the music was either spontaneously created, or perhaps singers were able to indicate pitch and tempo with hand gestures. The Kelsey Museum of Archaeology at the University

---

40. Sachs, *Rise of Music*, 57–58.
41. Sachs, *Rise of Music*, 62–63.

of Michigan has a papyrus that shows evidence of musical notation, though the resulting music and what is on the papyrus itself is Greek, not Egyptian.

The Kelsey Museum also has in its collections figurines, funerary artifacts, a variety of wind and percussion instruments, and pottery. These were all discovered through archaeological digs. In addition, there is an ostracon that has a list of tax payers, two of which play the flute. An ostracon is a piece of pottery (or stone), usually broken off from a vase or another earthenware vessel. In archaeology, ostraca may contain scratched-in words or other forms of writing that may give clues as to the time when the piece was in use.

According to paintings on pottery, male musicians are pictured playing almost any instrument available, while the only options for women was to play the harp and percussion instruments. By the Middle Kingdom (2074 BCE), ensembles of both genders were common, and during the New Kingdom (1539 BCE), it was even common to see female-only musical ensembles at rituals, celebrations, and wherever a song was needed.[42]

Ancient Israel

As we have seen, the Hebrew people were not the first to worship, but they were the first to worship Yahweh. We know the Israelites were never isolated from the surrounding cultures of their day, that they were part of a particular culture, and they contributed to that culture. In the Hebrew Bible we read about the people of God at worship. We know they sang psalms and offered various sacrifices. They worshipped in many places and at different times. They gave tithes and offerings. What else did they do in worship? How was their worship structured? Did the Hebrews adopt some of the worship practices of their pagan neighbors? Or, is it possible that Hebrew practices had some common cultural features found in all ancient worship?

The development of worship and song in ancient Israel stretches over a long period of time and in different contexts. Brueggemann has noted that given the present state of our knowledge, "Scholars believe it possible to trace, in a rough form, the ways in which worship was practiced in various contexts and then was vigorously adjusted and transformed under continuing contextual pressures to take a variety of new shapes."[43] How and when Israel emerged as a separate people is open to debate, but it came from very rich and varied cultures as we have seen.

The cultures of the Near East, Egypt, and various centers in Mesopotamia are prime sources from which Israel could draw in developing its own

---

42. Ancient Egyptian displays in the Kelsey Museum.
43. Brueggemann, *Worship in Ancient Israel*, 4.

distinctive worship practices. Though primitive in our understanding, the theologies of these cultures gave a sense of structure to the world and established the legitimacy of political power. "Israel adapted these narratives for liturgical enactment," writes Brueggemann, "in ways that featured Yahweh as creator God and that identified the Davidic king as human regent for the purposes of the creator God."[44]

From available archaeological information, we can come to some tentative conclusions about the roots of congregational song in Israel:

1. Religious rites, including sacrifices and offerings, have been part of the human scene from the earliest times.
2. Prehistoric people and ancient civilizations had some concern for and belief in a future existence, often one that was like their present world.
3. People have expressed their concerns about life and death and their relationship to deities in visual and structural artistic forms.
4. Hymns and sacred poems have been written by ancient people, but we do not know with certainty how they were used or if they were used in worship.
5. It is evident that the early Hebrews had some of the same religious concerns, ideas, and practices of their neighbors. However, Israel's worship was distinctive in its reference to Yahweh.

Genesis 1–11

Historically, the stories in the first eleven chapters of Genesis both precede and parallel the events of these other ancient peoples and civilizations we have studied. The Hebrews were part of the same culture. Many of the stories in these early chapters are similar to stories told by other people in other places. For example, what is common among all major religions of the ancient Near East, the religion of Israel excepted, is that the first rebellion against the Creator took place not among human beings, but in the world of the deities; all of those religions have the story of a rebellion against a creator.

The first eleven chapters of Genesis give us a portrait of the Hebrew worldview. A worldview is a set of fundamental beliefs through which we view the world and how we fit into it. These beliefs give direction to life, such as what we value, what is moral, what is true and false, and what our commitments need to be. All of us have a worldview but may not be aware of it.

---

44. Brueggemann, *Worship in Ancient Israel*, 4.

The Bible is the record of God's eternal search for us, just as God sought Adam and Eve after they sinned. How could humankind ever again have direct and immediate access to God? It was possible when God took the initiative and revealed himself to humankind. God does not reveal information, he reveals himself. The Hebrew Bible describes God in terms of what he does as perceived through human experience. Men and women experienced the mighty works of God and wrote them down when inspired by God. They have shared their religious experience with us and given us something by which we can measure our own experiences with God.

What we get from Genesis 1–11 is a worldview based upon a God who reveals Himself. There is no division between a natural world and a supernatural world as we think of today; the two are one. As we read earlier about ancient people, the Hebrews shared the belief that God was the source and cause of everything and he is present and active in his creation. The Hebrews believed the stories were true in explaining how and why certain things have happened. This following list is somewhat brief, but it gives an overview of the early Hebrew worldview: God is creator of humankind and everything else in the universe.

1. The garden of Eden is a garden sanctuary where there was immediate access to God and people could respond to him in perfect fellowship.
2. Humankind is responsible to God for naming animals and taking care of God's world and the creatures in it.
3. Sin, as the distortion of relationship and commitment to God, originated because people wanted to be like God and disobeyed him.
4. Humankind is separated from God because of this distortion and cannot be allowed to live in Eden.
5. People have to work hard and die because Adam and Eve sinned.
6. There are different languages because humans wanted to be like God and built a tower.
7. God punishes sin by sending a great flood that covered the earth and destroyed all life except what was safe on Noah's ark.

After Eden

Genesis 4 begins by telling us that Cain offered a sacrifice of the fruit of the ground while Abel offered a sacrifice of the firstlings of his flock. The Scripture says Cain's offering was rejected while that of Abel was accepted. While some commentators have made the difference between the two offerings a difference of kind, the writer of the New Testament book of Hebrews tells us that it was a difference of heart attitude: "It was faith that made Abel offer to God a better sacrifice than Cain's. Through his faith he won God's approval as a righteous man, because God himself approved of his gifts. By means of his faith Abel still speaks, even though he is dead" (Heb 11:4). Apparently, Cain harbored ill feelings toward his brother, feelings that rendered his offering unworthy and eventually led to murder.

It is interesting to note that there are no commands in the text for them to offer sacrifice. From the beginning, an offering to God was natural, and this was a long time before Moses instituted sacrifice. The editor of Genesis assumes the existence of an altar and a procedure for sacrifice without telling us how the idea originated.

There is nothing about a grain or fruit offering from the garden that would cause God to reject it any more than there is something about an animal offering that would cause God to accept it. The story does not indicate the offering of either man was for atonement. Most likely they were offerings of thanksgiving. However, the story does give us another basic biblical principle for worship: it is our faith that makes us acceptable to God and not what we offer to him. We feel compelled to give God our best, but even our best is not good enough to win favor with God.

Reading further in chapter 4 we discover Enoch was the first builder of cities (v. 17b). Lamech, his son, was the first to practice polygamy (v. 19). The sons of Lamech engaged in various activities (v. 20). In three successive verses the inventors of three significant phases of Hebrew life are named: Jabat, the father of all shepherds; Jubal, the father of musicians; and Tubalcain, the father of all mental artisans (vv. 20–22).

The biblical tradition of the early development of music is too brief to tell us much: "His brother's name was Jubal, the ancestor of all musicians who play the harp and the flute" (Gen 4:21). The Jubal narrative is very old and has a song associated with it in Genesis 4:23–24.

> Lamech said to his wives,
>
> "Adah and Zillah, listen to me:
>
> I have killed a young man because he struck me.
>
> If seven lives are taken to pay for killing Cain,
>
> Seventy-seven will be taken if anyone kills me."

A unique feature of the biblical story about the beginnings of music is that it was common humankind that invented music. Other ancient peoples had stories that told of gods or national heroes who invented music. For example, the Egyptian god Thot is supposed to have written books on music and acoustics as well as playing the harp. The Indian god Narada supposedly invented the harp.

We move on to Genesis 6 and read that Noah "had no faults and was the only good man of his time. He lived in fellowship with God" (6:9b-10). Living "in fellowship with God" implies a daily worship life style and Noah's obedience in building the ark was an act of worship. The record tells us nothing about how Noah worshipped.

In Genesis 8 we see that after the flood Noah built an altar to the Lord and "took one of each kind of ritually clean animal and bird, and burned them whole as a sacrifice on the altar" (8:20). There is no indication in the text of how Noah knew to build an altar or what made certain animals and birds ritually clean. Noah seemed to understand that God's grace required a response of gratitude and submission to God.

A natural inclination to worship someone or something is evident in the story of the Tower of Babel in Genesis 11. Most people think the mixing up of languages is the thrust of this story, but basically it is a story of worship. The people of Babel wanted to make a name for themselves. Since they felt secure in their achievements, the need for God was minimized.

Yahweh or Baal?

The Hebrews failed to subdue all of Canaan and there was constant flirtation with the Baal worship of the people living there. This may be because the Hebrews had difficulty believing God could sustain them in Canaan, for they had never known such fertility in Egypt. The Canaanite farmers attributed that fertility to the god Baal. There was no doubt Yahweh was God in the arid desert, but was He also God in Canaan?

The book of Judges in the Hebrew Bible details both the failures and the triumphs of the Hebrew people to subdue the land and its people. In Genesis the Canaanites are described as descendants of Canaan, the son of Ham and grandson of Noah. All through the book of Judges we read of the struggle for the hearts and minds of God's people and the struggle continued through the reign of the kings. The places of Asherah worship were commonly called "groves," and the Hebrew word "asherah" could refer either to the goddess or to a grove of trees. One of King Manasseh's evil deeds was that he "took the carved Asherah pole he had made and put it in the temple" (2 Kgs 21:7). Another translation of "carved Asherah pole" is "graven image of the grove."

Considered the moon goddess, Asherah was often presented as a consort of Baal, the sun god (Judg 3:7, 6:28, 10:6; 1 Sam 7:4, 12:10). The Law specified that a grove of trees was not to be near the altar of Jehovah (Deut 16:21).[45]

Despite God's clear instructions, Asherah and Baal worship was a perennial problem in Israel. As Solomon slipped into idolatry, one of the pagan deities he brought into the kingdom was Asherah, called "the goddess of the Sidonians" (1 Kgs 11:5, 33). Later, Jezebel made Asherah-worship even more prevalent, with four hundred prophets of Asherah on the royal payroll (1 Kgs 18:19). One reference of Jewish worship of Baal/Asherah is in the book of Jeremiah:

> The children gather wood, and the fathers kindle the fire, and the women knead [their] dough, to make cakes to the queen of heaven, and to pour out drink offerings unto other gods, that they may provoke me to anger. (7:18)

At times, Israel experienced revival. Gideon (Judg 6:25–30), King Asa (1 Kgs 15:13), and King Josiah (2 Kgs 23:1–7) all led notable crusades against Asherah worship.

We have a few clues in the Bible that inform us about Baal-Asherah worship as practiced by the Hebrews. A few of these worship elements also appear in the Hebrew worship of Yahweh.

1. Worship was near poles and trees (Deut 7:5, 12:2–3; 2 Kgs 16:4, 17:10; Jer 3:6,13; Ezek 6:13).
2. Planting sacred gardens (Isa 1:29). Apparently, people believed that dedicating a garden to a fertility god would cause him to bless their crops.
3. Sacrifices were made, usually bulls or sheep (1 Kgs 8:23).
4. At times firstborn children were sacrificed. The Bible calls this practice detestable (Deut 12:31, 18:9–10). In Numbers 3:11–13 God specifically appointed the tribe of Levi in place of the firstborn of the Israelites, so they had no excuse for offering their children.

A virtual catalog of the idolatrous practices of the Hebrews can be found in 2 Kings 23:4–19.

According to 1 Kings 14:22–24, the Hebrews put up stone pillars and symbols of Asherah on hills and under shady trees and had men and women prostitutes at these places of worship. The inspired writer concludes, "The

---

45. Barton, "Ashtoreth and Her Influence," 73–91.

people of Judah practiced all the shameful things done by the people whom the Lord had driven out of the land as the Israelites advanced into the country" (v. 24; cf. Isa 65:1–5).

The Hebrews also made offerings of food and drink to their God, but since Yahweh was not represented by a statue or in any visual form, these sacrifices were burnt up or poured out on the altar. The book of Numbers records the precise offerings of meat, grain and drink that were required by God twice each day, and more required on the Sabbath and Passover festivals (Num 28).[46]

Coda

From this brief study of prehistoric humans, we do not see them as brutes that barely rise above dumb animals. Though primitive and living thousands of years ago, we see them as human beings with an ability to have ideas that go beyond their everyday experience. They held a belief in an invisible and more powerful reality than visible reality. This is a worldview of gods and spirits, a world that has been diminished by our modern scientific views that would claim reality exists only in what is physical.

Prehistoric art and music could very well be primitive ways of dealing with the facts and mystery of life and death mentioned earlier. These ideas found artistic expression then just as they find artistic expression today. We shall now see how these religious and artistic ideas began to evolve over time.

Archaeologists suggest that humans have always worshipped as evidenced by ancient burial mounds found in many places of the world. When these sites were excavated, archaeologists inferred people had worshipped because of the artifacts found, the position of bodies, and the remains of what appeared to be an altar of some sort. Of course, we know nothing about the god or gods these people worshipped, how they worshipped or what they believed about an afterlife. However, the existence of ancient burial customs would seem to indicate that people have an inner awareness of some ultimate power or powers that are unconditioned by human experience. Worship seems to be a natural response to that awareness.

From available archaeological and biblical information, we can come to some tentative conclusions about the roots of congregational song in Israel:

---

46. Coogan, *Old Testament*, 139–41; 152–69.

1. Religious rites, including sacrifices and offerings, have been part of the human scene from the earliest times.

2. Prehistoric people and ancient civilizations had some concern for and belief in a future existence, often one that was like their present world.

3. People have expressed their concerns about life and death and their relationship to deities in visual and structural artistic forms.

4. Hymns and sacred poems have been written by ancient people, but we do not know with certainty how they were used or if they were used in worship.

5. It is evident that the early Hebrews had some of the same religious concerns, ideas, and practices of their neighbors. However, Israel's worship was distinctive in its reference to Yahweh.

2

Congregational Song in the Old Testament

Chenaniah, leader of the Levites in music, was to direct the music, for he understood it.

—1 Chronicles 15:22

In this chapter, we trace the development of congregational song among the Hebrew people who have settled their promised land through the Hebrew Bible or Old Testament. We start with the book of Genesis and close with the voice of the prophets and the decline of worship and song to YHWH.

In the last few verses of Genesis 11 and beginning with Genesis 12, we enter the realm of recorded history in the Bible and the lives of the Hebrew patriarchs. According to the Old Testament, the patriarchs are Abraham, his son Isaac, and his grandson Jacob. They are referred to as the three patriarchs of Judaism, and the period in which they lived is known as the patriarchal period. David, Moses, and Joseph are also known as patriarchs, but Abraham, Isaac, and Jacob are the men we are concerned with at this point.

The Old Testament affirms that the God who spoke creation into being made himself known to the patriarchs of Israel at particular times and in particular places. God spoke directly to Abraham, Isaac, and Jacob, though we do not know exactly how he spoke to them. In so doing, God initiated a relationship with Abraham that was later confirmed for Isaac, Jacob, and his descendants. The promise was to make of them a great nation. They were to possess the land of Canaan and be blessed above all other nations so that they would bless all people on the earth.

In the Time of Moses

In the pre-mosaic era, it seems that the head of a family or tribe would preside over worship, functioning as a priest for his family. Worship was centered primarily on sacrifice, which is found in many religions both then and now. This seems to be the practice of Abraham and his immediate family. During their lifetimes, three dfferent altars were erected throughout Canaan to mark the places where God had been made known to them under various names. Sacrifice was not offered just anywhere, but at those particular sites as a demonstration that the land belonged to God and that God would give the land to his people at a time of his choosing.[1]

We know nothing of any worship ritual Abraham carried out or whether his worship was accompanied by singing. Having been associated with the worship of Sumer, he would have some general understanding of music in worship. As we saw earlier, the worship in Sumer and Canaan included hymns and music. A liturgy uncovered by archaeologist George Barton at Ras Shamra, Syria seems to have been used for a spring festival in Jerusalem c. 1800–1600 BCE, the general time of Abraham and his meeting with Melchezedek.[2]

Barton points out that the evidence does not give a full demonstration of the location, but there is a high probability that this was a liturgical feast in Jerusalem. The liturgy included these elements: a call for the gods to come to the feast, preparation of a sacrifice, responses and recitations by the people that could have been spoken or sung, and words and actions calculated to ensure both a good harvest and the birth of children. This could be similar to the rituals Abraham performed.

When the children of Israel left Egypt, and "carried away the wealth of the Egyptians," (Exod 12:37) they did not forget to bring with them some of the country's musical instruments and a record of its musical system. This is apparent from the manner in which the victory over Pharaoh was celebrated and described in Exodus 15:1–18, the text of a hymn of praise sung by Moses and the Israelites. The hymn celebrates their deliverance from Egypt (15:1–12) and the anticipated conquest of the land of promise (15:13–16). The land is described as a "mountain, the place that you, LORD, have chosen for your home, the Temple that you yourself have built" (17b). The land is a sanctuary where "You, LORD, will be king forever and ever" (v. 18).

Immediately following (vv. 20–21), we read that after the Israelites had crossed the Sea of Reeds and the Egyptians had been drowned, "The

---

1. Gen 12:1–3, 7; 13:14–17; 15:1–8, 12–16.
2. Barton, "Liturgy," 61–78. See also Smith, *Rituals and Myths*.

prophet Miriam, Aaron's sister, took her tambourine, and all the women followed her, playing tambourines and dancing. Miriam sang for them: 'Sing to the LORD, because he has won a glorious victory; he has thrown the horses and their riders into the sea.'" It should be noted that although the Bible speaks of singing, voices are not described—merely the words of the songs are recorded.

The Sinai Event

The giving of the Law to Israel on Mount Sinai was the most momentous event in the Jewish people's history. The once-wandering Israelite tribe, under the leadership of Moses, had just escaped from Egypt and were creating a new kind of society. The Bible does not present the giving of the Law as one dramatic event, but as a lengthy process that begins on Sinai and ends forty years later. More and more laws keep coming all the time and Moses commits them to writing.

Tent of the Lord's Presence (Tabernacle)

How many times Moses went up Sinai to meet with God is debatable. Schwartz makes a claim for at least eight trips up the mountainside.[3] Regardless of the number, on one of those trips God told Moses, "The people must make a sacred Tent for me, so that I may live among them" (Exod 25:8). Unlike the deities of other ancient eastern Mediterranean peoples, the God of the Hebrews was incorporeal and invisible who made himself known through physical manifestations.

> When the king of Egypt let the people go, God did not take them by the road that goes up the coast to Philistia, although it was the shortest way. God thought, "I do not want the people to change their minds and return to Egypt when they see that they are going to have to fight." Instead, he led them in a roundabout way through the desert toward the Red Sea . . . During the day the Lord went in front of them in a pillar of cloud to show them the way, and during the night he went in front of them in a pillar of fire to give them light, so that they could travel night and day. The pillar of cloud was always in front of the people during the day, and the pillar of fire at night (Exod 13:17–18, 21–22).

---

3. Schwartz, "What Really Happened?" See also Zvielli, "Why Did Moses Go Up Sinai Twice?"

The Tent was considered to be the place where God's presence dwelled among the Israelites, where the divine and earthly realms met. The physical design of the tent represented a gradual move from the everyday world to the Holy of Holies where God lived, and it was entered only once a year by the High Priest.

The Covenant Box

God's presence was symbolized by a wooden chest known as the Ark of the Covenant, or the Covenant Box, the term that I am using. The Covenant Box was regarded by the Israelites as God's throne and it contained the stones upon which the Ten Commandments were written. Before it found a permanent home in Jerusalem, the Covenant Box was carried by the Israelites wherever they went. Furnishings included a table with twelve loaves of bread set out as an offering to God, a lampstand with seven lamps, an altar for incense, an altar for sacrifices, and a bronze basin for ritual washings. The Covenant Box was given a special place within the Tent, and when the Israelites moved from place to place, the Tent was taken down and carried by the Levites, with the Covenant Box, to the next camp site. The fact that the ark was the place of the Lord's presence among His people brought great assurance to the people of God. The Creator of the universe was living among His grumbling, complaining, bickering, and sinful people.

Detailed instructions for worship in the Tent are described in Leviticus 1–7. These instructions were given by God to Moses from the Tent erected at the foot of mount Sinai. The Lord had filled that Tent with his presence in a cloud that settled upon and covered the outside of the tabernacle, while on the inside it was filled with the glory of the Lord (Exod 40:34–38).

We have no direct evidence of singing during rituals in the Tent of God's Presence. However, the giving of the Law on stones, the repeated visits to Sinai, the Tent of Dwelling and its attendant furnishings, and the Covenant Box are all things the Israelites inherited from Mesopotamia and Egypt, so I think we can hypothesize that there was singing in the rituals in the Tent of Dwelling. Detailed information about music at the Tent is available only with regard to trumpets, which were purportedly used in connection with and during the cultic rites.

The tent of presence and the covenant box had long been the special venue for divine revelation. Moses was told to go to the tent to receive instructions from God (Exod 25:21–22, 33:6–11, Num 7:89, 12:4–10), and it was there that God gave him a song to write that would be a witness in the mouths of the children of Israel (Deut 31:14–15, 19–26).

Numbers 10:1–10 contains instructions for the use of trumpets.[4] They were to be made from "hammered silver" to call the people together and for "breaking camp" (v. 1). Then follows information about the various short and long trumpet blasts that told the people what to do. The trumpets were to be blown by Aaron's sons, the priests, a rule for all time (v. 8b). The purpose of trumpets sounding during sacrifices was "a reminder for you before your God: I am Yahweh your God" (10:10 CSB).

Wandering in the Wilderness

While wandering in the Valley of the Moabites, the people began to complain of thirst. God commanded Moses to bring all the people together and He would provide them with water. After getting water, the Israelites sang this song (Num 21:17–18):

> Wells, produce your water;
>
> and we will greet it with a song,
>
> The well dug by princes
>
> and by leaders of the people,
>
> Dug with a royal scepter
>
> and with their walking sticks.

Later, in the same chapter, the Israelites celebrated their victory over the Amorite king Sihon with a song (vv. 27–30).

In Deuteronomy 31 we find God giving instructions to Moses and Joshua when Moses is at the end of his life and Joshua will succeed him. YHWH met with the two men at the tent of meeting and told them that after Moses' death, the people of Israel would renege on the covenant that Yahweh had made with them, and worship the gods of the lands they were occupying. Moses was told to write down the words of a song and teach it to the community, so that it would "stand as evidence against them" (v. 19).

Just before the people cross the Jordan river, Moses is on the top of Mount Nebo, looking out on the promised land. Moses knows he will be unable to enter the land despite his leadership and dedication in leading the Children of Israel. After wandering 40 years in the desert and his goal almost reached, he is moved by God to sing. Deuteronomy 31:22 states that Moses did as he had been instructed, and in verse 30, "Moses recited the entire song while all the people of Israel listened."

---

4. Smith, *Music in Ancient Judaism*, 33–38.

Cantor Erik Contzius has pointed out in his blog that Moses implores heaven and earth to give ear to his song. He proclaims God's faithful and true nature. He describes God as the ultimate guide and protector of the people. The song is forty-three verses long, and we can only imagine the great joy Moses felt at seeing the land of Israel and the sorrow he must have felt at not being able to lead the people further.[5]

Music in Everyday Life

Music was important in the culture of ancient Israel. We discover that music was a part of everyday life as well as a part of worship. Whether at a marriage feast, at a funeral, or in the temple, music is used to express joy or sorrow, praise or prayer. The joy taken in music is evidenced by its prominent role in the celebrations of life. Apparently, music could spring to life spontaneously and effortlessly. The following passages do not directly relate to a worship practice but give us a glimpse of the many ways music was part of the daily life of the people of Israel.

Work tasks were often accompanied by music, evidenced by the songs or chants of workers bringing in the harvest or treading grapes:

> And gladness is taken away, and joy out of the plentiful field; and in the vineyards there shall be no singing, neither shall there be shouting: the treaders shall tread out no wine in their presses; I have made their vintage shouting to cease. (Jer 16:10)

Other events in life were celebrated with music, such as at funerals:

> David sang this lament for Saul and his son Jonathan, and ordered it to be taught to the people of Judah. It is recorded in The Book of Jashar. (2 Sam 1:18)

Victorious armies were met with the songs of women celebrating the return of Israel's warriors.

> The prophet Miriam, Aaron's sister, took her tambourine, and all the women followed her, playing tambourines and dancing. Miriam sang for them: "Sing to the LORD, because he has won a glorious victory; he has thrown the horses and their riders into the sea." (Exod 15:20–21)

> As David was returning after killing Goliath and as the soldiers were coming back home, women from every town in Israel came out to meet King Saul. They were singing joyful songs,

---

5. Contzius, "Why Do We Sing?," para. 14.

dancing, and playing tambourines and lyres. In their celebration, the women sang, "Saul has killed thousands, but David tens of thousands." (1 Sam 18:6–7)

Music was used to bid someone farewell:

> ... I would have sent you on your way with rejoicing and singing to the music of tambourines and harps. (Gen 31:27)

Or to welcome a loved one home:

> When Jephthah came to his house at Mizpah, behold, his daughter was coming out to meet him with tambourines and with dancing. (Judg 11:34a)

As in our own generation, music was used for personal enjoyment:

> David was playing the harp, as he did every day ... (1 Sam 18:10b)

> Their children run and play like lambs and dance to the music of harps and flutes. (Job 21:11–2)

> Men and women sang to entertain me ... (Eccl 2:8)

Music was used in a negative way, such as mocking and scorning others:

> They talk about me in the streets, and drunkards make up songs about me. (Ps 69:12)

> Those worthless nobodies make up jokes and songs to disgrace me (Job 30:9).

Festive occasions called for music, such as the crowning of kings:

> Zadok took the container of olive oil which he had brought from the Tent of the LORD's Presence, and anointed Solomon. They blew the trumpet, and all the people shouted, "Long live King Solomon!" Then they all followed him back, shouting for joy and playing flutes, making enough noise to shake the ground." (1 Kgs 1:39–40)

Music was also recognized as affecting the human spirit to soothe depression.

> His [Saul's] servants said to him, "We know that an evil spirit sent by God is tormenting you. So, give us the order, sir, and we will look for a man who knows how to play the harp. Then when the evil spirit comes on you, the man can play his harp, and you will be all right again." (1 Sam 16:15–16)

Singing to a person who is depressed is like taking off a person's clothes on a cold day or like rubbing salt in a wound. (Prov 25:20)

Old Testament Musical Instruments

The Old Testament seldom mentions the forms of music, the origins of instruments, and how they should be played. The way to play or make instruments was passed on by oral tradition rather than written record. Most of that oral tradition has been lost, leaving us with only the briefest of information found in the Bible. In addition, very few ancient musical instruments exist intact, so we must guess at how they looked and sounded.

Our present knowledge of ancient musical instruments is gathered from pictorial representations as well as remains from instruments discovered through archaeology. By comparing Scripture references with the artifacts of other cultures, historians and archaeologists have helped fill in many of the gaps in our knowledge of music in Bible times.[6] However, many biblical instruments are not explicitly described and we are unsure of how they were played in comparison to music instruments of today.

Musical instruments are placed in four basic groups according to the way the sound is produced: (1) string instruments, which use vibrating strings to produce the sound; (2) percussion instruments, in which the sound is produced by a vibrating membrane or metal shell; (3) wind instruments, which produce sound by passing air over a vibrating reed or passing air across an opening, and (4) wind instruments that produce sound by vibrating lips in a mouthpiece. Biblical instruments can also be placed in all four of these categories.[7]

Wind Instruments

Shofar

The instrument most frequently named in the Old Testament is the shofar and is the only instrument to have been used continuously in synagogues from antiquity to the twenty-first century. The word is often translated as trumpet. It is made of a ram's horn and is semi-circular in shape. Modern shofars can play at least two notes a third or fourth part, so the shofar is

---

6. Rabinovitch, *Of Jewish Music*, 13–17; Rothmüller, *Music of the Jews*, 5–6.

7. Vos, *New Illustrated Manners and Customs*, 209–13. See also Burgh, "Music and Musical Instruments," 1–5, and Campbell, "Critical Review," 48–51.

not a melody instrument. Its sounds are differentiated primarily by the rhythm patterns played. They could blow legato and staccato notes and trills, which made it possible to convey complicated signals to announce assembly, battle, and ambush.

The shofar was sounded on most important events like war, holidays and the anointing of a new king. It served as a signaling instrument in times of peace and war (Judg 3:27; 6:34; Neh 4:18–20). Since its chief function was making noise, the shofar announced religious festivals and warned of danger. The shofar held a prominent place in the life of Israel, as noted by its function in national celebration (1 Kgs 1:34; 2 Kgs 9:13).

Music played a role in the Sinai experience. When Moses went up the Mount to receive the tablets of law, the shofar was sounded, though the word is usually translated as trumpet. Its usage created awe and fear, for "all the people in the camp trembled" (Exod 19:16).

Other uses of the shofar are given in the book of Leviticus: proclaiming a special Memorial (23:23) and sending the "trumpet throughout your land on the day of Atonement" (25:9). The special memorial day is also called the Feast of the Trumpets and corresponds to the Jewish New Year. The day is calculated from the beginning of the Exodus, as a new era for the Hebrews began with that event.

Trumpet (hatsotsra)

There is some confusion about the identity of the trumpet when the word appears in Scripture, for some English translations translate the word *shofar* as trumpet. Further identification is difficult for at other times the word *yobel* is translated as trumpet. Yobel describes the sound made either by a shofar or a trumpet. In Numbers 10:1–10 God told Moses how to make two trumpets of hammered silver to use for calling the people together and for breaking camp.

> The LORD said to Moses, "Make two trumpets of hammered silver to use for calling the people together and for breaking camp. When long blasts are sounded on both trumpets, the whole community is to gather around you at the entrance to the Tent of my presence. But when only one trumpet is sounded, then only the leaders of the clans are to gather around you. When short blasts are sounded, the tribes camped on the east will move out. When short blasts are sounded a second time, the tribes on the south will move out. So short blasts are to be sounded to break

camp, but in order to call the community together, long blasts are to be sounded." (vv. 1–7).

The trumpets are to be blown by Aaron's sons, the priests, and a protocol was established for how and when they were to be blown:

> The following rule is to be observed for all time to come. When you are at war in your land, defending yourselves against an enemy who has attacked you, sound the signal for battle on these trumpets. I, the LORD your God, will help you and save you from your enemies. Also on joyful occasions—at your New Moon Festivals and your other religious festivals—you are to blow the trumpets when you present your burnt offerings and your fellowship offerings. Then I will help you. I am the LORD your God. (vv. 8b–10)

The shape of the hatsotsra was very similar to the shape of a modern bugle, except that it was one straight piece. Instruments such as these were common among the Egyptians, so it was not difficult for the Israelites to know how to make them. Priests played the hatsotsrah and others played the shofar, perhaps indicating different tones or sounds were used for warfare, such as signals.[8] When mentioned in the Bible it is only in plural (*hatsotsrot*). At times, both the shofar and the hatsotsra were played together, as Psalm 98:6 and Hosea 5:8 indicate:

> Blow trumpets (hatsotsrot) and horns (shofars), and shout for joy to the LORD, our king. (Ps 98:6)

> Sound the horn [shofar] in Gibeah, the trumpet [hatsotsra] in Ramah. (Hos 5:8a)

The Mishnah was published at the end of the second century CE and is an edited record of a complex body of material known as the oral Torah that was transmitted in the aftermath of the destruction of the Second Temple in 70 CE. In the Mishnah it is said that no less than two trumpets (hatsotsrot) were played in the temple (Mishna Arakhin, 2:3, 5) and they were played with psalters, harps and cymbals. There were never less than twenty-one trumpet blasts in the temple and never more than forty-eight. The Mishnah also described when and how many times they were used in temple services (Suka, 5:5, Tamid, 6:6).[9]

Mishna Rosh Hashana discusses the shofar used on Rosh Hashanah (the Jewish New Year festival). It was made from the horn of an ibex,

---

8. Shaked, "Music in the Bible."
9. Kulp, "Arakhin."

straight, and its mouth was overlaid with gold. There were two trumpets, one on each side of it. The shofar gave a long blast and the trumpets a short one, since the commandment for the ceremony was to play the shofar.[10]

Clarinet or Oboe

The Hebrew word *chaliyl* occurs in six Old Testament references. It was translated pipe or pipes in the King James Version, and flute in the New International Version. Based on archaeological work by Nelson Glück, some now think this instrument was a primitive clarinet, a single reed pipe with a mouthpiece. Others think the chaliyl was a double reed instrument that is the ancestor of the oboe. Whatever the instrument was, it would not have been a transverse instrument like the modern flute, but similar to a modern recorder.

The primitive clarinet was a popular instrument in Bible times. It is mentioned in Isaiah 5:12; 30:29; and Jeremiah 48:36. New Testament references include Matthew 9:23; 11:17; Luke 7:32; and 1 Corinthians 14:7. The clarinet probably was not used in the temple, but it was a popular instrument for banquets, weddings, or funerals.

Ugav

In Psalm 150 we read about the *ugav* (a small pipe), a word that is related to *Abbub*, meaning "hollow reed" in Phoenician and we know the Phoenicians had such an instrument called *Abobas*.[11] No one is certain what this instrument was.

Flute

The flute (mashrokitha) was actually a big pipe and had a mouthpiece. It probably had a sharp, penetrating sound, somewhat like an oboe. The flute was popular for secular and religious use, but it was not mentioned as an instrument of the first temple orchestra. It was sometimes allowed in the second temple. Because of its penetrating sound it was used in processions (Isa 30:29).

---

10. Kulp, "Rosh Hashanah."
11. Doukhan, "Music in the Bible," 18–25.

String Instruments

THE HARP (KINOR) AND LYRE (NEVEL)

The harp (kinnor) was a small lyre with at least seven or possibly eight strings and was considered to be the more sophisticated instrument. Its shape and number of strings varied, but all types of lyres produced a most pleasing sound. The lyre was used in secular settings (Isa 23:16), but was in sacred use too. It was the instrument David used to ease King Saul's depression. Generally, this instrument was played by stroking the strings with a plectrum, much as a guitar can be played with a pick. However, David seemed to prefer to use his hand instead (1 Sam 16:16, 23; 18:10; 19:9). Skilled craftsmen made lyres of silver or ivory and decorated them with lavish ornamentation.

The lyre (nevel) was frequently used for secular music, such as the merrymaking at Nebuchadnezzar's banquet. It was an instrument of ten or more strings and played by plucking the strings with the fingers.

Percussion Instruments

BELLS

One kind of bell had a name (metsilloth) that came from the Hebrew word meaning "to jingle" or "to rattle." This type of bell is mentioned only once in the Bible, where we are told that the Israelites attached these bells to the bridle or breast strap of horses. There is no evidence they were ever used as musical instruments. Bells (pa`amon) are also mentioned as part of the priests' garments, but there is no evidence they were used as musical instruments. Many times even the harness bells of the horses will be inscribed with the words "Dedicated to the LORD" (Zech 14:20).

CYMBALS

Cymbals (metziltayim or tziltzal) were made of copper and were the only percussion instrument in the temple orchestra. Cymbals were more likely small finger cymbals, something liked metal castanets, rather than the large cymbals we are used to seeing. They were used when the people were celebrating and praising GOD and joined with trumpets and singers to express joy and thanks to the LORD:

> David commanded the leaders of the Levites to assign various Levites to sing and to play joyful music on harps and cymbals. (1 Chr 15:16)

Asaph, David's chief musician, was a cymbal player.

> Asaph was appointed leader, with Zechariah as his assistant. Jeiel, Shemiramoth, Jehiel, Mattithiah, Eliab, Benaiah, Obed Edom, and Jeiel were to play harps. Asaph was to sound the cymbals... (1 Chr 16:5)

When the people returned from captivity, Asaph's descendants were called to join singers and trumpets in praise to the LORD.

> When the builders started to lay the foundation of the Temple, the priests in their robes took their places with trumpets in their hands, and the Levites of the clan of Asaph stood there with cymbals. They praised the LORD according to the instructions handed down from the time of King David. (Ezra 3:10)

Sistrum (menana)

The sistrum was a small U-shaped frame with a handle attached at the bottom of the curve. Pieces of metal or other small objects were strung on small bars stretched from one side of the sistrum to the other.

> David and all the Israelites were dancing and singing with all their might to honor the LORD. They were playing harps, lyres, drums, rattles (menena), and cymbals. (2 Sam 6:5)

The use of the sistrum goes back to ancient Egypt and has counterparts in other ancient cultures. It was merely a noisemaker, played by women on both joyous and sad occasions.[12]

Timbrel (toph)

A vibrating membrane produced the sound of this instrument. It is correctly translated as either timbrel or tambourine. It was carried and beaten by the hand. In very early times it may have been made with two membranes, with pieces of bronze inserted in the rim.

---

12. Vos, *New Illustrated Manners and Customs*, 209–13.

When Israel Had Kings

By the time of Saul, Israel's first king, music had come to be recognized as having an effect upon the lives of people. Part of the struggle Israel had with pagan gods may lie in the fact that many of these pagan cults had highly ecstatic worship services utilizing music.

Saul

When the prophet Samuel anointed Saul as king of Israel, Saul had an experience that demonstrates how music was a part of the ecstatic worship of prophets. Samuel told Saul he would have an experience that would prove God had chosen him to be king. Saul was to go to the Hill of God in Gibeah where he would meet

> a group of prophets coming down from the altar on the hill, playing harps, drums, flutes, and lyres. They will be dancing and shouting. Suddenly the spirit of the LORD will take control of you, and you will join in their religious dancing and shouting and will become a different person. When these things happen, do whatever God leads you to do. (1 Sam 10:5-6)

Everything Samuel had told Saul happened. The spirit of God took control of him and Saul joined in the ecstatic dancing. When Saul finished, he went to the altar on the hill.

This was not the only time Saul had an ecstatic experience. In 1 Samuel 19:2-24 both Saul's servants and Saul participated in the religious exercises of a group of prophets under the leadership of Samuel. Indicative of the limits to which these men would go is the statement in verse 24 that Saul

> took off his clothes and danced and shouted in Samuel's presence, and lay naked all that day and all that night. (This is how the saying originated, "Has even Saul become a prophet?")

Music was also recognized as affecting the human spirit to soothe depression. On one depressive day, Saul's servants told him to get someone to play the harp (*kinnor*) to drive away his melancholy.

> His servants said to him, "We know that an evil spirit sent by God is tormenting you. So give us the order, sir, and we will look for a man who knows how to play the harp. Then when the evil spirit comes on you, the man can play his harp, and you will be all right again." (1 Sam 16:15-16)

David was selected for this purpose, and the Scriptures relate that Saul was soothed by the music. Similar instances can be found in 1 Samuel 18:10 and 19:9.

David

When David became king, music and worship were raised to a new level. At the very beginning of his reign, David wanted to bring the Covenant Box from Kiriath Jearim to Jerusalem. They started back to Jerusalem amid great rejoicing: "They sang and played musical instruments—harps, drums, cymbals, and trumpets" (1 Chr 13:8b). However, Uzzah, one of the drivers of the cart carrying the Ark, put out his hand to steady the Ark, and was smitten by the Lord for touching it. David, in fear, left the Ark at the house of Obed-edom the Gittite, instead of carrying it on to Jerusalem, and there it stayed three months (2 Sam 6:1–11; 1 Chr 13:1–13).

Meanwhile, David prepared a place in Jerusalem for the Covenant Box and erected a tent for it. Then he assembled the people who were to bring the Box to Jerusalem. The musicians were all men and members of the priestly tribe of Levi. The men were divided into separate groups, with each group performing a special function. The ark was brought back with shouts, dancing, and sounds of music.

> David appointed some of the Levites to lead the worship of the LORD, the God of Israel, in front of the Covenant Box by singing and praising him. Asaph was appointed leader, with Zechariah as his assistant. Jeiel, Shemiramoth, Jehiel, Mattithiah, Eliab, Benaiah, Obed Edom, and Jeiel were to play harps. Asaph was to sound the cymbals, and two priests, Benaiah and Jahaziel, were to blow trumpets regularly in front of the Covenant Box. It was then that David first gave Asaph and the other Levites the responsibility for singing praises to the LORD. (1 Chr 16:4–7)

In the parallel passage of 2 Samuel 6, lyres, drums, and rattles are added to the musical ensemble and the chief musicians and David wore white linen robes. In addition, David wore an ephod, a linen apron that was a vestment for the high priest.

Although the Covenant Box was in Jerusalem, worship was conducted both there and at Gibeon. Asaph and the other Levites were put in permanent charge of the worship in Jerusalem, with the son of Jeduthun and sixty-eight men of his clan to assist Asaph. Two other men were placed in charge of guarding the gates to the tabernacle. Zadok the priest and his fellow priests were in charge of worship in Gibeon. They burned sacrifices daily as written in the Law, and Heman and Jeduthun were chosen to sing praises to the Lord. These two men were also in charge of the "trumpets and cymbals and the other instruments which were played when the songs of praise were sung" (1 Chr 16:37–42).

King David appointed men directly descended from Levi to be in charge of the music at the place of worship in Jerusalem after the Covenant Box was moved there. The musicians were divided into three choirs.

> They took regular turns of duty at the Tent of the LORD's presence during the time before King Solomon built the Temple. The family lines of those who held this office are as follows: The clan of Kohath: Heman, the leader of the first choir, was the son of Joel. His family line went back to Jacob . . . Asaph was leader of the second choir. His family line went back to Levi . . . Ethan of the clan of Merari was the leader of the third choir. His family line went back to Levi . . . The other Levites were assigned all the other duties at the place of worship. (1 Chr 6:32–48)

How was it possible to have such an impressive display of music? David had created an academy to train Levitical families in the singing of psalms before the LORD. "Four thousand," he said, "shall offer praise to the LORD with the instruments which I have made for praise" (1 Chr 23:5 NRSV). David and the chiefs of the service also set apart for the service "certain of the sons of Asaph, and of Heman, and of Jeduthun, who should prophesy with lyres (*kinnorot*), with harps (*nevalim*), and cymbals (*tsiltsilim*)" (1 Chr 25:1 NRSV).[13]

Though David was forbidden to build the temple, he began preparations for the construction by amassing materials and organizing various work groups. He also organized the worship that was to take place in the temple.

> King David and the leaders of the Levites chose the following Levite clans to lead the worship services: Asaph, Heman, and Jeduthun. They were to proclaim God's messages, accompanied by the music of harps and cymbals. This is the list of persons chosen to lead the worship, with the type of service that each group performed:
> The four sons of Asaph: Zaccur, Joseph, Nethaniah, and Asharelah. They were under the direction of Asaph, who proclaimed God's messages whenever the king commanded.
> The six sons of Jeduthun: Gedaliah, Zeri, Jeshaiah, Shimei, Hashabiah, and Mattithiah. Under the direction of their father

---

13. Doukhan, "Music in the Bible," 18–25.

they proclaimed God's message, accompanied by the music of harps, and sang praise and thanks to the LORD.

The fourteen sons of Heman . . . the king's prophet, these . . . sons and also three daughters, as he had promised, in order to give power to Heman. All of his sons played cymbals and harps under their father's direction, to accompany the Temple worship. And Asaph, Jeduthun, and Heman were under orders from the king.

All these twenty-four men were experts; and their fellow Levites were trained musicians. There were 288 men in all. (1 Chr 25:1–7)

Feasts and Festivals

The Jewish year was punctuated with great festivals that were celebrated in the temple. Some were timed to coincide with the changing seasons. Others commemorated great events in the life of Israel. All were occasions of wholehearted joy and thanksgiving for God's good gifts to his people, and at the same time sober gatherings to seek his cleansing and forgiveness. The purpose of the festivals was for worship: a time of God meeting with his people. There may have been many local festivals, but there were three national festivals during the year when all work stopped, and all men were required to attend.

We have no biblical passages that give us information about music used at these festivals, but based upon the worship practices we have record of, we can infer that these were joyous occasions accompanied by music. As N. T. Wright has noted,

> The great majority of Jews went up to Jerusalem for the festivals singing the psalms en route; the great majority of Jews heard scripture read regularly in their synagogues. In these ways they acted out, and thereby demonstrated to themselves, their belief that Jerusalem, and its Temple, were the center of the created order, the place where the creator of the world, who had entered into special covenant with them as a nation, had chosen to place his "name."[14]

---

14. Wright, "Jerusalem in the New Testament," 55.

Passover and the Feast of Unleavened Bread

These two festivals were celebrated together and combined both pastoral and agricultural elements. The Passover is a lambing festival from Israel's early days that was connected to the Exodus from Egypt and thereafter used to celebrate the Hebrews' deliverance. The Feast of Unleavened Bread originally was a feast of the barley harvest. Both festivals occurred in the spring, and we do not know when they were combined. The combined festival lasted for one week.

Five days before Passover, the national Passover lamb would be taken to the temple in procession to be the publicly sacrificed. The lamb was met by crowds of people waving palm branches and joyously singing Psalm 118 as they remembered God's miraculous delivery of their ancestors from the clutches of the Egyptian Pharaoh. One passage sung was,

> Oh Lord, please save us, Oh Lord, please save us. Oh Lord, send us prosperity, Oh Lord, send us prosperity. Blessed is He that comes in the name of the Lord. We have blessed you from the house of the LORD. (Ps 118:25–26)

Feast of Weeks (Harvest)

This festival was held in the summer at the beginning of the wheat harvest, which in theory followed seven weeks after the cutting of the first stalks of barley. Later, this festival was known as Pentecost and was celebrated fifty days after the Passover. Originally this was a celebration when the first fruits of the harvest were offered to God, but by 70 CE, and probably earlier, it was also a time to celebrate and remember the giving of the Law to Moses on Mount Sinai. In the Old Testament we find detailed instructions for calculating the time of year for the festival when the barley and the wheat were coming out of the fields. It was a time to come together with brethren and celebrate before Yahweh for the bountiful harvest he has given Israel.

> When you come into the land that the LORD is giving you and you harvest your grain, take the first sheaf to the priest. He shall present it as a special offering to the LORD, so that you may be accepted. The priest shall present it the day after the Sabbath. (Lev 23:9–11)

The Feast of Ingathering (Tabernacles)

This was an eight-day autumn festival at the end of the fruit harvest and is sometimes called the Festival of Tabernacles. It is also known as the Feast of Shelters. Historically, this feast commemorates the forty-year period during which the children of Israel were wandering in the desert, living in temporary shelters. The Hebrew word for this festival is *sukkot* and means "booths." The shelter (*sukkah*) could be built of any materials, but its roof had been of organic material and partially open to the sky. The decor of the interior of the *sukkah* could range from totally unornamented to lavishly decoration.

Sukkot, or the Feast of Tabernacles, is one of the three great pilgrimage feasts recorded in the Bible when all Jewish males were required to appear before the Lord in the temple in Jerusalem. Throughout the holiday, Jews today continue to observe this time by building and dwelling in temporary shelters in their backyards, just like the Hebrew people did while wandering in the desert. This joyous celebration is a reminder of God's protection, provision, and faithfulness.

As part of the ceremony, a priest would draw water from the pool of Siloam and carry it to the temple where it was poured into a silver basin beside the altar. The priest would call upon the Lord to provide heavenly water in the form of rain for their supply. During this ceremony the people looked forward to the pouring out of the Holy Spirit (cf. Joel 2:28–29).

Another part of the Feast of Tabernacles was the lamp-lighting ceremony. Every evening during the feast, a priest would light three huge torches on the lampstand in the temple courts to commemorate God's leading of their ancestors through the pillar of fire in the wilderness (Exod 13:21–22). People who gathered in the temple courts would also bring smaller torches and light them, and sometimes sing and dance all through the night. They probably sang, "Give thanks to the Lord, for he is good; his love endures forever" (Ps 118:1). Perhaps the entire temple courts were brightened with the three huge flames on the lamps and numerous smaller torches.

Jesus attended the Feast of Tabernacles and spoke these amazing words on the last and greatest day of the Feast: "If anyone is thirsty, let him come to me and drink. Whoever believes in me, as the Scripture has said, streams of living water will flow from within him" (John 7:37–38 NIV). The next morning, while the torches were still burning, Jesus said, "I am the light of the world. Whoever follows me will never walk in darkness, but will have the light of life" (John 8:12 NIV).

Associated with this feast was the Feast of Dedication. This was also an eight-day festival commemorating the cleansing of the temple and altar by Judas Maccabaeus three years after their defilement by Antiochus

Epiphanes. The prominent feature of illuminations in the festival gave it the name Feast of Lights. The observance of the Feast of Tabernacles is recorded in Exodus 23:16; 34:22; Leviticus 23:34-43; Numbers 29:12-40; Deuteronomy 16:13-15; Ezra 3:4; and Nehemiah 8:13-18.

Praise in the Temple

Information about the temple built by Solomon is found in 1 Kings 6-7 and 1 Chronicles 3-4. It was designed as a permanent house for God, not a building to hold large numbers of people. The temple measured about 90 feet long by 30 feet wide and 45 feet high. The First Temple was divided into two sections, with part of the inner section curtained off to form the sanctuary. In front was a large entrance porch, and along the sides were storerooms.

Music in the First Temple

The Hebrew Bible has little solid information about the use of music in the First Temple. The main passages that contain references to music are 1 Kings 10, the first 39 chapters of Isaiah, the book of Amos, and several passages in the psalms. The Chronicles contain a large quantity of information about music in the First Temple, but the first temple was destroyed in 720 BCE and many scholars believe 1 Chronicles was written about 350 BCE. This span of 250 years between the end of the First Temple era and the time of the writing of 1 Chronicles calls into question the credibility of Chronicles as far as musical practices are concerned. None of the music used in the temple was written down, so we will never know much about it. Apart from knowing the Levites were in charge of worship and the people sang with instrumental accompaniment, we have no certainty.

Apparently, Solomon did not change the existing music practice established by David his father (2 Chr 7:6, 8:14) though he did have some lyres and harps made for the singers (2 Chr 9:11). When the temple was finished, Solomon brought the Covenant Box, the Tent of the Lord's Presence and all of its equipment into the temple. Then Solomon called all the people together before the Covenant Box, and the Levites began the musical part of the service.

We find David's music academy at its historical height.

> The priests of every group had gone through the ceremony to make themselves clean and acceptable to the LORD. The Levite musicians, including Asaph, Heman, Jeduthun, and their sons

and relatives, were wearing robes of fine linen. They were standing on the east side of the altar, playing cymbals, small harps, and other stringed instruments. One hundred twenty priests were with these musicians, and they were blowing trumpets. They were praising the LORD by playing music and singing: "The LORD is good, and his love never ends." Suddenly a cloud filled the Temple as the priests were leaving the holy place. The LORD's glory was in that cloud, and the light from it was so bright that the priests could not stay inside to do their work. (2 Chr 5:11–14 CEV)

The temple emphasized God's presence: "Then have them make a sanctuary for me, and I will dwell among them" (Exod 25:8; *cf.* 2 Chr 6:7; Ezek 43:7). The sacrifices were the constant reminder of the ratification of the Sinai covenant and was a demonstration that Israel was to be separate from the surrounding culture.

The temple also had a symbolic character, ordained by God (1 Chr 28:19). The space used for worship was considered to be sacred, and the arrangement of the outer court, inner court, and Holy of Holies indicated the people were separated from a holy God. The furniture in the temple, such as the altar, lamp stands, incense, the laver, Bread of Presence, and Covenant Box all pointed to an encounter with God. There was nothing in furniture or arrangement of space that was selected at random or placed in a haphazard position.[15]

Temple worship was for all of Israel and not just for the Levites who were in charge of services. In the temple sanctuary Israelite worshipers could join with others, and in response to God's presence, sing a psalm in unison or antiphonally, they could shout words of praise or dance, and they could respond with litanies.

The basic instrumental ensemble used in temple music was probably harps, psalteries and cymbals (kinnor, nevel and metsiltaim). This professional ensemble had developed during the processions and festivities of the transfer of the Covenant Box from Shilo to Jerusalem by King David (1 Chr 16:5).

> When the Maccabees restored the rituals in the temple like in David's time, on he twenty-fifth day of the ninth month, the month of Kislev, in the year 148 . . . the anniversary of the day the Gentiles had desecrated the altar. On that day a sacrifice was offered on the new altar in accordance with the Law of Moses.

---

15. See Hurowitz, "YHWH's Exalted House," 63–110.

The new altar was dedicated and hymns were sung to the accompaniment of harps, lutes, and cymbals. (1 Macc 4:52–54)

The music was festive and the sound of some of the instruments played was very loud. Sources in the Talmud refer to the great sounds in the temple that were heard all the way from Jerusalem to Jericho.[16] The musicians sought to have an instrumental balance much like an orchestral director today would want. As with the modern orchestra, this was achieved by restricting the number of each instrument in the ensemble. Sources in the Mishna, the collection of mostly halakic Jewish traditions compiled about 200 CE and made the basic part of the Talmud, state that in the temple there should be between two to six psalters, two to twelve flutes, and no less than two trumpets, and nine harps, but only one cymbal.[17]

Temple musicians had their own ways of making contrast in music. One was using voices of different qualities and registers; another was by antiphony, a "question-and-answer" form of singing. Likely this was taken over from secular usage, in line with the tendency for secular practice to be incorporated into religion.

What did temple music sound like? It is impossible to say with certainty. However, there is evidence that the scale used by the ancient Israelites would correspond to our modern diatonic scale made up of seven pitches, rather than the pentatonic scale prominent today in the Middle East. Part of this evidence comes from the research into the ancient Ugaritic tablets that were discussed earlier and the work of Suzanne Haïk-Vantoura, though some scholars question both the research and the conclusions reached.

Our ears probably would not find this music sounding too strange, but these ancient scales were not tuned like present-day scales. There was no universal tuning in the ancient world and some notes might sound slightly out of tune to us because of this. Two kinnors playing together might sound slightly out of tune and a slight variance of distance between the finger holes of wind instruments could make a scale sound slightly out of tune as well as an ensemble sound a little out of tune.

The music in biblical times was based on the principle of cantillation and improvisation, guided by signs originally devised as textual accents, punctuations, and indications of emphasis. Their musical interpretation was dependent on a knowledge of the oral tradition through which the melodic formulae are transmitted. Today, cantillation refers almost exclusively to the ritual chanting of readings from the Hebrew Bible in American synagogue services. The chants are written and notated in accordance with the special

---

16. Shaked, "Music in the Bible."
17. Shaked, "Music in the Bible."

signs or marks printed in the Masoretic text of the Hebrew Bible to complement the letters and vowel points.[18]

A song was composed of short melodic formulas that were combined through improvisation and according to strict and complex artistic rules. We find an indicator of this procedure in a number of songs in the Scriptures that clearly appear to be put together from several earlier passages. For example, in David's prayer of dedication as the ark was set inside the tent at Jerusalem (1 Chr 16:8–36) we find a composite of Psalm 105 (vv. 1–15), Psalm 96 (vv. 2–13), and Psalm 106 (vv. 1, 47, and 48). This way of composing would require years of apprenticeship and training.

The music was then transmitted by the worship leader to the congregation, the singers and instrumentalists by rote, using hand signals (chironomy) to indicate the contour of the melody. This became especially formalized in the cantillation of the Torah, which was chanted in regular intervals every Monday and Thursday (the market days in Jerusalem) and on the Sabbath, as well as on the holy days.[19]

Music in the Second Temple

Following the tragic destruction of the Second Temple in 70 CE, the entire musical legacy of the temple, both vocal and instrumental, seemed to be forever lost. However, these hand signs were eventually systematized and transcribed by Aaron ben Asher in Tiberias in the ninth century CE. During the tenth century CE, at about the same time Western notation was starting to appear, this method of oral transmission was progressively replaced by written accent signs added above the Hebrew text by the Masoretes. These men were scribes and Bible scholars, based primarily in the Hebrew cities of Tiberias and Jerusalem, as well as in Babylonia, working between the seventh and eleventh centuries CE. The Masoretic Text is still the oldest complete copy of the Hebrew Bible that we have.[20]

Part of the reading tradition the Masoretes had preserved was a series of accents (te'amim), which occur throughout the entire Old Testament. The Masoretes did not realize the meaning or the significance of these accents, and for centuries there have been countless theories as to what their original meaning was. Most theories have started from the assumption that they were to emphasize precise points of grammar in the text.

---

18. Doukhan, "Music in the Bible," 19–20.
19. Doukhan, "Music in the Bible," 19–20.
20. Doukhan, "Music in the Bible," 23.

Leaving all these debates aside, Suzanne Haïk-Vantoura, a French musicologist, who was also Jewish, concentrated only on finding a musical meaning of these accents. Noticing the marks in the version of the Hebrew Bible she used to read, Miss Vantoura read in an encyclopedia that these signs of cantillation dated back to antiquity and that their real musical meaning was lost. This triggered her curiosity. Through countless experiments and a laborious process, she finally realized that all these symbols represent musical tones: the degrees of a scale, or else ornaments of one to three notes. The accents were, in fact, representations of hand gestures that had been used in ancient Egyptian music to denote both the pitch and the ornamentation of a melody. This is the system of hand gestures mentioned earlier that is known as chironomy.[21]

From research done on the Ugarit tablets and the psalm hand signs, we can assume there was some simultaneous sounding of notes that would form harmony, but not harmony in the way we think of harmony. In addition, archaeologists have uncovered pictures of harpists that show the player with both hands on two different strings, so some simultaneous sounding of notes is very likely.

Songs of the Temple

The basic worship materials for temple worship was the book of Psalms that contains praises, prayers, litanies, and meditations of Israel set to poetic form. The name of the book is derived from the Greek psalmos (plural psalmoi), which signifies primarily playing on a stringed instrument, and secondarily the composition played or the song accompanied on such an instrument. The book of Psalms is really more than one book, for it is divided into five books:

1. Psalm 1 through 41 (all except four attributed to David).
2. Psalm 42 through 72 (eighteen attributed to David).
3. Psalm 73 through 89 (one attributed to David).
4. Psalm 90 through 106 (two attributed to David).
5. Psalm 107 through 150 (fifteen attributed to David).

Each of these books ends with a doxology, and Psalm 150 forms a doxology for the entire Psalter. There are other groupings such as the Hallel (Pss 113–118), sung at the Passover and other festivals and the Songs of Ascent

---

21. Haïk-Vantoura, *Music of the Bible Revealed*.

(Pss 120–134) individual songs that were sung on the way to the temple. The final collection of materials put into the Psalter, as we know it, grew out of a long, partly obscure history. As years went by, some materials would be added and other materials would be omitted. The earliest texts would be those written and collected by David, and later collections would be those written by Asaph and the sons of Korah.

Authors of the Psalms

Though the psalm titles designate David himself as the author of seventy-three of the psalms, we have seen that the Levitical families assigned to musical service in the temple are associated with many of the other songs. The sons of Korah (1 Chr 6:31–38, 2 Chr 20:19) are responsible for Psalms 42, 44–49, 84, 87 and 88.

It is possible some psalms were written by unknown authors, and David's name was attached to lend credence and acceptability to the psalm. Psalm writing did not begin with David but was newly developed by him. I think we can assume that the Israelites must have been influenced by the hymns and psalms of the Babylonians and the Egyptians when they dwelt with these peoples. It would be impossible to determine who wrote the first psalm, but the form goes back to the beginning of Hebrew poetry.

Over forty references are made to the temple musicians in the books of Chronicles, and 1 Chronicles 25 refers to musicians who were to prophesy with music:

> David, together with the commanders of the army, set apart some of the sons of Asaph, Heman and Jeduthun for the ministry of prophesying, accompanied by harps, lyres and cymbals. (v. 1 NIV)

Many Old Testament scholars from different theological traditions refer to prophetic guilds attached to the temple who were responsible for the production of inspired psalmody. These men wrote psalms that were considered by the Hebrew people to be God's word to them. You could think of Asaph the prophet, whose sons could easily be his guild or school of prophets (1 Chr 25:2). Ross is of the opinion that there is no doubt the sons were offspring of Asaph, but the term could also mean guilds or schools these men formed.[22] The title of prophet given to Asaph in 2 Chronicles 29:30 could relate to his position of making music in the temple:

---

22. Ross, *Recalling the Hope of Glory*, 255–57.

> The king and the leaders of the nation told the Levites to sing to the Lord the songs of praise that were written by David and by Asaph the prophet. So, everyone sang with great joy as they knelt and worshipped God.

Psalm Titles

Many of the psalms have titles that give direction as to what instrument should be used. A few folk tunes were used as psalm tunes for everyone knew these secular tunes. Authorities have given different interpretations to the meaning of the Hebrew titles to the psalms. It is uncertain who wrote the titles, but it is ascertained that the compiler wrote the titles in the very earliest of psalter compilation as directions for playing and singing. Some psalms are signed "the Chief Musician" who could be either Asaph or David. The comment in 1 Chronicles 15:22 that Chenaniah should direct the music "for he understood it" seems to suggest there was some type of theoretical basis for the music and a body of song repertoire to be used in worship.

The meanings of certain psalm titles are difficult to translate. One difficult word in the psalms is *selah*. Nearly every biblical commentary gives a different possible meaning of the world. Since the psalms are actually songs set to music, many scholars concluded that it was not a sung word, but referred to directions for the accompanying musicians. However, in her book, *The Music of the Bible Revealed*, Suzanne Haïk-Vantoura, offered a different view. She stated that *selah* was not an instruction for musicians. She concluded that *selah* is part of the lyrics. No formal definition is given for selah, but she believed it was like the amen at the close of prayer. Selah stressed the importance or reality of what was said.[23]

It is interesting that this word, *selah*, was a focus of considerable speculation by a number of fourth- and fifth-century church fathers. They understood the term to refer to musical directions involving a pause, a modulation of voice, a change in instrumentation, or a change of meter or rhythm or melody. In Pope Gregory's mind, it was a reminder to singers and readers that they should pause and leave room for further inspiration of the Holy Spirit.[24]

---

23. Wright, "Jerusalem in the New Testament," 55.

24. Knust and Wasserman, "Biblical Odes," 351. See also Hurowitz, "YHWH's Exalted House," 66–110.

Old Testament Canticles

There are songs in the Old Testament that are not psalms. These songs are called canticles and are liturgical hymns. Taken from the books of the Old Testament other than the book of Psalms, canticles resemble the psalms in form and content. The canticles have a long tradition in the liturgy of the church, standing beside the psalms as a lyrical witness to God's goodness. The canticles more commonly used are those of

- Moses (Exod 15:1–18, Deut 32:1–43).
- Hannah (1 Sam 2:1–10).
- Isaiah (12:2–6, 20:1–6, 45:15–25, 55:6–11).
- Hezekiah (quoted in Isa 38:10–20).
- Jeremiah (31:1–10).
- Ezekiel (36:24–28).
- Habakkuk (3:2–19).

The Order of Temple Worship

We are not certain what order of worship was observed in the time of Solomon. Williamson[25] thinks the words of Isaiah 6:3, "Holy, holy, holy! The LORD Almighty is holy! His glory fills the world" could have been based upon some aspect of the regular liturgy of Isaiah's temple. We do know that worship was centered around the annual festivals that involved a pilgrimage to the temple (Ps 81:3, 122:1–4). This was still the practice as described in the Gospels. Temple worship in the time of Jesus was conducted daily and the temple was always open.

The actual daily service was varied according to different seasons and days. The titles of several psalm imply that certain tunes and instrument were to be used at specific times. The people sang from the psalms, accompanied by lyre and harp. Not less than two or more than six harps were to be used and not less than nine lyres, but there was no limit to the number of lyres. Two large silver trumpets were used, chiefly for announcing portions of the service (cf. Num 10). Apparently, there was a pair of large brass cymbals to which Paul referred in I Corinthians 13 as "sounding brass" and "tinkling cymbal." Possibly they were used to announce the beginning of the service.

---

25. Williamson, "Temple and Worship in Isaiah 6."

The sacred rituals were visible and tangible expressions of the relationship between the Hebrews and Yahweh. There were rules for the sacrifices and there were sacrifices for various occasions and situations. For example, there were burnt offerings, fellowship offerings, sin offerings, and trespass offerings. All of these grew out of the Sinai Event and point to the sacrifice the Christ was to make in the future (see Heb 10).[26] Temple worship features visible, outward actions such as bowing down (Ps 95:6, 138:2), lifting the hands (Ps 63:4, 134:2), clapping (Ps 47:1), or the festal shout (Ps 47:5, 89:15, and 100:1. Various movements of the people were included, primarily processions accompanied by dance (Ps 68:24–25, 100:4, 149:3, 150:4). There are indications that the Ark was carried in procession to symbolize Yahweh's ascension to his holy mountain and entrance into the sanctuary as king over his people (Ps 24:7, 47:5, 132:8).

The Shema

At some point in the service the priests recited the Shema, which is a declaration of faith in one God. The obligation to recite the Shema is separate from the obligation to pray and a Jew is obligated to say the prayer in the morning and at night. Originally, the Shema consisted only of one verse: Deuteronomy 6:4. In the development of the liturgy the prayer was expanded to three paragraphs from Deuteronomy 6:4–9, 11:13–21; and Numbers 15:37–41.

Worshipers pledge their allegiance to Yahweh, the great King and only God in an act of renewal of some kind. The Hebrew word translated "give thanks" (1 Chr 16:34; Pss 118:1, 136:1) and "thanksgiving" (Pss 100:4, 147:7), so common in Israelite worship, describes the worshiper's lifting his or her hands in affirmation, or confession, of loyalty to Yahweh. The worshiper pledges commitment with expressions similar to "You are my God" (Pss 16:2, 31:14, 140:6) or "I am your servant" (69:17, 116:16, 143:12).

Temple Musicians

Our biblical sources do not indicate women had any function at all in temple worship. Those who are mentioned are men, and that would be normal in a male-dominated society. Smith believes that

> it is a reasonable assumption that the musicians at the sacrificial rites were men . . . female participation in the offering of

---

26. Shaked, "Music in the Bible."

sacrifice to the Deity, the central act of the cult, would have been unlikely. The musicians were therefore probably men. The musicians at non-sacrificial rites . . . were not exclusively male. This is shown, for example, by Psalm 68:26, where the psalmist lists the participants in processions as "singers," "players," and "maidens, young girls who played hand drums."[27]

Psalm 137:2–6 gives us evidence that singing in the temple was accompanied by harps and that the instrumentalists sang as they played. These musicians may have been temple musicians prior to their captivity.

> On the willows nearby
> we hung up our harps.
> Those who captured us told us to sing;
> They told us to entertain them:
> "Sing us a song about Zion."
> How can we sing a song to the LORD
> in a foreign land?
> May I never be able to play the harp again
> if I forget you, Jerusalem!
> May I never be able to sing again
> if I do not remember you,
> if I do not think of you as my greatest joy!

Tambourines accompany dancing. String instruments of several types accompany singing, and praise is amplified with percussion instruments such as cymbals

Temple Singing

Singing was both vocal and choral; refusing to sing was not an option for temple worship. Throughout the psalms we find calls for the worshiper to "Sing joyfully to the LORD, you righteous" (cf. Ps 31:1) and the response "I will sing to the Lord." Among the many instructions on how to sing we find these: "Sing praise to the LORD, who rules in Zion!" (Ps 9:11); "sing to him with stringed instruments" (Ps 33:2); and "Sing a new song to him, play the harp with skill, and shout for joy!" (Ps 33:3).

---

27. Smith, *Music in Ancient Judaism*, 86.

We also find the happy responses of worshipers, such as: "I will sing with joy because of you. I will sing praise to you, Almighty God" (Ps 9:2). "But I will sing about your strength; every morning I will sing aloud of your constant love" (Ps 59:16). "I will shout for joy as I play for you; with my whole being I will sing because you have saved me (Ps 71:23). "O LORD, I will always sing of your constant love; I will proclaim your faithfulness forever" (Ps 89:1).

Singing could be antiphonal; that is, a response by the congregation to something sung by a choir or worship leader, such in Psalm 20:1–9. The king sings/speaks verses 1–4:

> May the LORD answer you when you are in trouble! May the God of Jacob protect you! May he send you help from his Temple and give you aid from Mount Zion. May he accept all your offerings and be pleased with all your sacrifices. May he give you what you desire and make all your plans succeed.

The congregation sings/recites verse 5:

> Then we will shout for joy over your victory and celebrate your triumph by praising our God. May the LORD answer all your requests.

The king sings/recites verses 6–8:

> Now I know that the LORD gives victory to his chosen king; he answers him from his holy heaven and by his power gives him great victories. Some trust in their war chariots and others in their horses, but we trust in the power of the LORD our God. Such people will stumble and fall, but we will rise and stand firm.

The Congregation sings/recites verse 9:

> Give victory to the king, O LORD; answer us when we call.

Several psalms have refrains or are prefaced by the word *hallelujah* that was used as a refrain. This probably means they were sung responsorial style. This kind of singing could be done away from the temple, but without instrumental accompaniment. "Some interpreters," states Leonard, "believe that the 'new song' (Pss 33:3, 96:1, 149:1), and the word *selah* often mentioned in the psalms, refer to outbreaks of improvised praise." According to Leonard, Hebrew songs probably were "a blend of prescribed structure and improvised expression." Worship incorporates extended praise, both structured and spontaneous, with no indication of time limitations. Psalms were performed according to certain prescribed musical pattern, some of which may be reflected in many of the superscriptions of the psalms. At the same time there was room for spontaneity.[28]

Litanies and Shouting

A litany is a series of praises or petitions that are recited by the worship leader and responded to in a recurring word or phrase by the congregation. Psalm 136 is an excellent example of a litany. After every line of text, the congregation would repeat "His love endures forever." There are many references to people shouting "hallelujah" or "amen" during worship. While it is not music technically, shouting is a congregational response.

Physical Responses

The Psalms give us all kinds of information about responding to God with the whole body, such as lifting the hands in prayer and adoration: "Raise your hands in prayer in the Temple, and praise the LORD!" (Ps 134:2). Clapping hands in joy and celebration: "Clap your hands for joy, all peoples!" (Ps 47:1a). "Praise his name by dancing . . ." (Ps 149:3a).

Climax and Blessing

God speaks through prophetic utterance, taking the people to task for unfaithfulness and calling them to rededicate themselves to the Lord (Pss 46:10, 50:7, 85:8). There is a climax where the Lord "appears" or "comes" in some way, perhaps in the ceremonial recitation of the covenant. Several psalms proclaim this manifestation of God's presence (e.g., 50:2, 67:1, 80:7, 96:13). A blessing is pronounced upon the worshipers, perhaps as an act of dismissal (Pss 24:5, 91:1–15, 112:1, 133:3).

The Prophets and Song

The root form of the Hebrew word for prophet"(*navi*') means to "announce" or "forth-tell." The prophets were spokesmen for God. Their task was that of statesman and moral teacher, religion having become a national more than an individual matter. This is not to say that the prophets were unconcerned with individuals. In fact, they were very much concerned with translating

---

28. Leonard, "Davidic Worship."

the requirements of the law into personal terms. The emphases and methods of the prophets changed as national conditions changed.

Since the time of the earliest prophets of Israel, the followers of Yahweh have been concerned about the power of music to affect human emotion and behavior. The earliest of these prophets were ecstatics who wandered about the country under a leader, gathering crowds with their music and furious dancing. This was done to stimulate religious fervor in themselves and to influence the onlookers in the strongest possible way. Later prophets used varied methods for conveying their revelations from God. Three literary forms were speeches or sermons, poems, and lamentations. In many instances, the prophetic messages were sung as well as spoken, continuing the practices of the earlier nevi'im. Hebrew poetry rhymes thoughts rather than sounds, and the poetic structure of the prophets (and the Psalms) is evident in modern English translations of the Bible, for the text will look like poetry rather than prose.

Two times music is associated with prophetic pronouncements. One is when King Saul was told he would meet a group of prophets "coming down from the altar on the hill, playing harps, drums, flutes, and lyres. They will be dancing and shouting" (1 Sam 10:5). The second is when the prophet Elisha is consulted by the kings of Israel, Judah and Edom, and he requests, "Now get me a musician." As the musician played his harp, "the power of the LORD came on Elisha . . ." (2 Kgs 3:15). The practice of prophesying to the accompaniment of instruments might be the context of this passage in Ezekiel 33:32 where God is warning the prophet how his message will be received:

> So my people crowd in to hear what you have to say, but they don't do what you tell them to do. Loving words are on their lips, but they continue their greedy ways. 32 To them you are nothing more than an entertainer singing love songs or playing a harp. They listen to all your words and don't obey a single one of them.

The Prophet Amos

Amos condemned the profaning of Solomon's Temple and warned of God's impending judgment on the Israelites. However, he was not condemning temple worship in and of itself. He was condemning the wrong attitude in worship and the assumption by the people that God was pleased because they supported temple ceremonies. By looking at what he condemned, we can get an idea of some of the things that were included in temple worship. For example,

> The Sovereign Lord says, "People of Israel, go to the holy place in Bethel and sin, if you must! Go to Gilgal and sin with all your might! Go ahead and bring animals to be sacrificed morning after morning, and bring your tithes every third day. Go on and offer your bread in thanksgiving to God, and brag about the extra offerings you bring! This is the kind of thing you love to do (Amos 4:4–5).

This indicates that animals were offered for sacrifice in the morning and tithes were brought every third day. Though the bread of thanksgiving, extra offerings, songs, burnt offerings, and grain offerings were a part of temple worship, we have no idea of their frequency. Note, too, that reference is made to Bethel and Gigal as other places of sacrificial worship.

> The Lord says, "I hate your religious festivals; I cannot stand them! When you bring me burnt offerings and grain offerings, I will not accept them; I will not accept the animals you have fattened to bring me as offerings. Stop your noisy songs; I do not want to listen to your harps. Instead, let justice flow like a stream, and righteousness like a river that never goes dry. (Amos 5:21–24).

For Amos, social justice and righteousness is more important before God than sacrifices.

The Second Temple Prophets

The Babylonian captivity had a great effect upon the lives, religious beliefs, and music practices of the Israelites. References to music in the book of Daniel show the influence of Babylonian music. In Daniel 3 are listed instruments named in Aramaic rather than Hebrew and they likely were similar, but not identical to, wind and string instruments used by the Jews.

The Jews were able to return to their homeland in 537 BCE after the overthrow of Babylon by Persia. A caravan of fifty thousand people began the journey back to Jerusalem and the rebuilding of the temple was started. It was finished in 516 BCE. Ezra 3:8–13 gives the details of the return home with instruments and singing. Among those returning were "two hundred male and female singers" (Ezra 2:65).

Nehemiah 12 gives the details of the dedication of the rebuilt temple. The musicians were divided into two groups; one group with instruments went to the right and one group, possibly singers, went to the left around the walls. The dedication was one of great pomp and ceremony.

> The Temple musicians and the Temple guards also performed their duties in accordance with the regulations made by King David and his son Solomon. From the time of King David and the musician Asaph long ago, the musicians have led songs of praise and thanksgiving to God. In the time of Zerubbabel and also in the time of Nehemiah, all the people of Israel gave daily gifts for the support of the Temple musicians and the Temple guards. The people gave a sacred offering to the Levites, and the Levites gave the required portion to the priests. (Neh 12:45–47)

The Prophet Malachi

By now, the temple was rebuilt, sacrifice and feasts had resumed; but the dramatic promises of the prophets like Haggai and Zechariah were still far from fulfillment. Unfortunately, this worship soon degenerated and was not acceptable to God as described in Malachi 1–2. In these chapters Malachi gives a harsh condemnation of contemporary worship practices. Worship was so repugnant that God wanted someone to close the doors of the temple so worship would cease. The people assumed that whatever pleased them would also please God.

What did Malachi see wrong with this worship? Had not the long years of captivity in Babylon taught the Jews the necessity of worshipping the Lord God? Now the captives were back home, Jerusalem had her walls rebuilt, and the temple and its worship system had been reestablished. What could be wrong? Malachi had a list of their offenses against God: the priests were offering improper sacrifices to God; they kept the best animals for themselves and offered God poor creatures.

> When you bring a blind or sick or lame animal to sacrifice to me, do you think there's nothing wrong with that? Try giving an animal like that to the governor! Would he be pleased with you or grant you any favors? (Mal 1:8)

The priests had failed in their task of instructing the people in righteousness:

> It is the duty of priests to teach the true knowledge of God. People should go to them to learn my will because they are the messengers of the Lord Almighty. But now you priests have turned away from the right path. Your teaching has led many

to do wrong. You have broken the covenant I made with you. (Mal 2:7-8)

They prayed, but God would not hear unless their hearts were right. They had laws to obey, but were disobedient. They refused to listen to God, they had defiled the temple with their marriage practices, and they refused to give a tangible expression of their love for God through their financial giving.

> You drown the Lord's altar with tears, weeping and wailing because he no longer accepts the offerings you bring him. You ask why he no longer accepts them. It is because he knows you have broken your promise to the wife you married when you were young. (Mal 2:13b-14)

Worship practices were so bad that God said, "I wish one of you would close the Temple doors so as to prevent you from lighting useless fires on my altar" (Mal 1:10).

Traditionally, the number of years between the book of Malachi and the book of Matthew is considered to cover roughly four hundred years, spanning the ministry of Malachi (c. 420 BCE) to the appearance of John the Baptist in the early first century CE, almost the same as the Second Temple period (530 BCE to 70 CE).

Around 19 BCE, Herod the Great began a massive renovation and expansion of the Second Temple area. The temple itself was torn down and a new one built in its place. The resulting structure is sometimes referred to as Herod's Temple, but it is still called the Second Temple because the sacrificial rituals continued without interruption throughout the construction process. This is the temple of the New Testament.

For You to Think about

1. Read the following passages that relate to the conquest of the southern kingdom in 586 BC: 2 Kings 25 and Jeremiah 35-47.
   - In what way do Psalms 74, 80 and 137 refer to this event? Be specific in your answers by referring to descriptive items in the psalms.
   - Why would this conquest be celebrated in worship?
2. What biblical principles can you infer for the use of musical instruments in worship today? Why or why not are these principles valid only for the Old Testament?

3

Congregational Song in the New Testament

> The New Testament begins and ends
> with outbursts of song.[1]

THE NEW TESTAMENT BOOKS are not primarily theological and historical treatises. Worship leaders should see the New Testament as books that are primarily addressed to worshipping communities. The books were composed, circulated, and read with the spiritual needs of the early believers always in view. References and quotations related to worship are scattered throughout the New Testament. As McGowan has so well stated,

> It should not . . . come as a surprise that words usually translated as "worship" in English versions of the New Testament are not primarily concerned with the conduct of Christian assemblies or communal rituals. Like their equivalent in the Hebrew Bible, these terms are concerned either with reverence and obedience or with bodily performances that enacted them . . .[2]

McGowan states that words commonly translated "worship" in both the Old and New Testaments are related to prostration. In Matthew 28:17 our translations read, "When they saw him (the risen Christ) they worshipped him . . ." McGowan notes that the disciples are not "singing, reciting prayer, or (only) experiencing a feeling or attitude; they are flat on their faces."[3]

> We cannot find a liturgy in the New Testament. What we do find is evidence of worship practices that became a fixed part of

---

1. Stapert, *New Song*, 14.
2. McGowan, *Ancient Christian Worship*, 6.
3. McGowan, *Ancient Christian Worship*, 6.

church worship in the late first and early second centuries and became the ideal forms of Christian worship along with "what kind of implied authority was deemed appropriate to establish it."[4]

The Influence of Temple and Synagogue

The two centers of worship in the New Testament gospels are the synagogue and temple. The origin of the synagogue is obscure and contemporary scholarship is divided over the identity of the synagogue and when it became an important worship center. Earlier, scholars had placed the synagogue within the Babylonian captivity when the Jews were separated from the temple and its sacrifices. Their view was that since the temple had been destroyed and thousands of Jews were taken into captivity, a new means of worship had to be devised, so the synagogue fulfilled that purpose. Since this occurred again following the destruction of the Second Temple in 70 CE, other scholars think the synagogue was a later development. Consequently, there is a danger of reading back into the New Testament worship practices that developed after 70 CE.[5] In addition to serving as a place of worship, the synagogue was a public social hall that gave identity to the Jews and enabled them to maintain the nonsacrificial aspects of the Law.

Jesus and the Synagogue

In Luke 4:16, Jesus is described as entering into the synagogue, "as his custom was." Not only is it recorded that he went there, but he also taught, preached, healed, and expounded the Scriptures in the synagogue. The stage for several confrontations between Jesus and the Jewish leadership of his day was the synagogue (Matt 12:9–13; Mark 1:21–28; 3:1–6; Luke 6:1–11). He taught in them (Matt 13:54), healed in them (Luke 4:33–35; Mark 3:1–5), and debated the interpretation of Torah in them (John 6:28–59). On the other hand, Jesus participated in the synagogue services by reading and teaching from the Scriptures:

> When Jesus finished telling these parables, he left that place and went back to his hometown. He taught in the synagogue, and those who heard him were amazed. "Where did he get such wisdom?" they asked. "And what about his miracles? Isn't he the

---

4. McGowan, *Ancient Christian Worship*, 12.

5. Bradshaw, *Search for the Origins*. See chapter 2 for a full discussion. See also Beckwith, "Jewish Backround."

carpenter's son? Isn't Mary his mother, and aren't James, Joseph, Simon, and Judas his brothers? Aren't all his sisters living here? Where did he get all this?" (Matt 13:53–56)

Scholars disagree on the nature of synagogue worship in the first century because information is scarce. The synagogue services were held on Saturdays and feast days. The fact that the synagogue continued after the captivity and after the temple was rebuilt and its services restored is significant.

Synagogue worship probably incorporated many aspects of temple worship, such as fixed prayers (the disciples asked Jesus for one, which resulted in the so-called Lord's Prayer or Model Prayer) and the reciting of the Ten Commandments. The Torah was read every service and the prophets were read as second lessons (Acts 15:21). After the readings followed the sermon (Acts 13:15). Regular times of prayer were observed daily in the synagogue. These set prayer times had existed in the temple and continue to exist in some form in twenty-first-century Catholic churches and monasteries.

The most outstanding features of synagogue worship that were different from temple worship were (1) the synagogue did not provide for sacrifices, and (2) laymen or scribes led the worship in the absence of the priesthood. The leader of worship was the presiding elder or ruler of the synagogue, chosen because of his character and for the esteem in which the Jews held him. Originally these scribes were priests and Levites, but eventually pious laymen devoted their lives to the study of the law. By the time of Jesus, they had become an official religious class of interpreters of the law. Ezra seems to have been the first scribe, or at least the first mentioned, in the Bible (Ezra 7:6; Nehemiah 8:1).[6]

At some point in the service is the reciting of the Shema. The first line of the Shema, "Hear O Israel, the Lord is our God, the Lord is One," (Deut 6:4) is repeated as a response throughout the prayer services. Jesus used the Shema as the beginning exhortation of the first of his two greatest commandments: "Jesus answered, 'The most important one says: "People of Israel, you have only one Lord and God. You must love him with all your heart, soul, mind, and strength"'" (Mark 12:29–30). Then, Jesus adds a verse from Leviticus 19:18: "The second most important commandment says: 'Love others as much as you love yourself. No other commandment is more important than these'" (Mark 12:31).

Jesus also refers to the Shema in John 10:30. A group of Jews in the temple in Jerusalem at the Feast of Dedication, or Hanukkah, asks him if he

---

6. Ross, *Recalling the Hope of Glory*, 356–60.

is Messiah, the anointed one of God. Jesus concludes his response with the words "I am one with the Father." The Jews immediately recognize this is an allusion to the Shema for "Once again the Jewish leaders picked up stones in order to kill Jesus" (John 10:32). Additionally, Paul reworks the Shema in relation to the risen Christ:

> We have only one God, and he is the Father. He created everything, and we live for him. Jesus Christ is our only Lord. Everything was made by him, and by him life was given to us. (1 Cor 8:6)

At some point the readings were related to a sermon, either an exposition of the law or a more devotional type talk. The ruler of the synagogue called on Jesus to speak. In Luke 4:21 Jesus said, "This passage of scripture has come true today, as you heard it being read." It was a most amazing statement, and the people of Nazareth were quick to see that in him, Jesus, they saw the Messiah of prophecy, as the following verses indicate.

Worship in the Second Temple

After a decree by the Persian King Cyrus in 538 BCE, some 50,000 Jews set out on the first return to the Land of Israel, led by Zerubbabel, a descendant of the House of David. One of the first tasks was to rebuild the walls of Jerusalem and to restore the temple and its worship, and it stood on the Temple Mount in Jerusalem from c. 516 BCE to 70 CE. In comparison with Solomon's Temple, the rebuilt temple lacked its grandeur and it underwent many partial renovations. Beginning in 20–19 BCE, the temple was almost completely dismantled, and its rebuilding commenced under Herod the Great. It is sometimes referred to as Herod's Temple and perhaps was completed around 62 CE. This is the temple Jesus knew.

Definitive information about what temple worship was like in the time of Jesus is scarce. According to Smith,[7] there are literary sources that span the years 450 BCE and 200 CE and he sorts them into three groups. The earliest group consists of the books of Psalms, Ezra-Nehemiah and Chronicles, and provides a picture of music at the Second Temple up to around 300 BCE. The second group consists of books in the Apocrypha of the Septuagint[8] that provides details from the last two centuries of the Second Temple. The third group consists of literature written during the time of, and shortly after,

---

7. Smith, *Music in Ancient Judaism*, 106–7.

8. The Septuagint is a Greek version of the Jewish Scriptures translated in the third and second centuries BCE by Jewish scholars for Greek-speaking Jews. This is the Bible the earliest Christians used.

Herod's Temple, and includes works by Josephus, small sections of the New Testament Apocrypha and the Mishnah. Of all the sources, the most valuable are the Mishnah and the literature belonging to the earliest group.[9]

The Mishnah is the collection of oral laws compiled and edited about 200 CE by Rabbi Judah ha-Nasi. Though the temple had been destroyed 130 years prior to its publication, in the world described by the Mishnah, the temple still exists and the laws that governed it are expressed in the present tense. However, there is no way for us to know whether what is being described is actually first-century temple worship.

According to Mishnah Tamid 7.3, worship at the daily sacrifices of burnt offering included a choir of at least twelve men aged between thirty and fifty, together with some Levite boys to "add sweetness to the song." The boys only sang and did not play instruments, and were not counted in the number of serving Levites. Apparently, the adult singers completed a five-year training period before being admitted to the choir.

A variety of instruments were used in the worship. At least two priests played metal trumpets, though that number could be increased for special feast days. There was only one cymbal. There were never less than two harps and never more than six. Never fewer than nine lyres, though their number could be increased indefinitely.

The musicians stood on a platform that divided the Court of the Priests from the Court of Israel. After the day's required sacrifices, a priest would sound the *agraphia*, after which the priests entered the sanctuary and prostrated themselves before the altar while the Levites began their music. Two priests blew the *shofar*, a Levite clashed his cymbal, and the choir began to sing the psalm text for the day or a section from the Pentateuch. At the end of each section, a trumpet sounded and the congregation prostrated themselves.[10]

Jesus and the Temple

Jesus also taught in the temple, attended the temple services, and even commanded a leper whom he had healed to go to the temple and submit to the cleansing rites required by the Mosaic Law (Matt 8:4). Jesus was not antagonistic to the temple as an institution, but he was antagonistic toward the corrupt practices associated with the temple. This explains his cleansing of the temple. Jesus condemned neither the temple nor its elaborate services.

---

9. Smith, *Music in Ancient Judaism*, 106–7.
10. *Tamid*, chapters 5 and 7. Foley, *Foundations of Christian Music*, 30.

Jesus Displaced Temple Worship

Jesus saw himself as the new temple, the place where people meet God. He was "greater than the Temple" (Matt 12:6) and at the Last Supper saw himself as the final sacrifice and Lamb of God.

> While they were eating, Jesus took a piece of bread, gave a prayer of thanks, broke it, and gave it to his disciples. "Take and eat it," he said; "this is my body." Then he took a cup, gave thanks to God, and gave it to them. "Drink it, all of you," he said; "this is my blood, which seals God's covenant, my blood poured out for many for the forgiveness of sins." (Matt 26:26-28)

Perhaps the encounter with the Samaritan woman in John 6:3-43 is the clearest statement Jesus made about the nature of worship. First, there was a discussion about living water versus the water in the well. Jesus very clearly identifies himself as the giver of eternal life:

> Those who drink this water will get thirsty again, but those who drink the water that I will give them will never be thirsty again. The water that I will give them will become in them a spring which will provide them with life-giving water and give them eternal life. (John 4:13-14)

The woman was confused, for Jesus was introducing a spiritual truth that was new to her. As Jesus told her about her personal life, the woman realized he was a prophet:

> "I see you are a prophet, sir," the woman said. "My Samaritan ancestors worshipped God on this mountain, but you Jews say that Jerusalem is the place where we should worship God." (John 4:19-20)

Like the Jews, the Samaritans believed the temple was where the people met God, but believed their temple on Mount Gerizim was the true temple, though it was no longer in existence. The proper place of worship seemed to be the most pressing theological issue for Samaritans. So, the woman wants to hear what this visiting prophet had to say about it. Jesus responded:

> Believe me, woman, the time will come when people will not worship the Father either on this mountain or in Jerusalem ... But the time is coming and is already here, when by the power of God's Spirit people will worship the Father as he really is, offering him the true worship that he wants. God is Spirit, and only by the power of his Spirit can people worship him as he really is. (John 4:21, 23-24)

Jesus directed her attention to the spiritual nature of worship that was not dependent upon physical location. It was not where worship took place; it was how one worshipped that was important. The woman asked Jesus about the Messiah: "I know that the Messiah will come, and when he comes, he will tell us everything" (John 4:25). Jesus responded immediately: "I am he, I who am talking with you" (John 4:26).

It was to this unnamed Samaritan woman that Jesus revealed himself as the Messiah. It is also the first of the "I am" statements in the book of John in which Jesus identified himself with the God who revealed himself to Moses in a burning bush. Jesus was placing himself at the center of a worship that was spiritual and eternal; not limited to time or place.

Jesus Reinterpreted Jewish Temple Worship

Jesus had a lot to say about the way people practiced worship. He had lived under the traditions of the Pharisees as he was growing up. He had seen the self-righteousness, legalism and hypocrisy that the religion of the establishment produced. Jesus had seen people perform righteous acts in order to impress others who were worshipping.

In the Sermon on the Mount, Jesus said when a person gives to those who are in need, they should not "make a big show of it, as the hypocrites do in the houses of worship and on the streets . . . But when you help a needy person, do it in such a way that even your closest friend will not know about it (Matt 6:2–3). Jesus also warned them not to be like the hypocrites, who "love to stand up and pray in the houses of worship and on the street corners, so that everyone will see them . . . But when you pray, go to your room, close the door, and pray to your Father, who is unseen" (Matt 6:5–6).

Neither were worshipers to disfigure their faces when fasting (Matt 6:16). The Law required fasting on certain occasions, like the day of Atonement (Lev 16:29–31; 23:27–32). People could fast at other times whenever a special petition was offered to God. The prophets Isaiah (58:3–7) and Jeremiah (14:12) had criticized hypocritical fasting in the Old Testament.

Jesus repeatedly ran afoul of the religious leaders because he was breaking their traditions. In his arguments, Jesus showed the inconsistencies in the traditions of the leaders. When he was accused of breaking the Sabbath by healing a man with a withered hand on the Sabbath (Luke 6:6–11), Jesus pointed out that it was lawful to pull a sheep out of a pit on the Sabbath; wasn't the life of a human of more value?

At another time, not only did Jesus heal on the Sabbath, he told the man to take up his bed and walk, and that was work which broke Sabbath rules

(John 5:8–18). He healed a woman with an infirmity and responded to criticism by saying, "Any one of you would untie your ox or your donkey from the stall and take it out to give it water on the Sabbath. Now here is this descendant of Abraham whom Satan has kept in bonds for eighteen years; should she not be released on the Sabbath?" (Luke 13:15–16). There were many other disputes, and in these Jesus was trying to show that human need took precedence over man-made rules and interpretations. Rules had turned worship into work and had taken all joy out of worshipping God.[11]

Earlier, in John 2:19, Jesus had said, "Tear down this Temple, and in three days I will build it again." He was referring to his body, but his hearers did not understand this. Later, during his trial before Pilate, this was one of the things Jesus was accused of. Destruction of the temple would be the destruction of religion, as the religious leaders knew it.

One of the most astounding examples of Jesus reinterpreting the worship of the temple is in connection with the Festival of Shelters found in John 7. The feast was a popular festival, rich in symbolism. Each day's activity included a water ceremony in which a procession of priests descended to the south border of the city to the Gihon Spring. There a priest filled a golden pitcher as a choir chanted Isaiah 12:3: "With joy you will draw water from the wells of salvation." The water was then carried back up the hill to the "Water Gate," followed by crowds carrying tree branches in memory of their temporary tents in the desert. The crowd would shake these branches and sing Psalms 113–118. When the procession arrived at the temple, the priest would climb the altar steps and pour the water onto the altar while the crowd circled him and continued singing. On the seventh day of the festival, this procession took place seven times.

Judaism saw this water ceremony on multiple levels. It was a plea to God for rain since the autumn in Israel is a time of threatened drought, and it was a source of rich symbolism. The feast was established as a memorial to the wilderness journey and God's provision of water from a rock. Pouring water over the altar of the temple represented the vision of the prophets Zechariah and Ezekiel who had visions of rivers flowing from the temple in a display of God's blessing (Ezek 47:1; Zech 14:8). Jesus' climatic appearance and astounding words should be understood against this background.

On the final day of celebration, Jesus steps into public view and makes his most stunning pronouncement of the feast. As the seventh water procession climbed the steep hill of south Jerusalem, verse 37 commences. "Now on the last day, the great day of the feast, Jesus stood and cried out, saying, 'If anyone is thirsty, let him come to me and drink.'"

---

11. Burge, *John*, 226–27.

As Robert Webber noted, the worship of the New Testament was born in the crucible of those events surrounding Jesus. These events "were recognized as the fulfillment of the Old Testament prophecies to Israel. At first there was no hint that a new people of God, one including the Gentiles, was being formed because of these events."[12]

New Testament Canticles

A canticle is a religious text, excluding the Psalms, taken from the Bible. The definition can be expanded to include non-biblical texts as well. Many composers have set the biblical canticles to music, creating a variety of moods and versions of each. The *Annunciation* canticle has also been a favorite subject of painters. These famous texts have been used through the centuries in various Christian denominations. We do not know the source of these canticles, but they may have been composed by an unknown person or persons, and used as hymns related to these events. Luke recorded them in his Gospel some sixty to eighty years later, so Luke or someone he knew could have written them. Even if not composed by Luke, they fit in well with themes found throughout Luke: joy and exultation in the Lord; the lowly person being singled out for God's favor; the reversal of human fortunes; and the fulfillment of Old Testament promises.

Neither is anything known about their preservation from their origin until Luke recorded them in his Gospel. The texts may have been preserved by Jewish Christians of Palestine. Or, Mary herself could have preserved the texts or someone near to her. It is possible, of course, that they underwent some elaboration between the time of origin and the time Luke wrote. They may have been used and developed as didactic hymns about the events they celebrate. The texts were written by Luke in Greek, but were translated into Latin by Jerome between 382 and 405 CE. The names of these canticles are taken from the first two words of its Latin version and can be sung in Latin or English as well as other languages.

Magnificat (Luke 1:46–55)

This is Mary's reaction the news that she will bear a son. Her reaction is that of a servant in this psalm of praise. There is no specific connection of the canticle to the context of Mary's pregnancy and her visit to Elizabeth. The loose connection between the hymn and the context is further seen in

---

12. Webber, *Ancient-Future Worship*, 41.

the fact that a few Old Latin manuscripts identify the speaker of the hymn as Elizabeth, even though the overwhelming textual evidence makes Mary the speaker.

The song is modeled on Hannah's prayer in 1 Samuel 2:1–10. Similar songs by women are by Miriam (Exod 15:19–20), Deborah (Judg 5:1–31), and Judith (Jdt 15:1–17).[13]

Benedictus (Luke 1:68–79)

Again, like Mary's canticle, it is largely composed of phrases taken from the Greek Old Testament and may have been a Jewish hymn of praise that Luke adapted to fit the present context by inserting verses 1:76–77 to give Zechariah's reply to the question asked in Luke 1:66: "Everyone who heard of it thought about it and asked, 'What is this child going to be?' For it was plain that the Lord's power was upon him."

Gloria in Excelsis Deo (Luke 2:14)

The text of the song begins with a slight variation on the words said by the angels as part of the announcement of the birth of Jesus to the shepherds in the field in Luke 2:14. The Latin Bible translated by Jerome uses *altissimis* (generally meaning "physically highest") instead of *excelsis* (meaning "lofty" or "high"). The song continues with verses added to make a proper doxology:

> Glory to God in the highest, and on earth peace
> to people of good will.
>
> We praise you.
>
> We bless you.
>
> We adore you.
>
> We glorify you.
>
> We give thanks to you for your great glory.
>
> Etc.

---

13. The book of Judith is part of the Apocrypha Scripture and appears in the Old Testament of Catholic Bibles. The nation of Israel treated the apocryphal books with respect, but never accepted them as true books of the Hebrew Bible. The early Christian church debated the status of the apocryphal books, but few early Christians believed they belonged in the canon of Scripture.

Nunc dimittis (Luke 2:29–32)

The *Nunc dimittis* is a canticle celebrating salvation that is sung by some Christian churches during evening services. The occasion is the presentation of the infant Jesus in Jerusalem. God has told a devout Jew named Simeon that he would not die until he saw the Savior; the *Nunc dimittis* puts the words of Simeon upon seeing the infant Jesus to song. It begins with the phrase *Nunc dimittis, servum tuum*, "now you have dismissed your servant," and continues with words of praise and joy.

Congregational Song in Acts, the Epistles, and Revelation

Nowhere do we find an order for worship in the New Testament, but we can find some clues of how the early churches worshipped. As we shall see in the following chapter, there are early documents that describe worship in the late first century and second century. However, in New Testament churches there was no fixed ordering of worship that all churches used. Differences in worship practices are related to the location of churches and the culture of their various communities.

We have no actual music that was used in the New Testament era, but we have plenty of evidence that music was used. Singing as part of worship is evident in Acts 16:53, that tells us Paul and Silas sang in the Philippian Jail and James 5:13 admonishes those who are merry to "sing psalms;" so, there must have been some song material available. The New Testament does preserve texts that may have been sung, but we can only speculate about what that music sounded like.

Not everything was spontaneous in worship. It is evident that there were worship materials that the churches used for teaching and singing. Where did they get those materials? We really don't know for certain, for the Greek translation of the Old Testament was the only Bible early Christians had and few, if any, personal copies of Scripture would be available. Many New Testament scriptural quotations are combinations of Old Testament passages, so it is possible that these combined passages were designed for the training of new gentile converts who would have little or no knowledge of the Old Testament. In addition, there were New Testament canticles, confessions and creeds, and hymns available both for worship and for training new believers.[14] Early church leaders may have created these materials for use in worship gatherings and the instruction of new believers.

---

14. Paul writes in 1 Corinthians 15:3–11. that he is passing on what he has received.

The Book of Acts

The book of Acts gives us some of the earliest examples of how Christians worshipped. We read that they assembled themselves for worship, new believers were baptized, the Eucharist was observed, intercessory prayers were offered, and they sang. What we don't find is who was the leader of worship.

Assemblies

In Acts, we see Christians meeting together for worship. After Peter's sermon on the day of Pentecost, some three thousand people responded in faith and were baptized, so by this time there was a recognizable group of believers. At the same time, Christians continued to worship in the temple.[15]

Baptisms

In Acts 8 is the account of Philip and the Ethiopian eunuch. Verses 36–37 indicate that a ritual was associated with baptism.

> As they traveled down the road, they came to a place where was some water, and the official said, "Here is some water. What is to keep me from being baptized?" Philip said to him, "You may be baptized if you believe with all your heart." "I do," he answered; "I believe that Jesus Christ is the Son of God."

Though verse 37 does not appear in all early manuscripts, there is still the implication of some type of baptismal formula.

The Eucharist

McGowan[16] suggests a ritual pattern for the Eucharist can be found, starting with many of the stories in the Gospels: taking bread, giving thanks, breaking the bread, and distributing the bread to be eaten. He cites an example

---

This is one evidence of pre-Pauline sources. Throughout the Epistles we find formulae that seem to be in common use and understanding, such as "faith, hope, and love," though not always in that order. Belief in the God who raised Jesus from death is another example. Romans 4:24, 8:11; 2 Corinthians 4:14; Galatians 1:1; and 1 Peter 1:21 are examples. A good source for further study is Hunter, *Paul and His Predecessors*. A second edition with updated material was published in 1961.

15. See Acts 2:46, 3:1–3, 3:8, 3:10, 4:1, 5:20–22, 5:24–25, and 5:42.
16. McGowan, *Ancient Christian Worship*, 26–27.

of this pattern in Acts 27:34-36, the remarkable story of Paul exhorting his frightened shipmates:

> I beg you, then, eat some food; you need it in order to survive. Not even a hair of your heads will be lost." After saying this, Paul took some bread, gave thanks to God before them all, broke it, and began to eat. They took courage, and every one of them also ate some food.

1 Corinthians 10-14

In 1 Corinthians 10-14 we find the most detailed account of worship rituals. In fact, Paul's account is the earliest record we have of the Last Supper. Paul is not concerned with giving an ordering of worship, but that worship be conducted in a worthy manner. Baptism and the Eucharist play a central role in Paul's teaching here. Baptism is a ritual that incorporates believers "into the one body by the same Spirit, and we have all been given the one Spirit to drink" (12:13). The Eucharist creates the body of Christ:

> The cup we use in the Lord's Supper and for which we give thanks to God: when we drink from it, we are sharing in the blood of Christ. And the bread we break, when we eat it, we are sharing in the body of Christ. Because there is the one loaf of bread, all of us, though many, are one body, for we all share the same loaf. (10:16-17)

Martin[17] uses the church at Corinth as an example since Paul devotes so much material to worship problems in that church (chapters 10 through 14). However, this does not mean we are to replicate the worship of the Corinthians in our churches today. What we look for are some biblical and theological principles that will pertain to our worship. Martin identified three elements that characterized Corinthian worship: the charismatic, the didactic and the Eucharistic.

The Charismatic Element

The charismatic element includes the offering of enthusiastic praise and prayer under the direct inspiration of the Spirit, whether in intelligible language or in ecstatic language: "Those who speak in strange tongues do not speak to others but to God, because no one understands them. They are

---

17. Martin, "Aspects of Worship," 6-7.

speaking secret truths by the power of the Spirit" (1 Cor 14:23). The Greek word used here is *glossa,* meaning "tongue or language." This word means either speaking in a natural language the speaker has learned or speaking in a language the speaker has not previously known and understood. The supernatural phenomenon that took place at Pentecost was the exercise of a gift whereby many people, from many countries, had gathered at Jerusalem and heard God's message in their own language.

1 Corinthians 14:26 discusses the reality of spiritual gifts and indicates that some have the gift of making psalms. There is some connection between speaking in tongues and making music. Exactly what the phenomenon of tongue speaking was for the Corinthian church is not clear. In verses 15–17 it seems some individuals were caught up in ecstatically inspired prayers and songs. While Paul does not censure this practice in worship, he insists that there must be an accompanying interpretation so that the church may benefit and be edified:

> I would like for all of you to speak in strange tongues; but I would rather that you had the gift of proclaiming God's message. For the person who proclaims God's message is of greater value than the one who speaks in strange tongues—unless there is someone present who can explain what is said, so that the whole church may be helped. (1 Cor 14:5)

There may be some connection between speaking in tongues and making music. It was, and is to some extent today, a Middle Eastern custom to express great joy in unintelligible song-speech. For Paul, such abstract expressions of joy and praise did not edify the church and emphasized worship that was intelligible.

The Didactic Element

This covers all worship in intelligible speech that aims at clarifying the will of God to the congregation.

> But in church worship I would rather speak five words that can be understood, in order to teach others, than speak thousands of words in strange tongues. (1 Cor 14:19)

If the Spirit gives gifts to every believer for the edification of the church, then this requires they be instructed. People cannot be brought to faith and repentance without some basic knowledge of what a faith relationship with

Christ is. Peterson has noted that "To be inspired is not enough: when Christians gather together words should convey meaningful truth."[18]

The didactic element also includes prophesying. Whether or not New Testament prophecy is the same as preaching today is open to debate, but preaching is important and primary in the proclamation of God's message,

Discerning truth was particularly important because there were always those ready to pollute the gospel. On the one hand, there were those who insisted a person had to follow the Jewish traditions to be a Christian. On the other hand, were those who were espousing some of the doctrines that later became Gnosticism. Consequently, if people were to bring a song and a prayer to worship, someone needed to be aware of what message was being proclaimed: "Two or three who are given God's message should speak, while the others are to judge what they say" (1 Cor 14:29).

Paul gave this instruction to the church in Thessalonica: "Put all things to the test: . . ." (1 Thess 5:21). John makes the same emphasis in 1 John 4:1: "My dear friends, do not believe all who claim to have the Spirit, but test them to find out if the spirit they have comes from God. For many false prophets have gone out everywhere."

The Eucharistic Element

The term "eucharistic" comes from the Greek word *eucharistia*, which means gratitude and/or thankfulness. This is the element of thanksgiving and praise in worship and included both prayer and singing. In 1 Corinthians 14:15–16 Paul refers to prayers of thanksgiving offered by both the mind and the Spirit so they are intelligible to those in the gathering.

That singing was included as a part of the church service is attested to by Acts 16:25, which tells that Paul and Silas sang in the Philippian jail. James 5:13 says those who are merry should "sing psalms." In 1 Corinthians 14:15–16 Paul refers to singing with both mind and Spirit.

The earliest biblical account of communion is in 1 Corinthians 10:14–22, where Paul urged believers not to attend pagan feasts and eat meat offered to idols. Those who participate in such affairs are partners with demons. He implies then that those who participate in communion are partners with Christ. Believers could not be partners both with demons and with Christ. He encourages believers to eat from one loaf to symbolize their unity with one another and with Christ. This introduces the next reference to communion in chapter 11:17–34. Paul mentions the divisions within their

---

18. Peterson, *Engaging with God*, 211.

fellowship. When they come together for communion they do not observe the Lord's Supper; they are observing their own supper.

The focus again is on both the vertical and horizontal aspects of worship. In communion, they not only meet with Christ, but they minister to one another. As Peterson points out that according to Paul, "those who disregard their responsibility to welcome and care for fellow believers cannot be worshipping or serving God acceptably."[19]

Ephesians 5:18–29 and Colossians 3:15–17

It is interesting in these passages that we speak the words of psalms, hymns, and sacred songs to one another, but sing them to God. Paul is emphasizing both the vertical and the horizontal aspects of worship: the vertical is person to God and the horizontal is person to person.

> Speak to one another with the words of psalms, hymns, and sacred songs; sing hymns and psalms to the Lord with praise in your hearts. (Eph 5:19)

> Christ's message in all its richness must live in your hearts. Teach and instruct one another with all wisdom. Sing psalms, hymns, and sacred songs; sing to God with thanksgiving in your hearts. (Col 3:16)

To determine the differences Paul wished to make between psalms, hymns, and spiritual songs is impossible. Psalms may have referred to the Old Testament psalms, while "hymns" and "spiritual songs" were Christian creations. Since the word *humnos* was used in Koine Greek to describe songs of praise and adoration to pagan gods, it would seem likely that New Testament "hymns" are expressions of praise and adoration to God. The more subjective, ecstatic expressions of religious experience could be spiritual songs. Regardless of how we interpret these words, it seems likely that they were songs of faith that most believers knew.

These verses include a discussion of how believers should live as children of God. The passages are not exactly duplicates of one another, but cover the same ethical requirements. In Ephesians 5:1–19, Paul gives three parallel sets of instructions: be wise, not unwise; be understanding, not foolish; and be filled with the spirit, not filled with wine. As Susan Hylen has observed,

---

19. Peterson, *Engaging with God*, 216.

A life of the Spirit results in singing and thanksgiving. "Psalms and hymns and spiritual songs" are not likely distinct kinds of songs, but suggests quantity and continual singing. Likewise, "singing and making melody" are synonyms. The description includes songs being sung both "to each other" . . . and "to the Lord" (5:19). The cumulative effect is that the life to which the reader is called is one of constant praise. Thanksgiving should likewise be abundant—"at all times and for everything"—and is given in the name of Christ and directed to God the Father.[20]

Daniel Block[21] writes that "these two texts are critical for understanding Paul's disposition toward music." He draws parallels between the two passages and summarizes what each passage teaches:

- Music provides an outlet for demonstrating that one is filled with the Spirit.
- Music is a means of promoting community in the body of Christ; we sing to one another.
- Music is an expression of thanksgiving to God; believers need to be thankful in all circumstances.
- Whether sung or played, music arising from a thankful heart brings great glory to God.

Block notes further that our interpretation must be within context. Paul's concern is greater and deeper than with just music alone. Too often we have directed attention on to the verses dealing with music without considering the entire passage.

The Book of Revelation

The temple and its worship had left such a profound influence upon John, or the writer of Revelation, that he re-coded the panorama of the redeemed church in heaven worshipping God in terms of temple worship. Revelation 5:8 and 14:2–3 describe the twenty-four elders and the redeemed church making music "made by musicians playing their harps." In Revelation 15:2 the church is pictured as battle worn from the great tribulation, standing victoriously on the "sea of glass" with the "harps God had given them."

The assembly sings the song of Moses and the Lamb. This is the Sabbath or rest of the church. The praise of God has the character of what we

---

20. Hylen, "Commentary on Ephesians 5:15–20," para. 9.
21. Block, *For the Glory of God*, 231–34.

know about worship in the temple. A Sabbath psalm is sung (Ps 92, cf. Ps 86) and the song of Moses (Deut 32; cf. Exod 15) is sung. By adding the Lamb's song to the song of Moses, John was expressing the Christian concept that Jesus was the fulfillment of all Old Testament expectations.

Confessions and Creeds

Jews in the synagogue would make a public confession of faith by reciting the Shema. Early Christians continued this practice of confessing faith. The language used suggests that confessions were a personal act. The following declarations would imply public confessions of personal faith in Jesus.

> If you confess that Jesus is Lord and believe that God raised him from death, you will be saved. For it is by our faith that we are put right with God; it is by our confession that we are saved. (Rom 10:9–10)

> This is how you will be able to know whether it is God's Spirit: anyone who acknowledges that Jesus Christ came as a human being has the Spirit who comes from God. (1 John 4:2)

Other confessions imply the content of belief held by a congregation and said in response to what God has done and said in Christ.

> And because of the proof which this service of yours brings, many will give glory to God for your loyalty to the gospel of Christ, which you profess, and for your generosity in sharing with them and everyone else. (2 Cor 9:13)

> Run your best in the race of faith, and win eternal life for yourself; for it was to this life that God called you when you firmly professed your faith before many witnesses. (1 Tim 6:1)

> My Christian friends, who also have been called by God! Think of Jesus, whom God sent to be the High Priest of the faith we profess. (Heb 3:1)

> Let us, then, hold firmly to the faith we profess. For we have a great High Priest who has gone into the very presence of God— Jesus, the Son of God. (Heb 4:14)

> Let us, then, always offer praise to God as our sacrifice through Jesus, which is the offering presented by lips that confess him as Lord. (Heb 13:15)

> If we declare that Jesus is the Son of God, we live in union with God and God lives in union with us. (1 John 4:15)

Martin has commented that when believers assembled for worship, "as they were reminded of all that God had accomplished on their behalf in the Gospel, they would break forth in some formula of grateful acknowledgment which was both a confession of their praise and appreciation, and an expression of their faith."[22]

To distinguish between confessions, creeds, and hymns is not always possible, for they may look very much alike. Creeds are confessions that have been extended with more descriptive words. For example, the confession "Jesus is Lord" (Rom 10:9) became extended until the confession of Christ took precedence over the confession of God.

> It is about his Son, our Lord Jesus Christ: as to his humanity, he was born a descendant of David; as to his divine holiness, he was shown with great power to be the Son of God by being raised from death. (Rom 1:3–4)

Another example of an extended confession is found in 1 Timothy 6:15–16 (CEV):

> The glorious God is the only Ruler, the King of kings and Lord of lords. At the time that God has already decided, he will send Jesus Christ back again. Only God lives forever! And he lives in light that no one can come near. No human has ever seen God or ever can see him. God will be honored, and his power will last forever. Amen.

In an age of rapid communication, we may find it difficult to appreciate the necessity of confessions and creeds. In a society that had few written materials available for the public, creeds and confessions were a means of teaching people what they believed and giving them words to articulate what they believed. As we shall see, the importance of creedal statements increased as more and more heretical ideas began to infiltrate the churches.

New Testament Hymns

Many early Christian hymns are part of what we now know as New Testament Scripture, and are so interwoven with other Scriptures as to be virtually indistinguishable from them. However, scholars disagree about which passages fit in this category. Some scholars have developed criteria

---

22. Martin, "Aspects of Worship," 15.

to identify those texts that are hymns or worship material. Von Dehsen, for example, has given these criteria:[23]

1. The passage contains vocabulary that is different from that of the surrounding context.
2. The passage is written in poetic form, that is, it exhibits rhythmical patterns and careful structure.
3. The content of the passage interrupts the context.
4. The name of the deity is absent and is replaced by a relative clause or a participle.
5. Words are used in the passage that are found nowhere else in the New Testament.
6. The cosmic role of God or Christ is emphasized.
7. Theological concepts and Christological doctrine are expressed in exalted and liturgical language.

First Corinthians 14:3–16 seems to indicate that speaking with tongues had expressed itself in the form of an inspired prayer-hymn. Verses 13 and 16 put praying and singing side by side and both activities are directly inspired by the Spirit and highly valued as contributions to worship. However, Paul is quick to point out that

> the person who speaks in strange tongues, then, must pray for the gift to explain what is said. For if I pray in this way, my spirit prays indeed, but my mind has no part in it. What should I do, then? I will pray with my spirit, but I will pray also with my mind; I will sing with my spirit, but I will sing also with my mind. When you give thanks to God in spirit only, how can ordinary people taking part in the meeting say "Amen" to your prayer of thanksgiving? They have no way of knowing what you are saying.

Hymn Fragments

New Testament scholars do not all agree, but fragments of what may be hymns are found in the following passages.

> Wake up, sleeper, and rise from death, and Christ will shine on you. (Eph 5:14)

---

23. von Dehsen, "Hymnic Forms," 8.

For there is one God and one mediator between God and humanity, Christ Jesus, Himself human, who gave Himself—a ransom for all, a testimony at the proper time. (1 Tim 2:5–6)

He appeared in human form, was shown to be right by the Spirit, and was seen by angels. He was preached among the nations, was believed in throughout the world, and was taken up to heaven. (1 Tim 3:16)

He has saved us and called us with a holy calling, not according to our works, but according to His own purpose and grace, which was given to us in Christ Jesus before time began. This has now been made evident through the appearing of our Savior Christ Jesus, who has abolished death and has brought life and immortality to light through the gospel. (2 Tim 1:9–10)

But when the kindness of God our Savior and His love for mankind appeared, He saved us—not by works of righteousness that we had done, but according to His mercy, through the washing of regeneration and renewal by the Holy Spirit. He poured out this Spirit on us abundantly through Jesus Christ our Savior, so that having been justified by His grace, we may become heirs with the hope of eternal life. (Titus 3:4–7)

For Christ also suffered for sins once for all, the righteous for the unrighteous, that He might bring you to God, after being put to death in the fleshly realm but made alive in the spiritual realm. (1 Pet 3:18)

Complete Hymns

There are other passages that seem to be full-blown hymns, but we must be aware that not all scholars agree. The first two hymns have their own set of problems, and both Martin and Bruce have written monographs on the Colossians passage.[24]

Philippians 2:6–11

He always had the nature of God,

---

24. Martin, "Early Christian Hymn," 195–205; Bruce, "Colossian Problems," 99–111. Martin has also written a monograph analyzing the hymnic material of Philippians 2:5–11: *Carmen Christi: Philippians 2:5–11*.

but he did not think that by force he should try to remain equal with God.

Instead of this, of his own free will he gave up all he had,

and took the nature of a servant.

He became like a human being

and appeared in human likeness.

He was humble and walked the path of obedience all the way to death—

his death on the cross.

For this reason, God raised him to the highest place above

and gave him the name that is greater than any other name.

And so, in honor of the name of Jesus

all beings in heaven, on earth, and in the world below

will fall on their knees,

and all will openly proclaim that Jesus Christ is Lord,

to the glory of God the Father.

Colossians 1:15–20

He is the image of the invisible God,

the firstborn over all creation.

For everything was created by Him,

in heaven and on earth,

the visible and the invisible,

whether thrones or dominions

or rulers or authorities—

all things have been created through Him and for Him.

He is before all things,

and by Him all things hold together.

He is also the head of the body, the church;

He is the beginning,

the firstborn from the dead,

so that He might come to have

first place in everything.

For God was pleased to have

all His fullness dwell in Him,

and through Him to reconcile

everything to Himself

by making peace

through the blood of His cross—

whether things on earth or things in heaven.

2 Timothy 1:1–3

For if we have died with Him, we will also live with him;

if we deny Him, He will also deny us;

if we are faithless, He remains faithful,

for He cannot deny Himself.

In analyzing this hymnic material, we get the impression that the emphasis is upon the work and significance of Jesus and is concerned with Jesus and not with God the Father. As Hurtado has pointed out, this would indicate "that singing/chanting songs in honor of Jesus was not an occasional, but a characteristic feature of early Christian worship."[25] Hurtado also states that in addition to the hymnic material in the New Testament, it is most likely that a big part of the earliest Christian hymnody involved the chanting of Old Testament psalms.

> I suggest that in the setting of early Christian worship, in which the Spirit was expected to inspire believers and bestow revelations, the Old Testament psalms, especially those that had already begun to be read as royal-messianic psalms in some pre-Christian Jewish circles, were "unlocked" as predictions of Jesus and as descriptions of his glory.

In a blog, Hurtado suggests that the singing involved in earliest Christian circles was likely much closer to simple chanting, rather than involving

---

25. Hurtado, *At the Origins*, 87.

any more complex musical patterns. "You don't need meter or rhyme to chant a text," he writes.[26]

It is this sense of Jesus' exalted power and his relationship to them as Lord that shaped the understanding of these early believers. In Colossians 3:16–17 we read that praise is offered to God in the name of Jesus and through Jesus. In Ephesians 5:19 we are to sing "to the Lord" who is likely the exalted Jesus, and throughout Revelation we have worship addressed to God and "the Lamb."

For You to Think about

1. What are some similarities and differences between worship in the temple and contemporary worship?

2. Use the criteria of von Dehsen and evaluate three of the hymns or hymn fragments discussed in the chapter. Then tell how you think the classification of these texts as hymns is justified or unjustified.

3. Which of the New Testament canticles could you use in the worship of your church, why would you use it, and how would you use it?

---

26. Hurtado, "On 'Hymns' in the New Testament," para. 3.

4

Congregational Song in the Early Church: 100–600 CE

> After manual ablution, and the bringing in of lights, each is asked to stand forth and sing, as he can, a hymn to God, either one from the holy Scriptures or one of his own composing...
>
> —Tertullian

STARTING WITH THE DESCRIPTIONS of congregational song in the book of Acts, this chapter surveys the places where early Christians worshipped and the difficulties of worshipping under Roman rule. Then, some of the writings of early Christians about congregational song are examined to discover the understandings and practices of early churches.

Christianity evolved from Judaism and the first Christians were Jews and Jesus was a Jew. Consequently, everything in Judaism is background for the faith and life of early Christians. There was the Greek Old Testament (the Septuagint), synagogue and temple worship, and music—a rich spiritual heritage. There was little or no heritage in terms of visual art, for the commandment to make no graven images was taken literally and seriously. The Jewish background to New Testament worship, at least what we can know for certain, was discussed in the last chapter.

The First Developments

In Acts 3 we see that the early Christians continued to worship in the temple until the differences between Jews and Christians became intolerable. At the same time, Christians started gathering together informally in homes for prayer and testimony. When they went to the synagogue it was to tell others about their new faith. Likewise, the apostle Paul made the synagogue a center of his missionary activities. It seems safe to assume that the early Christians adopted the musical practices of the synagogue, but little is known of what these practices were.

The New Testament book of James makes it clear that Jewish Christians continued to congregate, in some cases, in synagogues (Jas 2:2). We know that gentile Christians often met in homes (Rom 16:3–5) and in other unspecified places. It is little wonder, then, that the form of the synagogue service influenced the form of assemblies in the ancient church to some degree.

The first church was the church in Jerusalem and its membership consisted of Jewish followers of Jesus. The group meeting in the upper room following the resurrection of Jesus was the nucleus of this first church. Following the instructions of Jesus, some 120 men and women were waiting for the coming of the Holy Spirit.

On the day of Pentecost, and in response to the sermon of Peter, "about three thousand people were added to the group that day" (Acts 2:41). After Pentecost we learn that this group

- spent their time in learning from the apostles, taking part in the fellowship, and sharing in the fellowship meals and the prayers (Acts 2:42);
- continued together in close fellowship and shared their belongings with one another (Acts 2:44);
- met in the temple day after day (Acts 2:46);
- had their meals together in their homes, eating with glad and humble hearts, and praising God (Acts 2:46); and
- enjoyed the good will of all the people (Acts 2:46).

As a result, "the Lord added to their group those who were being saved" (Acts 2:47). Martin has suggested that

> in the earliest Christianity there were already two groups: an Aramaic-speaking congregation of Jewish messianists and also, maybe from the start, a Greek-speaking congregation led by the Seven and with Stephen as prominent as spokesperson for a missionary theology. So-called "hellenistic Christianity" on this view was part of the earliest church and not a later development due to the mission to Gentiles.[1]

The conflict between Jewish and Greek widows in Acts 6 would seem to substantiate this conclusion.

---

1. Martin, "Some Reflections," 43.

Christians in the Roman Empire

The church was born during the Roman Empire, one of the largest and most enduring in world history. Rome was a central hub of technology, literature, architecture, culture, and art in the ancient world. Rome was also the hub of commerce, trade, politics, and military might in the Mediterranean.

The engineers of the Roman age created an unparalleled network of roads in ancient history and the grand achievements of her road network led directly to the city of Rome and back out to her many territories. Approximately 50,000 miles (80,000 km) of roads spanned the Roman Empire, spreading its legions, culture, and immense influence throughout the known world. The old saying "all roads lead to Rome" simply could not have been more true.

Estimates of the height of Roman power in the first and second centuries describe an empire of some 2.2 million square miles with 60 million people who claimed citizenship of Rome (or as much as one-fifth of the world's population.) This is the secular context in which Christian worship practices begin to develop.[2]

Roman Religion

The Romans were polytheists in their religion, and many of their gods and goddesses were adapted from Greek religion. "Early Christian worship did not take place in a religious vacuum," according to Hurtado. "The Roman world was chock-full of religiosity, with a dizzying array of religious groups, movements, customs, activities and related paraphernalia."[3] He goes on to say that there was hardly any daily activity that was not connected with religion: "Birth, death, marriage, the domestic sphere, civil and wider political life, work, the military, socializing, entertainment, arts, music—all were imbued with religious significance and associations."[4]

Roman religion is associated with sacred places and objects. Though the gods were available to answer prayer at any moment and at any place, there was special power in a temple where the god lived. So we find temples to various Roman gods, sacred images, rituals, and sacred meals in abundance.

---

2. Two of the best Internet sources for the Roman Empire are "The Roman Empire in the First Century" (http://www.pbs.org/empires/romans/empire) and "Illustrated History of the Roman Empire" (http://www.roman-empire.net).

3. Hurtado, *At the Origins*, 7.

4. Hurtado, *At the Origins*, 9.

Emperor Worship

The nature of Roman religion expanded to include the Emperors themselves. Julius Caesar, having claimed to be a direct descendent of Aeneas, the son of Venus, was among the first to deify himself in such a manner. At first, such a system of human divinity was largely rejected by the masses, but the popularity of Caesar helped pave the way for future leaders. Thus, there were temples built and dedicated to various emperors. As the Imperial system gained hold, it was common practice for the Emperors to accept divine honors before their deaths. These living "gods," in some cases, required sacrificial rituals as signs of loyalty and ingrained themselves with the older more traditional pagan gods. Caesar was known as "the son of god" and people were required to confess, "Caesar is lord."

This statement of loyalty to Caesar, the requirement of a sacrifice to the emperor, and the forced belief in the complete pantheon of Roman gods became a significant source of conflict with early Christians. Every trade guild had a patron god, with sacrifices and rituals performed at public meetings. The instructions about meat offered to idols in 1 Corinthians 8 become clearer when we think about the social-religious climate of Rome.

Christian Persecution

Since Christians refused to worship either the emperor as lord or any of the Roman deities, they were regarded as atheists and this led to their persecution. The first major incident of Christian persecution took place in 64 CE when Nero was emperor. The fire that ravaged Rome in that year, and the subsequent building of Nero's golden palace on the destroyed property, was wildly unpopular in Rome. Many placed blame directly on Nero, accusing him of intentionally lighting the fire in order to build his palace. Nero tried to pin the blame for that fire on the city's small Christian community, regarded as a distinct, dissident group of Jews, so he burned many of them alive. Both Peter and Paul were said to have been martyred as a result. This move played on people's fears that Christian intention was the complete destruction of the Roman world as they waited for the judgment day.[5]

Under Domitian (51–96 CE), just a generation later, some sources indicate another persecution was directed at Christians. He was the first emperor to officially assume the title "God the Lord." He insisted others should hail his greatness with acclamations like "Lord of the Earth." Jews, and presumably Christians, refused to worship Domitian. The wholesale

---

5. Hurtado, *At the Origins*, 19–28.

persecution of Jews that followed is well documented; persecution of Christians is not.

Domitian ruled in an almost tyrannical reign of terror in which many perished, not just Jews and Christians. Political enemies, "divisive" groups, and individuals of all kinds met terrible fates. Many scholars think the beast that the author of Revelation describes, as well as the events in the book, are perhaps best interpreted as hidden allusions to the rule of Domitian.[6]

By the later third century Christian persecution from imperial sources was beginning to decline but one more great persecution was still to occur. Under the Eastern Emperor Diocletian, beginning in 303 CE and lasting for eight years, he and his successor Galerius began a systematic purge of Christians. While many perished, most were displaced from home and property. This final persecution against the now massive religion would soon be supplanted by the coming of Constantine and would not yet gain Imperial favor, but certainly complete tolerance.

Emperor worship and spasmodic Christian persecution would continue until late in the Western Empire until the reign of Constantine in the early fourth century CE. Constantine supposedly converted to Christianity or at least made it an acceptable part of Roman religion, eliminating the emperor deification altogether. Later Emperors such as Julian attempted to revive the old ways, but by 392 CE, Emperor Theodosius I banned the practice of pagan religions in Rome altogether and Christianity was, without question, the official religion of the state.

Christian Meeting Places

Early Christians had no temples or shrines, no images of God or of Jesus, no public religious processions, and no priesthood or sacred images. By Roman standards, early Christian worship would seem plain and unimpressive. As long as the Romans did not recognize Christianity as a religion distinct from Judaism, there were no problems in having public meetings.

House Churches

In the opening pages of the book of Acts we find believers meeting for worship both in the temple and in homes (Acts 5:42). At first, they probably met in homes to celebrate the Lord's Supper. Once it was evident to the Romans that Christians were not a sect of Judaism, they came under suspicion and

---

6. Galli, "Persecution in the Early Church."

meeting in homes of believers who had the economic resources to provide space large enough to hold 30 to 40 people was about their only option.

Some of these houses of worship were entirely converted into places of worship. The oldest surviving house that was modified clearly to serve as a church is the house church at *Dura Europos*, a remote Roman outpost on the Euphrates River on the eastern borders of present-day Syria. A British soldier digging trenches during the First World War rediscovered it. Excavations began in 1928 and a city of many peoples and religions began to emerge, as well as the world's earliest identified site of Christian worship. The house had been rebuilt in 231 CE after an earthquake and was modified for Christian usage circa 241 CE. After it was extensively remodeled at ground level, it no longer served as a residence.

By removing a wall from the original living room, a space had been created that was large enough for gathering the whole congregation in one room. At the center of the house is an open-air court. The court was not used for worship, but the meeting hall, baptistery, and sacristy all look into the court for light and air. There are no windows on the perimeter walls and only a single door to the street for entry. There was room for approximately seventy worshipers.[7]

The Catacombs

The catacombs are the ancient underground cemeteries, primarily in Rome, that were used by the Christian and the Jewish communities. The Christian catacombs, which are the most numerous, began in the second century and were popular until the first half of the fifth century. Christians gathered here to celebrate funeral rites and the anniversaries of the martyrs and of the dead.

In exceptional cases, during the persecutions, the catacombs were used as places of momentary refuge for the celebration of the Eucharist. They were not used as secret hiding places of the early Christians. This is only a fiction taken from novels or movies. After the persecutions, especially in the time of Pope Saint Damascus (366–84 CE) they became real shrines of the martyrs, centers of devotion, and for Christian pilgrimage from every part of the empire.

There were cemeteries in the open above ground, but Christians preferred underground cemeteries. The Christians rejected the pagan custom of cremation, so they preferred burial, just as Christ was buried.

---

7. Young, *Dura Europos*.

They sensed a moral obligation to respect the bodies that one day would be raised from the dead.

This genuine belief of the Christians created a problem of space, which greatly influenced the development of the catacombs. The areas owned by the Christians above ground were very limited in extent. Since tombs in open-air cemeteries were seldom reused, the space available for burial would have been quickly exhausted. The catacombs came as the solution to the problem; and it proved to be economical, safe, and practical. In fact, it was cheaper to dig underground corridors and galleries than to buy large pieces of land in the open. As the early Christians were predominantly poor, this way of burying the dead was decisive.

But there were other reasons too for choosing the catacombs. The Christians felt a lively community sense: they wished to be together even in the "sleep of death." During the persecutions, such out-of-the-way areas were very convenient for community meetings and for the display of Christian symbols. Since Roman law forbade the burial of the dead within the city walls, all catacombs are located outside the city, along the great consular roads, generally in the immediate suburban area of that age.

Church Buildings

In 313 CE Constantine issued the Edict of Milan that recognized the Christian faith as a legal religion. In addition to freedom from persecution, believers were enabled to build church buildings, to recover any buildings previously built, and to openly evangelize. Christianity now was a public religion as opposed to a private one. The Edict recognized Christianity as one religion among many, so it was an act of toleration and did not establish Christianity as the official state religion. Christians were now free to build church building without government interference.

Generous stipends for new property were granted both by the state and the Emperor himself. Christians soon found themselves meeting in beautiful buildings accompanied by increased ceremonials and rich vestments. Another development was the "Christianization" of many pagan festivals and customs.

Christians did not want anything that would link them to paganism, so the design of these new church buildings could not be anything like the Roman temples. At the same time, the buildings needed an architecture that was recognizable in the Roman world. Totally new architectural forms would not be as effective as architectural forms that were common in Roman life. The Roman building known as the basilica was the perfect choice for these new churches. This is still the basic floor plan for Catholic, Anglican, and Lutheran churches.

Roman cities would regularly have a basilica as a central public building. It was like our City Hall, a center of public power. These basilicas regularly had an architectural form of a rectangle with an apse. The apse was a semi-circular projection, usually off the short wall of the rectangular building. The Roman basilica was the site of the law court and the apse is where the magistrate would sit and dispense the law.

The basilica would be somewhat bare in decorations, so building additions were added on the long sides of the basilica so the church formed a cross. Gradually, these churches began to be adorned with lavish artistic decorations that reflected a Christian mysticism, a spiritual meaning or reality neither apparent to the senses nor obvious to the intelligence.[8]

Ordering of Worship and Song

During this tumultuous time, and in spite of sometime persecution, the church flourished. Perhaps the most significant happening was the development of liturgy or an ordering of worship. This is important, for the liturgy was responsible later for the architecture of churches, the symbolism of mosaics, the forms of sculpture, and the forms of music.

Christians could and can worship corporately without any order at all, but an ordering of some kind seems necessary. In fact, we will give worship an order whether we plan to do so or not. Just as most of us need a certain degree of order in our daily living to function properly, order in worship is necessary for proper functioning. In fact, the apostle Paul argued for order in worship in 1 Corinthians 14:40: "Everything must be done in a proper and orderly way."

In both the Old and New Testaments there are several words translated "worship" that describe both the attitude and the action of worship. Three words are used most often. The principal Old Testament word is *shachah*, which means "bow down," "kneeling before," and "prostrate oneself." The idea is the reverential attitude of mind or body, or both, combined with attitudes of religious adoration, obedience, and service. Another word is *sharath*, which means "to minister" or" to serve." A third word is *abad*, which means "to work for another" or "to serve as subjects of another." This word was used to describe the work of the Levitical priests.

The New Testament also has three principal words for worship. One is *proskuneo*, which means "kiss (the hand or the ground) toward," in the

---

8. For more information, see Stringer, *Sociological History of Worship*.

oriental fashion of bowing prostrate upon the ground. The translators of the Septuagint equated the Greek *proskuneo* with the Hebrew *shachah*. A second word is *latreuo*, which means, "to serve." The third word is *leitourgia*, used in the Septuagint to describe the service or ministry of the priests relating to the prayers and sacrifices they offered to God.

The Liturgy

The technical term for the ordering of worship is "liturgy," and the activities that take place within the order are "rites" or "rituals." The word liturgy is derived from the Greek word *leitourgia*. In both the Septuagint and the New Testament, this word is used to describe worship order. A related word is *leitourgeo*, which refers to Christians serving, whether by prayer or by instructing others. Just as we need order in daily life, we also need rituals, such as shaking hands and waving good-bye.

Consequently, we can define liturgy as the work of the people, or what people do and say as they worship God. Liturgy is what many churches refer to as an Order of Service, which is a description of how the various rituals are ordered. Ordering of worship, or liturgy, is centered in the two basic rites of the Christian faith, viz. baptism and the Lord's Supper or Eucharist.

Psalm Singing

The oldest tradition of Christian music is psalm singing. Like everything else about the relation between Jewish and early Christian worship, we have no knowledge of what Jewish materials were part of Christian worship. Accordingly, the earliest Christian singing was Jewish singing. Of course we immediately think of psalm singing. The word *psalmos* used in the New Testament in Ephesians 5:19 and Colossians 3:16 does not necessarily refer to the Old Testament psalter. The word "psalm" means songs that are performed with an accompanying plucked string instrument. So, what did they sing?

We know psalms were sung in the temple, so some writers have made an immediate connection between the two. There is nothing in the literature to suggest that early Christians believed their worship was connected to temple worship. They did continue to worship in the temple and at the same time have their own distinctive Christian worship, and it is possible the temple could be a source for Christian song. Another possible source of psalm singing is the synagogue, but we are uncertain how psalms were used there, if at all.

According to McGowan, the earliest explicit reference to the use of the biblical psalter in Christian gatherings is from a second-century apocryphal work titled *Acts of Paul*. In this work the "psalms of David" are included along with other songs sung in a Eucharistic meal. The meal was shared "according to custom," whatever that custom was. From other early sources we discover that music was an integral part of the liturgy. Music accompanied the solemn reading of Scripture and there was hymn and psalm singing, as well as singing a joyous "Alleluia."[9]

Early church music was sung in unison since many writers refer to congregations singing with one voice. The words could be psalms or hymns that were sometimes sung antiphonally. The diary of Egeria indicates hymns, antiphons, and psalms were sung by monks, virgins, and lay people. There are references to women singers, choirs of virgins, and perhaps female cantors. This was controversial in many places since women singers were prominent in some heretical groups.

The Christian theologian Tertullian tells us that by the late second century psalm-singing was a regular part of Sunday worship: "The Scriptures are read, psalms are sung, sermons are delivered, and petitions offered." He also describes worship in his native North Africa: "After manual ablution, and the bringing in of lights, each is asked to stand forth and sing, as he can, a hymn to God, either one from the holy Scriptures or one of his own composing . . ."[10]

Nearly all the church fathers speak of psalm-singing in the most glowing words. St. Basil, a theologian prominent in efforts to settle the Arian dispute, wrote of music being an invention of the Holy Spirit to teach Christian doctrine in an understandable manner. A psalm would drive away demons and the congregation would remember the teaching of the psalms they had sung even if they forgot the sermon. Basil was of the opinion that the suitable instrument for accompanying Psalm sings was the psaltery.[11]

St. Chrysostum wrote that God had given the psalms to create the better attitudes of mind and soul, since secular songs would invite demons. There was no need for an instrument to make the mind and spirit function in harmony with each other. When a Christian had submitted to the Holy Spirit, he would then create a spiritual melody.[12]

St. Jerome gave a definition for Paul's psalms, hymns, and spiritual songs. A hymn declared the majesty and power of God, and had an "Alleluia"

---

9. McGowan, *Ancient Christian Worship*, 111–12.
10. Tertullian, *Apology*, 39:17–18.
11. Dowley, *Introduction*, 33.
12. Willis, *Church Music and Protestantism*, 42, 213.

affixed to the end of it. Psalms affect the seat of emotions to produce the right kind of moral action. The Christian should sing more with the heart than with the voice.[13]

Early Writings on Worship and Song in the Church

Distinctively Christian worship practices began to be developed toward the end of the first century and the beginning of the second. The materials available to us are scant, but what we have indicates worship practices began to become ritualized in the second century (100–199 CE). Churches probably began developing fairly set worship patterns toward the end of the first century. Full-blown liturgies would come later.

The Didache (c. 100 CE)

The Didache,[14] with the subtitle "The Teaching of the Twelve Apostles," is an early handbook of an anonymous Christian community. The unknown author is one of the earliest to write about worship outside the pages of the New Testament and was probably written before many of the New Testament books. Scholars have differed widely over its date, placing it from between the middle of the first century to the end of the second.

The document reflects a very early period in the development of Christian worship. It is a manual of sixteen short sections of basic teachings that instruct believers in how to live as Christians. It could very well have been used for instructing new believers. The Didache includes how to show one another the love of God, how to practice the Eucharist, and how to take in wandering prophets.

Some of the instructions read like paraphrases or near quotations from New Testament writings. For example, the Didache has this: "Bless those who curse you, and pray for your enemies, and fast for those who persecute you. For what reward is there for loving those who love you? Do not the heathens do the same? But you should love those who hate you, and then you shall have no enemies" (1.3). This is very similar to the words of Jesus in the Sermon on the Mount. In the sections following there are references from the Ten Commandments and Proverbs.

---

13. Sachs, *Rise of Music*, 250–51.
14. Lightfoot, "Didache." See also Hawkins, "Didache."

Section 7 is titled "Concerning Baptism" and gives rubrics for the administration of the rite. After explaining "all things," the believer is baptized "in the name of the Father, and of the Son, and of the Holy Spirit, in flowing water." If no running water is available, other water is permitted. If there is very little water, baptism can be accomplished by "pouring water three times on the head in the name of Father and Son and Holy Spirit." There is no description of the "all things" that are explained, but the implication is some kind of pre-baptismal training was required. Additionally, "both the baptizer and the candidate for baptism" are to fast one or two days before the baptism.

Section 9 is titled "Concerning the Eucharist" and includes rubrics for the observance, prayers, and possible congregational responses. The cup is associated with "the holy vine of David" and God made this known "through Jesus your servant." The congregation perhaps responded with "To you be the glory forever."

The broken bread seems to be associated with the feeding miracles of Jesus. The leader says "the broken bread . . . scattered over the hills," but was gathered together and became one. Therefore, "let your church be gathered together from the ends of the earth into your kingdom." The congregation may have responded with "To you be the glory forever." Only those who had been baptized were eligible for the Eucharist: "Allow no one to eat or drink of your Eucharist, unless they have been baptized in the name of the Lord. For concerning this, the Lord has said, 'Do not give what is holy to dogs'" (9:5).

Section 10 is titled "After the Eucharist," and consists mainly of prayers. The Eucharist may have included a fellowship meal that concluded with the bread and wine for the rubric states "After the Eucharist when you are filled, give thanks this way . . ." (10:1) One prayer relates the Eucharist to eternal life, for thanksgiving is given to God because He "gives spiritual food and drink and life eternal through Jesus . . ." (10:3). These may be the earliest Eucharistic prayers.

Perhaps the most interesting section is number 14, which refers to Sunday worship:

1. On the Lord's day, gather yourselves together and break bread, give thanks, but first confess your sins so that your sacrifice may be pure.

2. However, let no one who is at odds with his brother come together with you, until he has reconciled, so that your sacrifice may not be profaned.

3. For this is what the Lord has said: "For from the rising of the sun to its setting my name is great among the nations, and in every place incense is offered to my name, and a pure offering; for my name is great among the nations, says the Lord of hosts . . . For I am a great King, says the Lord of hosts, and my name is reverenced among the nations."

McGowan notes that this is not an imitation of the Last Supper recorded in the Gospels, because there is no mention of "the death of Jesus, or his body and blood . . ."[15]

These brief extracts would seem to indicate an early connection between the Eucharist and the sacrifice of Jesus, an idea developed later in the Mass. Bishops and deacons were to be appointed, but their duties are not given. Regular Sunday preaching or instruction may not have been possible, for there are instructions about prophets or teachers "who come among you." Instructions are given for telling who a true prophet is, and who is not, as well as what courtesy to extend to the true prophet. Therefore, worship seems to be primarily the Eucharist and the attendant prayers.

Pliny the Younger (c. 61/63–c. 113 CE)

Pliny the Younger was the governor of Pontus and Bithynia from 111 to 113 CE. We have a whole set of his correspondence with the emperor Trajan on a variety of administrative political matters. Two letters are the most famous, in which Pliny encounters Christianity for the first time.

The Lord's Supper was a very mysterious event to the nonbeliever, and it was this mystery and secrecy that prompted Pliny to make an investigation and to give his findings to the Emperor Trajan. His report is dated 96–97 CE and gives us some insight into early Christian worship and the difficulties some believers were facing.

> They [the Christians] asserted, however, that the sum and substance of their fault or error had been that they were accustomed to meet on a fixed day before dawn and sing responsively a hymn to Christ as to a god, and to bind themselves by oath, not to some crime, but not to commit fraud, theft, or adultery, not falsify their trust, nor to refuse to return a trust when called upon to do so. When this was over, it was their custom to depart and to assemble again to partake of food—but ordinary and innocent food. Even this, they affirmed, they had ceased to do after my edict by which, in accordance with your instructions, I

---

15. McGowan, *Ancient Christian Worship*, 36.

had forbidden political associations. Accordingly, I judged it all the more necessary to find out what the truth was by torturing two female slaves who were called deaconesses. But I discovered nothing else but depraved, excessive superstition.[16]

What songs were sung and the oath that was taken are unknown. However, Pliny's comments indicate that there was congregational singing of other texts in addition to the psalms. Perhaps the oath was similar to a reciting of the Ten Commandments or like a Church Covenant recited in unison as in our own day. Pliny then relates that after this, they depart and meet together again for a harmless, common meal. This meal was probably an agape meal or "love feast" that was a common Jewish custom.[17]

Justin Martyr (110–65 CE)

Another early Christian writer was Justin Martyr, whose writings can be dated around the middle of the second century. In the *First Apology* (apology in the sense of defending the faith), Justin gives us a great deal of information about the structure of Christian worship. Of interest is his use of the word "eucharist" (from the Greek *eucharistia*, thanksgiving) to describe the Lord's Supper. This term became one of the commonly accepted words used in the church. Written to the Emperor Antoninus Pius, Justin was making a defense of the faith when believers were under threat of arrest. Here is his account of Christian worship:

> And on the day called Sunday there is a meeting in one place . . . and the memoirs of the apostles or the writings of the prophets are read as long as time permits. When the reader has finished, the president in a discourse urges and invites [us] to the imitation of these noble things. Then we all stand up together and offer prayers. And . . . when we have finished the prayer, bread is brought, and wine and water, the president similarly sends up prayers . . . to the best of his ability, and the congregation assents, saying Amen; the distribution, and reception of the consecrated [elements] by each one, takes place and they are sent to the absent by the deacons.[18]

---

16. Richardson, *Early Christian Fathers*, 90. See also Tripp, "Letter to Pliny."
17. Whiston, "Letters of Pliny the Younger."
18. Martyr, "First Apology 67."

Bradshaw[19] raises some questions about our acceptance of Justin's account as a picture of the church in Rome. The main concern is how accurate his account is, given he is writing to non-Christians. Is he using terms that would communicate more intelligibly to religious outsiders rather than terms actually used by Christians. Does the reference to "the memoirs of the apostles or the writings of prophets" really mean the use of readings were very flexible or did he think this was unimportant to his readers?

This concern should probably be extended to many of these early sources. One important thing to consider is whether all churches had a similar or exact liturgy, or do we only have descriptions of isolated congregations?

Hippolytus (c. 215 CE)[20]

The *Apostolic Tradition* of Hippolytus of Rome was composed in Rome around 215 CE. It apparently preserved older second-century practices that were in danger of falling into disuse or losing out to innovations. Hippolytus, a presbyter of the Roman church at the time, was so distraught over the innovating practices of his former friends, Pope Zephyrinus and his successor Callistus, that he rejected papal authority. He continued with this stance through the rules of Callistus's successors, Urban and Pontius. In the time of Pope Pontianus, both Hyppolytus and Pontianus were exiled to Sardinia, from all accounts an extraordinarily unhealthy place, where they were forced to work the mines. Shortly afterward, in 235 CE, both died there. The two were martyrs, and their bodies were both brought back to Rome, where they were honorably buried.

Most of Hippolytus' works are lost to us. The Greek original is wholly lost but for fragments in the heavily edited excerpts in the *Apostolic Constitutions*. In chapter 1 he states his purpose in writing is to "keep the tradition which has lasted until now, according to the explanation we give of it, and so that others by taking note of it may be strengthened."

Hippolytus was fearful that traditional, older second-century practices were in danger of falling into disuse or being eliminated by innovation. He was bold in stating "we have arrived at the essence of the tradition which is proper for the Churches."

In chapter 2 directions are given for the election of a bishop followed by an attending bishop giving a prayer of blessing on the new bishop in chapter 3. Chapter 4 includes prayers of the assembled body and includes words that are included today in various liturgies:

---

19. Bradshaw, *Search for the Origins*, 111–12.
20. Easton, *Apostolic Tradition of Hippolytus*, 33–61.

> Bishop: The Lord be with you.
>
> And all reply: And with your spirit.
>
> The bishop says: Lift up your hearts.
>
> The people respond: We have them with the Lord. (4.3)

There follows a lengthy prayer that serves as a confession of faith and includes the words of institution of the Eucharist.

Chapters 5 and 6 are prayers for bread and wine, cheese, and olives. The reference to bread and wine relates to communion, but there is no indication of how the cheese and olives are part of the ceremony.

Chapters 7–14 give instructions for ordaining deacons and the laying on of hands to other church leaders. Instructions are given also for the examination of leaders on their moral character and doctrine.

Church leaders are to "inquire concerning the works and occupations of those are who are brought forward for instruction" (chapters 15 and 16). Some people could be rejected outright. For example, "A magus [magician] shall not even be brought forward for consideration" (16.13).

A catechumen was anyone receiving instruction in the basic doctrines and discipline of Christianity before baptism and admission to communicant membership in a church. They were expected to "hear the word for three years. Yet if someone is eager and perseveres well in the matter, it is not the time that is judged, but the conduct" (17:1–2). Rules of conduct are clearly spelled out and extensive preparations were required before baptism. These instructions were given for baptism in chapter 21:

> At the hour in which the cock crows, they shall first pray over the water. When they come to the water, the water shall be pure and flowing, that is, the water of a spring or a flowing body of water. Then they shall take off all their clothes. The children shall be baptized first. All of the children who can answer for themselves, let them answer. If there are any children who cannot answer for themselves, let their parents answer for them, or someone else from their family. After this, the men will be baptized. Finally, the women, after they have unbound their hair, and removed their jewelry. No one shall take any foreign object with themselves down into the water.

After each catechumen to be baptized has gone down into the water, "the one baptizing shall lay hands on each of them, asking, "Do you believe in God the Father Almighty?" The expected answer was, "I believe." Between the second and third immersions, more questions were asked that are clearly creedal. There follows in the remaining twenty-one chapters detailed instructions for a community meal that included the Eucharist, prayers to be said, and hours of the day and evening when prayer were to be offered.

This is a fascinating document to read. However, there is no way of knowing whether every church followed the same pattern of prayer and worship. Some of the baptismal language seems to relate baptism with spiritual regeneration. One reference is to an unbaptized catechumen who is martyred. He was regenerated by the blood of his sacrifice. The age of the children to be baptized is not given, but the baptism of infants with sponsors declaring faith is certainly indicated.

Eusebius (264–339 CE)

Eusebius was from Caesarea was also known as Eusebius Pamphili. Eusebius was a Roman historian, exegete, and Christian polemicist of Greek descent who became the bishop of Caesarea about 314. In addition to Pliny the Younger, Eusebius, in his *Commentary on Psalm 64*, speaks of Christians "writing psalms and odes."[21]

John Chrysostom (c. 347–c. 407 CE)

Chrysostom was famous as an orator and moralist, wrote that God had given the psalms to create the better attitudes of soul and mind, and that secular music would invite a visitation from demons. Instruments were not needed for making the mind and spirit function in harmony with one another. When a Christian had submitted to the Holy Spirit, he or she would then create a spiritual melody.

Jerome (c. 342–420 CE)

Jerome was one of the great scholars in the fourth century who gave a definition for Paul's psalms, hymns, and spiritual songs. The earliest reference we have of a hymn book in the Latin church is found in Jerome's "Commentary on Galatians." In the preface Jerome refers to a book of hymns written by Saint Hilary that was used in the Diocese of Poitiers in 356 CE.

A hymn declared the majesty and power of God, and had an "alleluia" added to it. Psalms from the Old Testament affected the seat of emotions to produce the right kind of moral action. The moralist who examines these two types of song and also examines the harmony of the universe

---

21. Eusebius, quoted in Wagner, *Introduction to the Gregorian Melodies*, 6–7.

sings a spiritual song. The Christian should sing more with the heart than with the voice.[22]

Augustine (354–430 CE)

Probably the best recognized early church father, Augustine wrote that music touched his emotions deeply. He taught that the singing of devotional songs could fan the flames of religious fervor and devotion. Borrowing some ideas from Aristotle, he said different types of music could affect the different passions of the body in some mysterious way. Augustine's own conversion was due in part to singing; not just the sound of voices, but with the message conveyed in music from the psalms. Augustine defined the hymn as "praises to God with singing."

Augustine was the first Christian theologian to voice the ethical and moral problems of the church in connection with music. He had learned in his Greek education that music could produce specific behaviors. For example, soldiers were not to listen to music written in one particular key because it would cause them to be effeminate. These Greek presuppositions caused him believe music posed a possible threat. However, he was aware of the powerful influence of music and declared it should be harnessed and put in the service of God. Augustine believed the sensual and worldly influences of music should be combated.

His problem with congregation singing was whether the Spirit of God was working through the medium of music, or was he responding to music because of the way it made him feel. He comments in one of his Confessions that he never loved the results of sin; he simply loved the experience of sinning for its own sake. Similarly, could he love music for its own sake, simply for the experience of music? Music that could not move him toward a deeper experience of God was suspect. This dualism is still present in the minds of some twenty-first-century Christians in their thoughts about contemporary Christian songs.

The Pilgrimage of Egeria (384–85 CE)[23]

Egeria (also translated as Etheria) was a Galician woman who made a pilgrimage to the Holy Land about 381–84 CE. She wrote an account of her journey in a long letter to a circle of women at home which survives in fragmentary

---

22. Strunk, *Source Readings*, 59–75.
23. McClure and Feltoe, *Pilgrimage of Etheria*.

form in a later copy. Egeria was probably a Spanish nun, and her visit to the Holy Land was only fifty years after the death of Constantine, making her work the earliest surviving account of the area. Her descriptions, particularly that of Jerusalem, are written with an attention to detail. This makes her the prime source of early Christian pilgrimage and worship.

The text is a narrative, apparently written at the end of Egeria's journey from notes she took while traveling, and addressed to her "dear ladies." These women may have been members of her spiritual community back home. In the first part of the text, she describes the journey from her approach to Mount Sinai until her stop in Constantinople. Along the way, she made excursions to Mount Nebo and St. Thecla's martyrium. The second portion of the text is a detailed account of the liturgical services and observances of the church calendar in Jerusalem. Upon her return to Constantinople, she planned to make a further trip to Ephesus.

Egeria describes a service that is held each weekday before the cave where Jesus was buried and resurrected outside Jerusalem. Services are held just before daybreak, at daybreak, and the sixth, ninth, and tenth hours of the day. These services include the singing of psalms, hymns, and antiphons in response by both people and clergy, with prayers being said after each hymn and antiphon. As the day begins to break they begin to sing the matin hymns. She also describes preparations for baptism and the instruction given to those awaiting baptism. The instruction emphasizes the learning of the "Creed," but there is nothing to tell us about this creed.

At the tenth hour, or the Service of Lights, people bring their own candles for illumination, and vesper psalms and antiphons are sung for a good while. A deacon reads names for commemoration, during which many boys stand, "responding 'Kyrie eleison,' as we say, 'Lord, have mercy upon us.'"[24]

On Sunday the people congregate before sunup outside the Church of the Resurrection that is near the cave. Hymns and antiphons are sung and a priest brings a censer of incense, filling the air with a sweet smell. A Gospel is read and a procession leads from the cave to a cross outside of the church, with everyone processing and singing hymns.

At dawn, they proceed to the Church of the Resurrection that is at Golgotha "behind the cross." There, all things are done "according to the use which is customary everywhere on the Lord's day."[25] One or more sermons are preached and the service lasts well into the afternoon. Seemingly to assure her sisters, she writes, "This is very plain, that suitable psalms or antiphons are always said; those at night, those in the morning, and those

---

24. McClure and Feltoe, *Pilgrimage of Etheria*, 47.
25. McClure and Feltoe, *Pilgrimage of Etheria*, 48.

through the day, whether at the sixth hour or ninth hour or at vespers, being always suitable and intelligible as pertaining to the matter in hand."[26] The mention of hymns for matins and vesper indicates the texts would be "suitable" for the theme of the service and were part of weekly, repeated worship. Everything described by Egeria points to structured services.

Early Hymnody

The City of Rome fell in 476 CE and the Empire split into East and West. The Western Empire had its capital in Ravenna, Italy; the Eastern Empire had its capital in Constantinople. Justinian (527–563 CE) united the Eastern and Western empires in 540 CE and continued to maintain both Ravenna and Constantinople as capitols. However, he changed the name of Constantinople by restoring its Roman name of Byzantium, and the new empire is referred to as the Byzantine Empire. Justinian started a huge building campaign in Byzantium to make it the New Rome.

The church imitated the Empire and divided into the Roman (Western) church and the Orthodox (Eastern) church. Differences existed between Greek-speaking Christians of the eastern Mediterranean and Latin-speaking Christians of Italy and farther west. Outstanding differences were:

- The struggle between Rome and Constantinople over which one would be the capital city of the church.
- The rise of papal power in Italy. After the decline of the empire, the pope in Rome exercised much of the same power as the former emperors had, and eastern Christians did not look upon this with favor.
- The rapid growth in the West contrasted to controversy within the church in the East.
- The loss of territory and population in the East after the rise of Islam.
- Differences in the development of liturgy.

Hymns and psalms were prominent in both the Latin and Greek churches. While we have information about people who wrote hymns, many of these texts are no longer extant. Even less information is available to tell us what music was used for hymn and psalm singing and what it sounded like.

---

26. McClure and Feltoe, *Pilgrimage of Etheria*, 49.

Greek Hymns

Early hymn writers were Greek, wrote in Greek, and lived in areas represented by the Orthodox churches of today. However, the division of the church into east and west resulted in the death of Christian hymnody and poetry in the Greek-speaking world—the very region where it had originated. Consequently, the largest body of ancient hymnody survives from the Latin church.

Singing was accepted in the Greek churches, but where did the hymns originate? Were they compiled in any form? In 1909, a collection of hymns, originally in Greek, but contained in a fifteenth- or sixteenth-century Syriac manuscript, was discovered near the banks of the Tigris River. These hymns are entitled *The Odes of Solomon* and were bound together with another work, *The Psalms of Solomon*. The "psalms" have been identified as belonging to the Old Testament period, but the "odes" were definitely written in the New Testament period. Scholars reach this conclusion after a careful study of the text. The joy of the believer in Christ and other Christian feelings of emotion are expressed in the texts. A "hallelujah" appears at the end of each ode that sets it off in song form. No music is available to enlighten us as to the music used. What phase of Christianity these "odes" represent or who used them also remains a mystery. The probable date of composition is towards the end of the first century.[27]

In 1922 a papyrus was uncovered in Oxyrhynchus, Egypt, that contained the words and music of a third-century hymn. It is a short vocal piece composed in the general style of pre-Christian Greek music. The *Oxyrhynchus Hymn* (P. Oxy. XV 1786) is the earliest-known manuscript of a Christian hymn—dating from the third century CE—to contain both lyrics and musical notation. It is now kept at the Papyrology Rooms of the Sackler Library, Oxford. The text, in Greek, poetically invokes silence so that the Holy Trinity may be praised. This is an English translation of the text:[28]

> Let it be silent
>
> Let the Luminous stars not shine,
>
> Let the winds (?) and all the noisy rivers die down;
>
> And as we hymn the Father, the Son and the Holy Spirit,
>
> Let all the powers add "Amen, Amen."

---

27. Lang, *Music in Western Civilization*, 23.

28. Strunk, *Source Readings*, 5, 9–75. See also Sachs, *Rise of Music*, 250–51; Holleman, "Oxyrhynchus Papyrus," 1–17.

Empire, praise always, and glory to God,

The sole giver of good things, Amen, Amen.

The music for this hymn, both its pitch and rhythm, has been transcribed into modern notation. This is the earliest example of Christian church music that we have. Since it survives only as a small fragment we have no idea whether or not it is typical of Christian music of the time. It is not until the eighth century that we have another fragment of written music and no complete Christian manuscript with identifiable music notation until the ninth century.[29]

John Mason Neale (1818–66) translated "The Day of Resurrection," one of the surviving Greek hymn texts that is contained in many hymnals today. It was written by John of Damascus, a monk who lived in the Mar Saba monastery in the Judean desert. John devoted his life to scholarly study and writing, but is best remembered for his hymns.

Latin Hymns

Hilary of Poitiers (c. 310–66 CE)

Hilary was the first Latin hymnist who desired to make the singing of hymns popular. Hilary was exiled to Asia Minor in 356 CE because he was attacking the Arian heresy. His stay in Asia exposed him to Greek hymns that he tried to imitate upon returning home. These hymns were written in the rhythm of Roman marching songs in an effort to make the singing popular. His hymns were not successful because of their difficulty in being sung. None of his hymns appear in our English hymnals.

Ambrose of Milan (340–97 CE)

Ambrose was of greater significance than Hilary and is reputed to have produced the first Christian hymns to be written in Latin. He is also credited with starting liturgical hymn singing. While Ambrose was bishop of Milan, the conflict between Arians and the Christian orthodox grew worse. The Empress Mother, Justina, ordered Ambrose to allow Arians to use the church and its vessels for services. When Ambrose refused, he had to take shelter in the church to escape the authorities. His faithful members kept vigil day and night to maintain possession of their place of worship.

---

29. This short hymn can be heard on YouTube at https://www.youtube.com/watch?v=i1SEj1xGFi8.

To help his flock keep their long vigils, Ambrose wrote doctrinal hymns to strengthen their morale. The effectiveness of his hymns can be seen in the life of Augustine whom Ambrose baptized. Augustine attributed his conversion to Ambrose and his hymns.

An early hymn by Ambrose, which still appears in some church hymnals, is "O Splendor of God's Glory Bright." It is a Christological hymn written to teach correct doctrine opposed to the doctrines sung by the Arian heretics.

> O splendor of God's glory bright,
>
> Who bringest forth the light from Light;
>
> O Light of light, light's Fountain-spring;
>
> O Day, our days enlightening.

Prudentius (c. 348–413 CE)

Prudentius was the first Christian poet to unite classical scholarship and religion. Many of his poems and hymns survived throughout the Middle Ages, but only one hymn has found any lasting place in our hymnals. His hymn "Of the Father's Love Begotten," translated by John Mason Neale, appears in most of our hymnals. This hymn also was intended to promote the orthodox doctrine of Christ in opposition to the Arian doctrine. It affirms Jesus as the source and end of all things and is based on Revelation 1:8.

> Of the Father's love begotten
>
> ere the worlds began to be,
>
> He is Alpha and Omega—
>
> He the source, the ending he,
>
> of the things that are, that have been,
>
> and that future years shall see
>
> evermore and evermore.

Heretical Hymns

Hymn singing was not confined to the faithful orthodox. There were three prevalent heresies that also employed hymns to propagate the teachings of the groups: Gnosticism, Arianism, and Manichaeism.

Gnosticism

Tradition says Gnosticism was founded by Simon Magus, who is mentioned in Acts 8, after his rejection by the apostle Peter. Gnosticism was not a "school" of philosophy, but the general expression of common ideas. There were both secular and "Christian" versions. As a mixture of Greek and Oriental thinking, it led to very strange conclusions by some early Christian leaders. These leaders were enthusiastic, but their attempts to adjust the Christian message to the prevailing thought of the day, and to make it more acceptable, were declared heretical. Today, there is a renewed interest in Gnosticism among many Christian scholars.

Gnosticism troubled the church for some 150 years. It was a philosophy that taught that "matter" is intrinsically evil and "spirit" is intrinsically good. Being material, the body was considered to be evil, while virtue and goodness was attained by the pursuit of "knowledge." Since evil exists in the world, the God of the New Testament could not have been the Creator since God is good. Messiah's body was only an appearance, or, according to other Gnostics, only a human body he used temporarily (the same teaching existed in Manichaeism). For the Christ to possess a physical body would mean he was sinful. Consequently, the major teachings both of Judaism and orthodox Christianity were opposed. Two Gnostics who resorted to hymn singing in order to preach their "gospel" were Marcion and Valentinus.

Arianism

The other major heresy was Arianism. Founded by Arius (c. 250–336 CE). This was the belief that Jesus was a creation of God, therefore not fully divine. He was to be worshipped as being exalted above the rest of creation, but not as equal to God. The Council of Nicaea (325 CE) condemned his teachings and banished him to what is today Croatia. While in his banishment, he composed songs to teach his particular beliefs and taught them to everyone. The people sang his songs lustily, whether they understood or believed the teachings or not. There is no doubt about the influence of Arius' hymns.

When Chrysostom was bishop of Constantinople, in 398 CE, the Arians were not allowed to worship within the city walls, but they would come to town on a Saturday or Sunday evening and hold festivals and hymn sings on the streets that attracted huge crowds. Their hymns set forth Arian doctrines and hurled taunts at the orthodox believers and general confusion ensued. In a counterattack, Chrysostom organized his own hymn sings that resulted in bloodshed between the two groups. After that, Arians were banned completely by law.[30]

Manichaeism

As Gnosticism began to wane, a Neo-Gnostic movement developed under the inspiration of the Prophet Mani. The Manichaean movement became a world religion, spreading to Europe, Central Asia and China. It survived as a living religion in the Orient up until the present century. Manichaeism is a heresy that combined Persian religious beliefs with Christian beliefs. It taught absolute dualism of contrasting forces—the "kingdom of light" and "the kingdom of darkness." God is part of everything; thus, everything is a part of God. Physically, Jesus was an apparition. He was merely an aid to the good principle in every person that helps him or her overcome the evil principle that is also a part of everyone.

A large body of Manichaean psalms, hymns, and prayers is available in English. The *Acts of John*, an apocryphal (noncanonical and unauthentic) Manichaean writing, composed about 180 CE, supposedly is an account of the travels and miracles of St. John the Evangelist. The ninth-century patriarch of Constantinople, Photius, identified the author of the Acts of John as one Leucius Charinus. Nothing is known about him, but the book reflects heretical views that denied the reality of Christ's physical body and attributed to it only the appearance of materiality. The Acts of John likewise has one hymn containing Manichaean formulae to evade demons who could impede a person's journey to heaven. The book was condemned by the second Council of Nicaea (787 CE) because of its subversion of orthodox Christian teachings.[31]

The *Acts of John* is a compilation of four other apocryphal books that was substituted by the Manichaeans for our book of Acts. One of the four books is titled "The Dance of Jesus," a description of the hymn sung at the close of the Last Supper. The hymn is accompanied by a circle dance of some sort led by Jesus. M. R. James translated the text where Jesus is reported to have said,

> Before I am delivered up unto them (viz. the Jews) let us sing a hymn to the Father, and so go forth to that which lieth before us. He bade us therefore make as it were a ring, holding one

---

30. Newman, *Manual of Church History*, 1:393–94.

31. For the most complete information about Gnosticism, see the archives of The Gnostic Society, www.gnosis.org.

another's hands, and himself standing in the midst he said: Answer Amen unto me.[32]

This is one part of the text as translated by G. R. S. Mead:

Glory to Thee, Father!

(And we going round in a ring answered to Him:)

Amen!

Glory to Thee, Word!

Amen!

Glory to Thee, Grace!

Amen!

Glory to Thee, Spirit!

Glory to Thee, Holy One!

Glory to Thy Glory!

Amen!

We praise Thee, O Father;

We give Thanks to Thee, O light;

In Whom Darkness dwells not!

Amen![33]

While this perhaps sounds strange to our ears, there is ample evidence that a similar ritual was performed in many places for several centuries. It might even be possible that the popular song "Lord of the Dance" has its roots deep in this Manichaean hymn.[34]

For You to Think about

1. Study carefully both the descriptions of and prescriptions for worship given by the *Didache,* Pliny, and Justin Martyr. Then, summarize what you have read as answers to these questions.

    - How will worship take place (what are appropriate things to be acted, said and sung)?

---

32. Quoted in Van Unnik, "Note on the Dance," 1.
33. Mead, "Hymn of Jesus," 76–77.
34. Dilley, "Jesus as Lord."

- Who determines what is said, sung, and acted in worship?
- In what order should they be sung, said, or acted?
- How much variation is allowed from week to week?
- What are the biblical and theological criteria that inform the discussion?

2. Study the creeds and confessions in this chapter. Using them as a model, write a confession of faith that you could use in your church.

3. Which of the New Testament canticles could you use in the worship of your church, why would you use them, and how would you use them?

5

Congregational Song in the Western Church

> No others shall sing in the Church, save only the canonical singers,
> who go up into the ambo and sing from a book.
>
> —Council of Laodicea

BETWEEN 476 CE WITH the "fall" of the Western Roman Empire and 1517 CE with the publishing of Martin Luther's Ninety-five Theses, the pope and the church in Rome were able to unify Western Europe in a manner unparalleled since Roman times. The church touched everyone's life, no matter what their rank or class, or where they lived. With the exception of a small number of Jews, everyone in Europe was thought to be a Christian, from the richest king down to the lowest serf. This is because everyone was baptized shortly after birth, and from the moment of its baptism a few days after birth, a child entered into a life of service to God and God's church. As a child grew, it would be taught basic prayers, would go to church every week barring illness, and would learn of its responsibilities to the church.

Every person was required to live by the church's laws and to pay heavy taxes to support the church. Disobedience could result in discipline by the civil authorities. In return for this, people were shown the way to everlasting life and happiness after lives that were often short and hard. In addition to collecting taxes, the church also accepted gifts of all kinds from individuals who wanted special favors or wanted to be certain of a place in heaven. These gifts included land, flocks, crops, and even serfs. This allowed the church to become very powerful, and it often used this power to influence kings to do as it wanted.[1]

The central idea of this period was the promise of salvation through the church and mediated through its Sacraments. The word "sacrament" is

---

1. Lord, *Music in the Middle Ages*, 27.

from *sacramentum*, a Latin word for an oath of allegiance. The Eucharist (or communion or the Lord's Supper) was the most important sacrament. The word "Eucharist" is from *eucharistia*, a Greek word which means "thanksgiving." The church has seven sacraments and they are essential for a person to retain their spiritual relationship to God. Through administration of the sacraments, the clergy had power to forgive sins and to determine a person's eternal destiny.

Congregational song in the western church was sparse, but later development of song was influenced by several major events: the standardization of the liturgy, the development of the Mass, Gregorian chant, the influence of monasticism, and cathedral churches.

Standardization of the Liturgy

By 590 CE, when Gregory became pope, liturgy varied in different localities. If Gregory could unify the liturgy around a common language and structure it would help unify the church as well as increase the authority and prestige of the papacy and the church in Rome. Gregory's ambition was difficult to attain, for there was more than one liturgy being used. The major liturgies were associated with cities and influential bishops of those cities:

The Roman liturgy, used in the churches around the Mediterranean. The Roman rite was used principally in Rome and became the official rite of the Catholic Church after the ninth century. Its form was fixed in 1570 after numerous minor changes in emphasis and ceremony. The Roman liturgy was simpler and less ornate and symbolic than the Eastern liturgy. However, there were still some local variants in the Roman liturgy that lasted until the Council of Trent in the sixteenth century.

The Gallican liturgy, used primarily in Gaul (present-day France), in one sense identifies all the Western rites outside of Rome. It refers to the liturgical music sung as part of worship in the Western church in Gaul until it was replaced by Roman chant following the late eighth century.

The Mozarabic liturgy, found in Christian churches in Moslem Spain. *Mozarabes* were Christians under Moorish- (Islamic) occupied Spain. This chant style centered in Seville, Toledo, and Saragossa. Moslems generally did not concern themselves with such details of other religions as what chants they used. The rite and chant form continued in use under the Muslim conquest, but was replaced with the Roman rite after the Christians regained Spainish territory. The Mozarabic Chapel in the Toledo Cathedral still uses the Mozarabic rite and music.

The Ambrosian liturgy, was compiled by St. Ambrose and used in the church in Milan, Italy. It is characterized by different categories of chant, different chant texts, and different musical styles than the other chants. By the eighth century, this chant was normative across northern Italy, perhaps reaching into southern Italy as well. Though the many local variants of the Roman rite were standardized by the Council of Trent, Milan and the part of northern Italy that formed its archdiocese was allowed to retain this rite because of its antiquity.

The Celtic liturgy and its music traces its roots back to the establishment of Christianity in Britain by St. Patrick in the fifth century CE. In the absence of central authority, the diocese and churches of Britain, Wales, Scotland, and Ireland developed local rites and chant forms that were replaced beginning in the seventh century by St. Augustine of Canterbury, who installed the Roman rite.[2]

The Influence of Charlemagne

In spite of Gregory's lofty goal, he lacked both the authority and power to enforce the Roman liturgy upon those churches using a different liturgy. That goal was not achieved until some 200 years later by Charlemagne, King of the Franks. On Christmas 800 CE, Pope Leo III crowned Charlemagne as Emperor of the Holy Roman Empire. His was an empire that included most of western Europe and northern Italy. The reasons for this event go beyond this present study. According to Graves, "The coronation of Charles sparked much debate during the middle ages." He then added:

> At issue was what relationship of the church to state. Did the act of crowning the emperor show the pope's superior authority as giver of the empire to King Charles? Charles didn't think so. He continued to rule as the divinely appointed protector of the church, appointing bishops as well as counts to office.[3]

The real emperor of Rome was the Byzantine Empress Irene, in Constantinople, whom Pope Leo III could not accept because of her gender. This posed a potential political problem for Charlemagne, for he was head of a rival empire. In order to expand his influence, Charlemagne used his power to demand, often harshly, that all churches and monasteries use the Roman liturgy. Just as Pope Gregory had desired, the common liturgy and

---

2. More detailed information on various liturgies is available at www.liturgica.com.
3. Graves, "#203," para. 6.

language of the Roman Mass helped unify both western Europe and the Roman liturgy.

> He was not only the first, but possibly the greatest of the emperors from the eighth through the nineteenth century. He restored education, improved law, supported the church, backed ... attempts to produce an accurate Bible and in many other ways did much that was good. In France, his name was blended with his greatness, and he is known as Charlemagne.[4]

On 23 March 789, Charlemagne issued an *Admonitio generalis* ("General Correction," also known as the capitulary) to the Frankish clergy that covers educational and ecclesiastical reform within the Frankish kingdom. The work covers the goals of the king in eighty-two chapters. The more interesting part for our purposes begins in chapter seventy-two, which calls for schools to be established to teach the psalms, music and singing, and grammar. Schools were to teach boys how to read and write so they could help spread the Christian faith.[5]

The Development of Gregorian Chant

Gregory's concern for standardization of the liturgy extended both to the structure of the Mass and the liturgy that surrounded it. This included music, for the Council of Laodicea (363–64 CE) had formulated regulations concerning who was to sing in the church services:

> Canon 15: No others shall sing in the Church, save only the canonical singers, who go up into the ambo (pulpit) and sing from a book.
>
> Canon 23: The readers and singers have no right to wear an orarium (*stole*), and to read or sing thus habited.[6]

We can learn a few things here. The singers (and readers) probably were minor clergy, such as a subdeacon. This is because they had no right to wear a stole (orarium) and could not read or sing if wearing one. The number is not given, but those who were to sing would go to the ambo or pulpit and sing from a book. This would indicate an available body of song or chant large enough to be bound in a book. The reason for these regulations is not clear, but it may have been that "undesirable" persons wanted

---

4. Graves, "#203," para. 8.
5. Charlemagne, "Admonitio Generalis."
6. Synod of Laodicea, "Canons of the Synod," 132, 143.

to sing, those who could not sing well. After this Council, congregational music was completely in the hands of a clergy choir.

Since congregational music became nonexistent, singers took on a new importance, some being promoted to high church positions on the merits of their singing rather than on other qualifications. Many priests were neglecting their pastoral ministry because they had to spend so many hours practicing music. Gregory's task was daunting, but out of all this ferment evolved what is known as Gregorian chant, named after Pope Gregory. His actual role in the development of the chant is uncertain, but his influence was great. The earliest church music of which we have record is Gregorian chant, and Pope Gregory is traditionally credited for having ordered the simplification and cataloging of music assigned to specific celebrations in the church calendar. The legend goes like this:

> In the house of the Lord, like a most wise Solomon, knowing the compunction which the sweetness of music inspires, he compiled for the sake of the singers the collection called "Antiphoner," which is of so great usefulness. He founded also the School of Singers who to this day perform the sacred chant in the Holy Roman Church according to instructions received from him. He assigned to it several estates, and had two houses built for it, one situated at the foot of the steps of the Church of the Apostle St. Peter, the other in the neighborhood of the buildings of the patriarchal palace of the Lateran . . . By a clause inserted in his deed of gift, he laid down under pain of anathema that these estates should be divided between the two portions of the School in payment for the daily service.[7]

Another important factor in the standardization of worship liturgy was the establishment by Gregory of the *Schola Cantorum* in Rome, a school for training singers. This would ensure that all churches would have both the same texts and the same music. The use of Latin and one system of music would unite churches of different nationalities and languages. Gregory collected the whole repertoire of chants available at the time in his *Antiphonale Missarum*, and these chants were a model and standard for worship in Roman Catholic church until the synod of Vatican II was held in the twentieth century.

A chant is halfway between speech and singing, and the melodic rhythm is dependent upon the rhythms of the text. Chants are monophonic [one voice] vocal music, meaning they are sung in unison without accompaniment of instruments. In general, the chants were learned by rote. Priests

---

7. This is an excerpt from the life of St. Gregory by John the Deacon, c. 872, and quoted in Wyatt, *St. Gregory and the Gregorian Music*, 12.

would follow the chant sung by the choirmaster until they learned the melody, which took many years of experience. There was no notation that indicated exact pitch until around 1000 CE. However, the resulting body of chant music is the first to be notated in a system that led to our modern musical notation. Gregorian chant has these characteristics:

1. Chant is not in a major key or a minor key, but in *modes* (though there are some modes which can sound like a modern scale).
2. Rhythm was derived from the rhythm of the Latin words.
3. Melodies are step-wise without wide leaps.
4. Chants have the range of a medium male voice.
5. Gregorian Chant has no meter at all, though it does have rhythm groups of two or three notes.

Types of Chant

Chants are classified by how they are written and sung and are labeled according to their primary structure. However, there may be other elements included as well, for the text, the phrases, words, and eventually the syllables, can be sung in various ways.

Syllabic Chant

The simplest type of chant is the syllabic as each syllable is sung to a single note. Simple chants are often syllabic throughout with only a few instances where two or more notes are sung on one syllable. For example, hymns are usually syllabic as in the tune Old Hundreth to which we sing the Doxology.

Neumatic Chant

A neumatic chant is more embellished than simple chants but not as ornate as the melismatic chants. The melody may be mostly syllabic but at times having a group of three or four notes for one vowel.

Melismatic Chant

Melismatic chants are the most ornate chants in which elaborate melodies are sung on long sustained vowels, as in this familiar refrain of the Christmas carol, "Angels We Have Heard on High." The refrain has the words, "Gloria in excelsis deo." All of the notes on the syllable "o" of *Gloria* are called a melisma. A melisma can range from five or six notes per syllable to over sixty in the more complex chants.

The Music Notation of Chants

The earliest chants were learned by rote from a singing teacher and it was long and arduous. There needed to be a way to indicate how long sounds were to be made and what the pitches would be. There also needed to be an easier way of learning new music.

Notation refers to how music is put into written form. The earliest form of Western notation is called neumatic notation. The word "neumatic" comes from the Greek word *neuma*, which means a "sign." Neumes are free-form wavy lines above the text to be sung that indicate pitch, the general inflection of the voice and how the melody moves up and down. However, neumes do not generally indicate rhythm. "These early neumes appeared in the ninth century," according to Apel, "and contained general information concerning the melodic contour, yet the intervallic distance between each note was indistinguishable.[8] In other words, exact pitches could not be determined by a neume, so the chants still had to be learned by rote.

In general, music historians have thought music notation using neumes began about the ninth century. However, Levy refers to the eightieth chapter of Charlemagne's *capitula* to an injunction that all clerics fully learn the Roman chant which his father Pepin ordered substituted for the Gallican chant. Levy posited the theory that there was some form of music notation in existence during the late eighth century for this transition to take place.[9] We may never discover exactly how music notation as we know it was developed.

The situation began to change around 1000 CE. There are examples of music writing that gives a clearer visual indication of pitches and the distance between pitches. Scribes imagined horizontal lines that represented lower or higher pitch and to a certain extent various degrees of length to indicate the duration of the pitch.[10] Instead of wavy lines, square notes were written on two horizontal lines.

---

8. Apel, *Gregorian Chant*, 181.
9. Levy, "Charlemagne's Archetype of Gregorian Chant," 82.
10. Levy, "Charlemagne's Archetype of Gregorian Chant," 1–30.

Guido d'Arezzo

Guido d'Arezzo was a medieval music theorist whose principles served as a foundation for modern Western musical notation. He was educated at the Benedictine abbey at Pomposa, and apparently developed his principles of staff notation there. He left Pomposa in about 1025 because his fellow monks resisted his musical innovations, and he was appointed by Theobald, Bishop of Arezzo, as a teacher in the cathedral school and commissioned to write the *Micrologus de disciplina artis musicae* ("A Short Treatise on the Discipline of Musical Art").

Guido is credited with the innovation of music notation. His new system used square notes written on four parallel lines. Guido added one red line and one yellow line to the already customary two-line staff. Since music could now be written down, musicians would learn new songs without having to hear them first.

Around 1030 CE a new method to teach singing was also invented by Guido. The hymn to St. John the Baptist was used by Guido to teach the scale. In listening to the monks singing this hymn, Guido observed that the first syllable of each line of the hymn formed one of the *sol–fa* syllables of the scale as we know it, and that taken successively they formed a six-note scale: *doh–re–mi–fa–so–la* (C–D–E–F–G–A).

> *Ut querant laxis.*
>
> *REsonare fibris*
>
> *MIra gestorum*
>
> *FAmuli tuorum*
>
> *SOLve polluti*
>
> *LAbii reatum*

The scale names given by him have remained to the present. The seventh tone, *si* (now called *ti*) was formed from the two initial letters of the two last words, "Sancte Joannes" (J is I in Latin). In time "doh" was used instead of "ut" and "ti" was added.[11] "These aspects of the new notation produced ramifications for both the literacy and transportation of music," wrote Strayer. Music could be learned without hearing it, music could be memorized more easily, and music could be transported to and learned in distant cities.[12]

---

11. Reisenweaver, "Guido of Arezzo," 30–31.
12. Strayer, "From Neumes to Notes," 10.

The Development of the Mass

When Gregory became pope, the idea that the Lord's Supper was a sacrificial offering of Christ upon the altar of the church had become firmly established and the worship service centered on this act. The name of the Supper had been changed to Mass, taken from the parting words of the priest: "*Ite, missa est*" (Go, you are dismissed).

At first, worship in the churches seemed to be rather simple. Scripture was read, psalms sung, and prayers offered. Gradually, a formal pattern of worship occurred. One of the earliest accounts is given by Justin in his *Apologia*. The Synaxis or non-eucharistic part of the service included

- an opening greeting by the leader of the congregation and response by the congregation;
- Scripture reading;
- Psalmody—singing or chanting psalm verses;
- Scripture reading;
- Sermon;
- The unbaptized are dismissed.

Distinct from this was the communion service:

- Offertory where the bread and wine were taken and put together on a table.
- Prayer of thanks to God for the wine and bread.
- The bread is broken (fraction).
- Communion with bread and wine distributed to the congregation.[13]

This division was necessary in practice because people who had never been baptized were excluded from the Eucharist. In many places it seems non-baptized people could not even enter the sanctuary of a church. Many of the older European cathedrals have separate buildings called baptisteries for the baptism of babies and new believers. Two outstanding Italian examples are the cathedrals in Florence and Pisa. The baptistery of the Pisa cathedral even has a huge tank of water in which baptisms were done by immersion. A smaller baptismal font is attached for the current form of baptism.

As liturgy developed, the first part was called the Liturgy of the Word and the second part the Liturgy of the Table. That twofold pattern

---

13. Justin Martyr, *First Apology*, in Roberts and Donaldson, *Ante-Nicene Fathers*, vol. 1.

is followed today in Catholic, Anglican, and Lutheran churches, as well as many other churches with less formal worship. For example, the Mass in contemporary American Roman Catholic churches begins with a Gathering Rite, followed by the Liturgy of the Word, the Liturgy of the Eucharist, and a Dismissal Rite.

The Mass has two sets of texts. One set is called the Ordinary and those texts never change, except with a few adjustments for certain special occasions or seasons of the year, and are said or sung at every Mass. The other set of texts is called the Proper. These texts change from service to service, and are proper (or appropriate) for a particular season of the Church Year. There are many musical settings of each Ordinary text, for they are set to individual melodies. The Ordinary and Proper elements are present in every Mass.

The Ordinary of the Mass

The ordinary of the Mass, as sung by the choir, has five main sections. The priest recites everything the choir sings immediately before or during the singing. This is necessary for the ritual to be effective spiritually. If there is no choir, the priest may sing the text. The following are the main sections of the Ordinary in the order they occur, and they are named after the first Latin word of the text.

Kyrie (Kyrie eleison, "Lord, have mercy")

The *Kyrie* is borrowed from the Eastern liturgy and introduced to the Latin liturgy in approximately 550 CE. *Kyrie* is the Latin spelling of the Greek word *kurios,* meaning "Lord." You may recall that Egeria heard a *kyrie* sung in Jerusalem in the fourth century. For her, it was a different element in the service, for she commented, "As the deacon says the names of various people, a number of boys stand and answer always, Kyrie Eleison, as we should say, Miserere Domine."[14]

In the Mass, the textual sequence is *kyrie eleison* (Lord, have mercy) three times, then *Christe eleison* (Christ have mercy) three times, followed by *kyrie eleison* three times. The music associated with these texts could be quite lengthy though the texts are very short.

---

14. McClure and Feltoe, *Pilgrimage of Etheria,* 47.

GLORIA

This is a version of the song sung by angels at the Christ's birth:"Glory to God in the highest" (Luke 2:14). Additional words of praise have been added and it is sometimes referred to as the "great doxology."

CREDO

This text is "*Credo in unum Deum . . .*" (I believe in one God) and is taken from the Nicene Creed. It is called "Nicene" because it was originally adopted in the city of Nicaea in 325 CE. It is a statement of faith widely used in many churches today other than Roman Catholic. Creeds were important to early Christians, for very few people could read or write. Memorizing a creed was a way for people to learn their beliefs. Also, there were many heretical groups vying for the attention of the people who had their creeds, and creeds authorized by the church were a way of combatting false teachings.

SANCTUS

According to the Catholic Encyclopedia, the earliest reference to the Sanctus as part of the liturgy is by Clement of Rome (d. 104 CE). Sanctus is the Latin word for "holy" and is based upon Isaiah 6:3:

Holy, holy, holy!

The Lord Almighty is holy!

His glory fills the world.

AGNUS DEI (LAMB OF GOD)

The text is based on the saying of John the Baptist: "Behold the Lamb of God, who takes away the sin of the world" (John 1:29). The *Agnus Dei* comes between the Lord's Prayer and the Communion and sounds the theme of sacrifice and adoration. Both Anglican and Lutheran liturgies have retained the Agnus Dei in their eucharistic rites.[15]

---

15. For further information, go to the online *Encyclopedia Britannica* (http://www.britannica.com/topic/) and search by each title.

The Proper of the Mass

The commemoration and adoration of saints are assigned specific calendar days in the Liturgical Year, as well as the assignment of more familiar events like Christmas and Easter. These are referred to as "feast days." In the Proper of the Mass, texts can change daily depending upon the feast day of the year. For example, texts proper for Easter are different from the texts proper for Christmas. In addition, there are many other short texts that are chanted on single notes called reciting tones or are simply spoken. The texts sung by the choir are the Introit, Gradual, Alleluia or Tract, Sequence, Offertory, and Communion.[16] They are listed below in the order in which they occur.

INTROIT (FROM THE LATIN *INTROITUS*, "ENTRANCE")

This word is taken from the Latin *introitus*, meaning "entrance." It is part of the opening of the worship service for many Christian denominations as clergy and choir enter the sanctuary. In its most complete version in the Western church, it consists of an antiphon, a psalm verse, and the *Gloria Patri* that is spoken or sung at the beginning of the celebration.

GLORIA PATRI

The *Gloria Patri* is a doxology or short hymn of praise to God. Here is the traditional English version still used today:

> Glory be to the Father,
> and to the Son:
> and to the Holy Ghost;
> As it was in the beginning,
> is now, and ever shall be:
> world without end. Amen.

---

16. For further information, go to *Encyclopedia Britannica* and search for each section by name: http://www.britannica.com/topic/.

Antiphon

This is music sung antiphonally by a divided choir or choir and congregation. Usually, a psalm verse would be set to a Gregorian chant. The pattern of singing would be:

Antiphon, Verse one;

Antiphon, Verse two, etc.

The antiphon text would be related either to the feast day or the psalm text. Gradually, psalm verses were dropped from various places in the Mass and only the antiphon was sung. The English word "anthem" is derived from the antiphon and designates a composition for a church choir.

Gradual

The hymn sung immediately before the reading of the Gospel is called a "Gradual." The name is derived from the Latin word *gradus*, meaning a step. In the very earliest churches, there was a raised pulpit (called an ambo) on either side of the sanctuary. The Epistle was read from one, and the Gospel from the other. After the Epistle had been read, the Gospel would be brought to the altar, censed, and blessed, then taken in procession, with lights and incense, to the ambo. While this was happening, a cantor would lead the people in the singing of a psalm or antiphon from the step (*gradus*) of the ambo. So this psalm was called the 'Gradual'. When ambos went out of fashion, both the reading of the Epistle, and the singing of the Gradual was from the Chancel step.

Alleluia (praise Yah)

The Alleluia (also spelled Halleluiah) comes from the Old Testament Hallel psalms, Psalms 113–118. The word *hallel* means "praise." An alleluia verse is generally added to the Gradual throughout the year.

Tract

The *Tract* (from *tractim*, without interruption) is taken from Scripture, very often from a psalm, and is sung without an antiphonal response, hence the idea of singing without interruption. In some seasons, the Tract is substituted for the alleluia.

Sequence

The Sequence derives its name in the ninth century from the Latin prose texts written over the wordless musical extension, or melisma, of the final "ah" of the Alleluia. The "ah" could be a very long series of notes without words. Without music notation, it was difficult to remember the notes and their sequence. As a memory help, words were added to this note pattern. Eventually, these notes and extra words were separated from the alleluia and sung like a hymn. In order to identify the original alleluia chant, the sequence was given the chant name.

Offertory

The offertory has a double function in the Mass. The people offer their monetary gifts while the priest is preparing to offer Christ on the altar as an unbloody sacrifice. Offertory is an antiphon and was once probably a psalm or a collection of psalms.

The Liturgical Year

The liturgy is organized in an annual cycle that is an enactment of the life, burial, and resurrection of Jesus the Christ. The various events in the Year provide the liturgical material for the Proper of the Mass. According to the United States Conference of Catholic Bishops, the liturgical year is made up of six seasons:

> **Advent:** four weeks of preparation before the celebration of Jesus' birth.
>
> **Christmas Time:** recalling the Nativity of Jesus Christ and his manifestation to the peoples of the world.
>
> **Lent:** a six-week period of penance before Easter.
>
> **Sacred Paschal Triduum:** the holiest "Three Days" of the Church's year, where the Christian people recall the suffering, death, and resurrection of Jesus.
>
> **Easter Time:** fifty days of joyful celebration of the Lord's resurrection from the dead and his sending forth of the Holy Spirit.
>
> **Ordinary Time:** divided into two sections: one span of 4–8 weeks after Christmas Time and another lasting about six months after Easter Time. This is a time when the faithful

consider the fullness of Jesus' teachings and works among his people.[17]

In order to know what day of the month and week these events take place the Secretariat of Divine Worship of the United States Conference of Catholic Bishops publishes the Liturgical Calendar for the Dioceses of the United States of America. This calendar is used by authors of lessons and other liturgical aids published to foster the celebration of the liturgy. The calendar consists of Holy Days, Feasts, the start and end day of the Catholic seasons (Advent, Christmas, Lent, The Triduum, Good Friday, Holy Saturday, and Easter Sunday). The Catholic calendar starts on the first day of Advent, which is four Sundays before Christmas. The other seasons are calculated based on this date.

The Influence of Monasticism

Vast monastic settlements for both women and men were becoming the focus of both the religious and scholarly life of the church. The expansion of monasticism was the main force behind the unprecedented artistic and cultural activity of the eleventh and twelfth centuries. New orders were quickly founded and monasteries and convents were established throughout Europe.

The earliest monastery adhered to the Benedictine Rule, established by St. Benedict in 529 CE. This document governed the daily lives of monks and nuns and was strict—its main theme being absolute obedience to the Abbot, or head of the monastery. Benedict required monks to spend time in reading, and this kept theology and culture alive through centuries when almost the entire continent was illiterate.

Other orders were also established, particularly the Cistercians and the Carthusians. These monastic orders differed from the Benedictines and one another mainly in the details of their religious observation. In general, they followed the Benedictine Rule, but differed in how strictly they applied their rules. The first nuns also adhered to the Benedictine Rule, and, as with the men, several different orders of nuns were founded.

Though monasteries were landowners from their inception, in the tenth century they began to acquire substantial gifts of cash, precious liturgical objects, land, and livestock. Monasteries, in turn, provided a haven from the world for pious men and women, as well as for social outcasts in

---

17. This can be read on the conference website at http://www.usccb.org/prayer-and-worship/liturgical-year/.

need of assistance. Monastic centers provided a fiercely intellectual environment, requiring literacy of brothers and sisters and establishing major libraries. Monastic complexes were also patrons and sources of tremendous art and architecture, such as frescoes and wall paintings.

One of the major contributions of the monastic members was their achievement in scholarship, providing important books about hymns, the lives of saints and theologians, and theology. The monasteries became repositories of knowledge: in addition to the Bible, the liturgical texts, and the writings of the Latin and Greek church fathers, their scriptoria copied the works of classical philosophers and theoreticians, as well as Latin translations of Arabic treatises on mathematics and medicine. Glowing illuminations often decorated the pages of these books and the most eminent among them were adorned with elaborate bindings.

Monks

A monk was a member of a group of religious men who lived a simple life apart from general society. Monks were clean shaven and were distinguished by a tonsure, the top back part of the head from which a circle of hair had been removed. Tonsures were a symbol of their renunciation of worldly fashion and esteem. A tonsure might also indicate that a monk had received clerical status.

Any man, rich or poor, noble or peasant could become a monk. Every candidate for admission to the order of the Benedictine monks took the vows of obedience, poverty, and chastity. Having once joined he remained a monk for the rest of his life. The medieval monks lived under strict discipline. They could not own any property; they could not go beyond the monastery walls without the abbot's consent; they could not even receive letters from home; and they were sent to bed early. A violation of the regulations by a monk brought punishment in the shape of private admonitions, exclusion from common prayer, and, in extreme cases, expulsion.

Nuns

Many women were placed into convents by their families. The church received a dowry from the parents of the nuns, and any jewelry that belonged to the girl was added to the wealth of the convent or nunnerie. Older women also became nuns, many widows choosing this way of life after the death of their husband. Many convents and nunneries only accepted women who were from wealthy backgrounds. Every candidate for admission to a nun's order took the vow of obedience. The solemn vows were taken four years later. Having once joined, a woman remained a nun for the rest of her life. The medieval ceremony for the consecration of nuns was similar to a wedding: a ring was placed on the nun's finger, she wore a wedding crown or headdress, and a ring was placed on her finger. Thereafter, a nun would be seen as married to God.

Hildegard of Bingen (1098–1179 CE)

The first composer, whose name we know for sure, is a product of this monastery system. Her name is Hildegard of Bingen and she lived in a time when very few women could write. Yet, she produced theological and visionary writings, founded a convent, and composed music. In spite of this, she was practically unknown until the 1990s.

Hildegard was the daughter of a knight, and when she was eight years old she went to the Benedictine monastery at Mount St. Disibode to be educated. The monastery was in the Celtic tradition, and housed both men and women (in separate quarters). When Hildegard was eighteen, she became a nun. Twenty years later, she was made the head of the female community at the monastery. Within the next four years, she had a series of visions, and devoted the ten years from 1140 to 1150 to writing them down, describing them. This included drawing pictures of what she had seen, interpreting and commenting on their significance.[18]

She wrote seventy-two songs, including a play set to music. Musical notation had only recently been developed to the point where her music was recorded in a way that we can read it today. Her compositional style is like nothing else we have from the twelfth century. The play set to music is called the *Ordo Virtutum* and show us a human soul who listens to the Virtues, turns aside to follow the devil, and finally returns to the Virtues, having found that following the devil does not make one happy.

She also left us about seventy poems and nine books. Two of the books contain medical and pharmaceutical advice, dealing with the workings of the human body, and the properties of various herbs. These books are based on her observations and those of others, not on her visions. She also wrote a commentary on the Gospels and another on the Athanasian Creed.[19]

---

18. Kiefer, "Hildegard Bingen, Visionary."
19. Kiefer, "Hildegard Bingen, Visionary."

Worship in the Monastery

The religious services in the monastery revolved around what is known as The Divine Office or Liturgical Hours. The Benedictine Rule required all monasteries to observe the divine office (*opus Dei*), a practice that may have been derived from the hours of prayer observed by Jews or the nightly services held by early Christians. There are eight divine offices:

- *Matins* (from the Latin *matutinus*, "morning"): the long night office before dawn called "vigils."
- Lauds (from the Latin *laudate*, "praise"): Psalms 148–50 and originally sung at dawn.
- Prime (from the Latin *primus*, "first"): the first of the offices sung at 6:00 a.m.
- Terce (from the Latin *tertius*, "third"): the third hour at 9:00 a.m.
- Vespers (from the Latin *vesper*, "evening"): the oldest of the hours, held in the evening between 4:00 and 6:00 p.m. Vespers was originally called *lucernarium*, the lighting of the laps.
- Compline (from the Latin *completorium*, "after supper"): held at the eighth hour at the end of the day before retiring for the night.

The hours were rigorously observed in the monasteries, but as individual churches adopted the Offices, several hours would be combined. The liturgy consisted of psalms, antiphons (short texts sung before and after a psalm or canticle), Scripture readings, hymns, versicles (sentences sung by the choir and priest), and collects (prayers for the day). At Matins and Laudes, Old Testament canticles were used. New Testament canticles were used at Laudes (Benedictus), Vespers (Magnificat), and Compline (Nunc Dimittis).

The Offices were gradually added to the services of the church, with some offices combined. Reese believes these hymns were generally syllabic, and divided between liturgical and non-liturgical hymns. Liturgical hymns were rarely used by a choir during Mass, but frequently during the Offices. Nonliturgical hymns were written expressly for singing outside the church and for private devotions.[20]

---

20. Reese, *Music in the Middle Ages*, 170–73.

Cathedral Churches

A cathedral is any Christian church where the bishop has his headquarters and contains the bishop's chair or throne. The term comes from the Greek word *cathedra*, which means "chair." Generally, cathedrals are larger buildings than ordinary churches. A bishop is responsible for a group of churches called a diocese, from a Greek word that means "administration." Each diocese is divided into parishes and each parish has a church designated as the parish church. When there was only one church in a parish, membership was determined by residency, with everyone within the parish boundaries considered to be members whether they attended or not. A similar definition of church membership exists in many countries that have a state church, such as England.

The cathedral was the center of life in the town. Everything of importance seemed to take place in the cathedral. People would go to the cathedral for weddings, baptisms, and confirmations as well as worship. The cathedral and its grounds also functioned as a community center for meetings and entertainments, such as liturgical plays.

Nearly every cathedral had a school. The original function of these schools was to train priests, but later, boys of noble families were admitted in preparation for high positions in church, business, or state. Perhaps one hundred students would be enrolled in a school, but most cathedral schools were small and accepted only twelve students at a time. The number twelve was probably chosen because Jesus had twelve disciples. Students were taught to sing because many parts of the religious services were chanted or sung rather than spoken and students were also part of the cathedral choir.

> Some cathedral schools were referred to as choir schools or song schools and the students often served in the cathedral's choirs . . . their studies covered far more than just choral work. They learned to read and write in Latin and received religious instruction . . . They were expected to stay in school until around the age of 11 or 12.[21]

In the traditional rendering of the Gregorian chant, some parts were sung by a soloist and answered responsorial by a choir singing in unison. In the Gothic period, the choir still chanted in the way it had done for centuries, but the solo parts began to be performed simultaneously by two or more individual singers. The distinction between solo voice and choir was replaced by the opposition of a group of individual singers and a massed chorus.

---

21. Newman, *Growing Up*, 119.

Early Polyphony

When several skilled soloists were available, the way was open for an art of much greater complexity than before. Since the music was still intended for church performance, it was mandatory that any newly composed music use one of the traditional sacred melodies; and a special part called the tenor, a term derived from the Latin tenere, meaning "to hold," was reserved for it. This melody was also known as the cantus firmus, or "fixed song," implying that it could not be changed.

Organum is a polyphonic (many-voiced) setting of chant in which two voices moving at the same time, note against note. One voice part is the chant melody. The second voice is newly composed. It is similar to a duet or the soprano and alto lines in a hymnal with music. This is in contrast to the single note melody in Gregorian chant. Organum was probably improvised before it was written down. The earliest written form of organum is found in the treatise *Musica enchiriadis* (c. 900 CE), meaning "Musical Handbook." Here, we find examples of a plainchant melody combined with another part singing the same melody in parallel motion a perfect fourth or fifth below.

Notre Dame Cathedral

During the late twelfth and early thirteenth centuries a large number of composers and singers were working under the patronage of the Notre Dame Cathedral in Paris. This school is important because it is where a large body of the earliest polyphony was written that gained prestige and wide acceptance. All of the composers are anonymous except two: Leonin (late twelfth century) and Perotin (early thirteenth century). Both of them are mentioned in a thirteenth-century treatise by an anonymous Englishman studying in Paris.

According to the treatise, they excelled in their craft. Leonin is credited with the composing the *Magnus liber organi* ("Great Book of Organa"), which contains a series of two-part organa for the entire liturgical year. Pérotin, the apparent successor to Léonin, is cited for his three- and four-voice organa, as well.

Another development of the Notre Dame School was rhythmic modes. These were set patterns of long and short sounds indicated by notes. The duration of each note is not determined by its form (such as quarter note, half note, etc.), but rather by its position within a group of notes. The rhythmic modes of Notre Dame polyphony were the first step towards writing music like music today.

To trace all of the interesting developments in music is beyond the scope of this book. However, in the 1300s, composers began to experiment more freely, resulting in a movement known as Ars nova (or "New Art"). Two very inventive composers, Guillaume de Machaut and Francesco Landini, were the dynamic of this movement. They had moved away from the "ancient" sound of medieval music that used only the white notes of the piano as opposed to our modern music uses both white and black keys of the piano. Though there was new musical freedom, the main emphasis of composers was music for the church.

In terms of the liturgy, there were no major developments until the late 1500s. As Metzger observed, "As early as the eleventh century, liturgical unity had been elevated to the level of an ecclesiological principle by the Gregorian reform, promoted by Pope Gregory VII. From that time on, the popes attributed to themselves a liturgical competence for all the churches. At the level of practice, liturgical unity was understood as uniformity."[22]

Hymns in the Western Church

Hymns have been mentioned throughout this chapter and are an integral part of the Western church. Medieval hymns are simply songs the church attached to its liturgy from time to time during the Liturgical Year. Though hymns could be sung at any service at any time during the year, they frequently become attached to a particular part of the liturgy or to a specific time of the year and become inseparable from the Proper of the Mass. Though hymns were sung, there was no congregational singing during the Mass, for hymns in Mass lay in the province of choir and clergy.

When reference is made to hymns, at any point in history, it is always to the texts and not to the music. Hymn texts are strophic; that is, each stanza of the text is set to the same music, as are hymns today. The early texts of the Western church are religious poetry, patterned after Latin poetry, so hymn texts are metrical; that is, they have a regular pattern of accented and unaccented syllables. We cannot know for certain what tunes were used for each hymn, but some hymn texts were sung to medieval secular tunes.[23]

The congregational song of the present-day church, regardless of style, label, or practice, began to take shape at this time in history and evolved out of liturgical as well as non-liturgical elements. The liturgical elements are hymns attached to the Mass, tropes, and sequences. There are also many

---

22. Metzger, *History of the Liturgy*, 122.

23. For information about the literary forms of these hymns see Kaske et al., *Medieval Christian Literary Liturgy*, 72–74.

non-liturgical elements that were not part of the church and its worship. These would include Laudes and Geisslerlieder. The characteristics of tropes, sequences, laude, and Geisslerlieder as congregational songs are all found in the songs of the church today.

Tropes and Sequences

Tropes and sequences are important for our study, for this is a new form of hymnody. As mentioned earlier, when choirs had difficulty remembering notes that had a vowel sustained over a great many melody notes, but no text, new words were added with a syllable set to each note as a memory device. One form of adding new words to a melody is called a trope. The trope is an interpolation of the original text and is based upon a short musical passage. An example of a troped kyrie could be: "Lord (Ruler of heaven and earth) have mercy." The words in parentheses would be sung to the long melisma over the "e" of kyrie.

The trope has been identified with texts of great variety, in both poetry and prose. It was written for the purpose of amplifying and embellishing a complete liturgical text. The trope forms a unit only in connection with a liturgical text, and when separated from that text has little or no meaning. In the example of a troped kyrie given above, he words "Ruler of heaven and earth" would make no sense if sung by themselves apart from the kyrie text.

The distinguishing mark of the sequence is its precise attachment to the Mass and to specific times of the year. Eventually, a common poetic form developed that matched the musical structure. The text was organized into pairs of rhyming couplets that could vary in length. One syllable was set to one note of music. Later, texts were set to newly composed music instead of chant melodies and the lengths of the couplets were equalized. The sequence is an independent unit, complete in itself.

The sequence used in contemporary Catholic churches that is nearest to a hymn form is the *Dies Irae*, attributed to Thomas of Celano (d. c. 1256). Its structure is comparable to a stanza-form hymn. The sequence probably reached its highest point in development with Adam of St. Victor (d. 1192), a monk whose works are in the form of hymns. The difference between sequences and hymns lies in the fact that the music changes for each pair of verses in the sequence, while poetic structure remains the same. Hymns keep the poetic structure the same music for each stanza.[24]

Sequences became extremely popular and were sung to some well-liked tunes. These melodies were identified in manuscripts by the Latin

---

24. For more detailed information, see Reese, *Music in the Middle Ages*, chs. 9–11.

word *incipit* (or sometimes the French word *timbre* was used) to help singers remember the source of the music and the first word of its text. As an example: suppose you were going to sing the "Alphabet Song." Its tune is the same as "Twinkle, Twinkle, Little Star." In the medieval program you would list it as "The Alphabet Song," *Incipit: Twinkle, Twinkle.* The separation of text and tune with the tune having a different title than the text is still in use in most modern hymnals. The title is at the top of the page. Usually, the name of the music will be found at the bottom of the page.

To give you an example, my church denomination had a hymn text writing competition to discover new material to include in a proposed hymnal. I was given the winning text by the publisher and asked to write music to fit the words. I wrote six different tunes that fit the text, each one named for a train stop between central London and my train stop of Petts Wood, the nearest my home. The title of the hymn text was "Free to Be Me." The title of my tune selected for the hymnal was CHISLEHURST, the train stop just before mine.

Tropes and sequences were never considered to be part of the liturgy, but were merely attached to it. As the number of sequences arose, steps were taken to eliminate them as the real texts of the liturgy were being obscured. The Council of Trent (1546–63 CE) banned all but five sequences still in use today. The same Council banned tropes altogether.

Laudes, Geisslerlieder, and *Leisen*

Laudes were Italian religious devotional poems and were very popular from about the mid-thirteenth to the sixteenth century, especially in Italy. Laude were exhortations to a moral life or of events in the lives of Christ and the saints. Laudes included poems of praise, meditations, invocations, exhortations, descriptions of sacred scenes, narratives, monologues, dialogues, and various mixtures of these types. The language exhibited fervor and sudden and uncontrolled expressions of intense emotion.[25]

Though there were many writers of lauda poetry, the composers were often unknown. Laude were simple and popular in style, and at times lauda texts were sung to folk melodies. The earliest laude, from the thirteenth century, were monophonic (single-line) compositions. By the sixteenth century the laude appear in polyphonic settings, usually in chordal style.

Geisslerlieder is the name given to a group of sacred songs sung by the flagellants of the thirteenth and fourteenth centuries who sought to appease the wrath of an angry God by penitential music accompanied by

---

25. Black and Gravestock, *Early Modern Confraternities*, 131.

the whipping of their bodies. In many respects they were German counterparts to the Italian laude. The music was simple, sung in the vernacular, often call-and-response, and closely related to folk songs. Some of the flagellant songs survived into the seventeenth century as folk songs in Catholic parts of central Europe.

Leisen were a type of hymnody developed from the Mass. These songs were of a folk nature similar to sequences and were based upon the congregational response "*Kyrie eleison*." Gradually they were lengthened into poems, with the *Kyrie* inserted at various places in the text. They were never a part of the Mass, but were used for popular occasions.[26]

The Coming Reformation

As we have studied so far, the worship structure of the Western church was pretty well established by 1100 CE. Worship was officially authorized for parish churches, for monastic churches, and for private chapels in the homes of nobility. Originally the language of worship was in the language of the people wherever they lived. After the establishment of the Roman rite as the official worship service the language used was Latin. The Mass as the continuing sacrifice of Christ was the main service of worship, and cycles of worship were organized around the Church Year.

The Mass was centered in the observance of the Lord's Supper. The ritual was mystical in the sense that the Mass was the vehicle through which God gave His grace to people. The bread and wine became the virtual blood and body of Christ through the miraculous action of the priest. The Mass was a sacred drama performed by the clergy for the congregation to observe. It was an allegory of the Christ Event. Each part of the liturgy, priestly vestments, utensils, and gestures of the priest were given meaning from the life of Christ. Not only was the Mass beneficial in conveying God's grace to the living, it was also a way grace could be mediated to those who were dead.

The role of the congregation was passive and devotional. As in the Eastern churches, the principal worship activity took place behind a choir screen. There were no icons in the Western churches, and in English churches the screen is called the "Rood Screen." Seldom did the people know what was happening behind the screen. It seems that the Epistle and Gospel readings may have been proclaimed from the top of the screen. In order for the people to know that the bread and wine had been blessed, a bell was rung. Then, the consecrated bread was raised so everyone could see it.

---

26. Hooper, *Church Music*, 36–37.

Temporal Power of the Church

Medieval culture was preoccupied with the question, "How may I find salvation?" The Roman church supposedly could destine a soul to hell or heaven at the signing of a decree. By claiming such great spiritual power, the church managed to accumulate great temporal power. A very important practice of the Roman church that increased religious dissatisfaction was the granting of indulgences. Originally these were intended to commute the penance required of a penitent sinner. The dangers of this practice increased as papal power increased and money was required in payment for indulgences.

Parallel with indulgences was the conversion of penance into a sacrament that was supposed to remove guilt and eternal punishment from the sinner, but did not free him or her completely from purgatory. If for any reason sufficient penance had not been made in this life, the penalty would be continued after death. This created a sense of uncertainty and fear in the hearts of the people.

By claiming such great spiritual power, the church managed to accumulate great temporal power. As a result, it came to be preoccupied with temporal affairs. This Romanist concept led to great unrest and a strong dissatisfaction with the secularized church for not adequately serving religious needs. The well-integrated doctrine and the ecclesiastical and civil hierarchies could not disguise the fact that the inner core of the Roman church was corrupt.

There was wide spread dissatisfaction with the wealth of the church and the low moral standards of the clergy. The esteem of the church was hurt as some church leaders violated the biblical laws they were entrusted to uphold and lived no differently than the secular merchants and political figures.

Desire for Piety

Throughout the Middle Ages many Roman Catholics had been asking how they might commit themselves to a more pious way of life, as well as criticizing the monks and priests of their day for being comfortable, lazy, hypocritical, and illiterate. The laxity of monks and priests (sometimes including popes) ranged from owning large estates to eating sumptuous meals to slacking in their spiritual duties to keeping mistresses.

Many individuals had attempted to break publicly with the Roman See but had met with defeat and sometimes with death. Tait reports that many of these Catholic martyrs "called themselves 'evangelicals,' dying for a life-giving message of free grace in Christ."[27] With its weakened influence, the church found its papal authority increasingly challenged, both locally and nationally. These challenges to papal authority flourished and were considered by the church to be heretical, but critics became more outspoken and numerous.

Though the influence of the Catholic Church was weakening, there was ever increasing popularity of religion throughout all parts of Europe. Religion began to change. Preachers, like Savonarola of Florence, called for sinners to repent. One movement, that grew in part from the German mystic, Eckhart, grew in western Germany in the Rhineland area. This movement believed in direct revelations from God without the church as an intermediary.

The communal and sacramental faith of the Catholic Church was challenged in Belgium, Luxembourg and the Netherlands by a movement known as the "devotion moderna" ("modern devotion" in Latin). This group emphasized individual and practical faith as opposed to the communal and sacramental faith of the Catholic Church. The Devotio Moderna established communal houses for women and men devoted to the experience of imitating Christ in Northern European towns and cities; initially, it constituted a "middle way" between the parish and the mostly rural religious orders of the day. They detested knowledge without virtue, so they established dormitories and schools for the spiritual formation of youth.[28]

This is not to say that religion alone was the determining factor in the coming Reformation. Other pressures and desires were a part of this movement too, although they were probably influenced by religion. There was economic prosperity in the hands of a few aristocrats that produced strife among the lower classes. Geographic boundaries were being lengthened, resulting in expanding commercial ventures at home and abroad. These changes brought about a corresponding increase in the use of money, banking, and the spirit of capitalism. Nationalistic sentiments began to rise as states were created, and resentment towards a foreign pope were rampant.

John Wycliffe and Jan Hus

During the fourteenth century, British philosopher John Wycliffe (1328–84), a professor at Oxford University, began formalizing his attacks on the Roman church. Both in his teachings and writings, Wycliffe attacked the Eucharist,

---

27. Tait, "Road Not Taken," 12–15.
28. Jensen, "Devotio Moderna."

calling it a source of superstition. Wycliffe claimed the Bible to be the final authority for faith, superseding even that of the pope.[29]

Wycliffe never took his teachings beyond England, but by a strange twist of fate they proved even more influential in far-off Bohemia than at home. The English king married a Bohemian princess, and consequently many Czech students came to Oxford, picked up Wycliffe's ideas and took them home.

Jan Huss (1372–1415), a Bohemian scholar, read these works and accepted and taught many of Wycliffe's ideas. Consequently, Huss was burned at the stake in 1415, being condemned by the Council of Constance for his criticisms of the church. Huss preached that

- The Scriptures should be interpreted literally;
- The Catholic doctrines of purgatory and the Mass were unscriptural;
- That church and state should be separate; and,
- The Scriptures should be made available to the people in their native tongue.

Ironically, the same Council ordered Wycliffe's body to be exhumed and desecrated the same year.

Congregational singing was still unknown in the churches, though the people were used to singing religious songs in the vernacular. The followers of John Huss, the Bohemian Brethren, were among the first to use congregational singing, for Huss believed the people ought to share in the singing; and he, and his disciples after him, wrote hymns to be used for this purpose. These hymns were nearly sermons in verse, valuable for teaching but poor for singing. Both Huss and Wycliffe attracted a small following, but any major opposition to the Christian church was still a century away.[30]

For You to Think about

1. Listen to a Gregorian chant on YouTube. Describe your feeling responses to the music.
2. Search YouTube for some examples of leisen and geisslerlieder. What are your responses to the music?
3. If you have never attended a Catholic Mass, a good introduction would be to view this twenty-five-minute YouTube video that explains the Mass while it is being offered: https://www.youtube.com/watch?v=cooqalRkEJs.

29. Roberts, "John Wycliffe."
30. Tomkins, "John Hus."

6

Congregational Song in the Reformation

Next to the Word of God, music deserves the highest praise.

—Martin Luther

THE IDEAS ABOUT WORSHIP and song of Luther, Calvin, Zwingli, and the Anabaptists, and the psalters and psalmody that taught and reinforced those ideas, are studied in this chapter. In order to gain a balanced view, this is followed by how congregational song was affected by the Catholic Counter-Reformation.

During the Renaissance (c. 1400–1600 CE) the demands of society shifted and became based on money instead of allegiances. The church had a difficult time adjusting to this new way of thinking. For example, the parish priests and monks had long served as the religious teachers of the peasants, but as the commercial class began to grow, the priests found that they knew very little about the needs of this new class of people.

Contributions to Church Reform

Other factors outside the church also made the Reformation possible, for it is only one of the important developments within the Renaissance (c. 1400–1600 CE). This was a time in history that witnessed the discovery and exploration of new continents, the growth of commerce, and the invention of potentially powerful innovations such as paper, printing, the mariner's compass, and gunpowder. For scholars and thinkers of the day, it was primarily a time when Greek and Roman learning and wisdom were revived after a long period of cultural decline and stagnation.

The invention of the printing press had resulted in an emphasis upon people learning to read and brought about the revival, study, and use of the Greek and Hebrew languages. This made it possible to make new Bible translations into the common languages and printed Bibles were available to the public for the first time. The invention of the printing press also made possible the spread of Protestantism through the mass publication of documents written by reformers.

One of the earliest characteristics of the Renaissance is an intellectual movement initiated by secular scholars known as humanism. Arab scholars had preserved the writings of the ancient Greeks in their libraries, and when Italian cities traded with the Arabs, ideas were exchanged along with goods. When the Christian Byzantine empire fell to Muslim Turks in 1453, Byzantine Christian scholars made a logical move to Italy and brought with them the fruits of their scholarship.

Humanism had some significant features. First, the subject of study was human nature with all of its varieties and achievements. Second, humanists believed the truth found in all philosophical and theological schools of thought had unity and compatibility. Third, humanism stressed the dignity and worth of mankind. This was in direct contrast to the medieval ideal of human unworthiness and the need of penance. Fourth, humanism fostered free enquiry, scholarly criticism of ideas, and the possibilities of human thought and creation.

During the fifteenth century, humanists expanded the study of texts to include Greek. Consequently, Greek texts both of ancient works and the New Testament could be read in their original language for the first time. Greek textual studies opened up new ideas for the humanists, particularly the more precise understanding of Greek philosophy. Humanists also read biblical texts in their original languages though they did not believe the Scriptures were authoritative.

Humanism was a strong cultural force and there were some similarities between the reformers and the humanists. Both groups were critical of the monastic system. Both humanists and reformers thought theological study had degenerated into irrelevant and quibbling arguments. Both groups promoted an understanding of the Bible based on a close scrutiny of the text in the original languages.

However, the humanists thought human nature was able to be perfected through education, while the reformers thought humanity was hopelessly lost and in need of redemption. Humanists thought all religions had the same universal truth and could be found equally in the Bible as well as in secular and pagan literature. The Reformers thought God was revealed only in and through the Scriptures.

The Lutheran Reformation

Into such a challenging milieu stepped a man named Martin Luther. He had a tenor voice and skill in performing on the lute, and perhaps even tried his hand at composing. He was a brilliant scholar and had received the Doctor of Theology degree because of his mastery of theological subjects and the biblical languages. Luther recognized the need of people to be able to read the Bible in their own language, so he translated the New Testament into German in 1522 and the whole Bible appeared in 1534.

There is some evidence that Luther came in contact with the Bohemian Brethren. His views were similar enough to theirs for him to be accused of being a Hussite. It may be that he was also influenced by the congregational singing of the Brethren as he was quick to see that one way to win the battle with the church was to have people sing their religion.

In 1522 a German pastor, Michel Weisse, was sent by the Bohemian Bishop Lucas, along with Johann Roh, to explain the views of the Brethren to Luther. They were appointed again in 1524 to report on the practices and the holiness of life of the Bohemian Brethren. Weisse was editor of the German Brethren hymnal of 1531 that contained 155 hymns that were either original or translations he had made. Roh was editor of the hymnal of 1541, and also the editor of a German edition in 1544 which had thirty-two hymns either written or translated by him. Many hymns of these two men passed into Lutheran hymnody.[1]

Changes in the Mass

Luther realized there were some changes that needed to be made in the Mass, but desired to change as little as possible at first. In 1523 he made the minimal changes necessary to express the new faith. This *Formulae Missae* was in Latin and all references to the sacrificial nature of the Mass were eliminated and restored the meaning of the Lord's Supper to a more commemorative act of worship. Luther quickly realized that his congregation did not understand Latin, so how would they know he had eliminated the unbloody sacrifice emphasis of the Mass?

Thus, in 1526 he came out with a Mass in German except for the *Kyrie eleison*. He dispensed with the choir and assigned all singing to the congregation. He would call frequent rehearsals for the congregation to learn new hymns, called "chorales." Luther also translated other parts of the litany that

---

1. Julian, *Dictionary of Hymnology*. See entries under each name and "Lutheran Hymnody."

had previously been sung by a choir in Latin into German and set them to tunes the congregation could sing. Scripture readings had a more prominent place and the sermon was given greater emphasis. Luther, unlike other reformers, left the structure of the Mass intact.

Musical Reforms

Luther believed that under God, music was of supreme importance. He held regular teaching sessions with students at meal time, and his comments were recorded by his students as "Table Talks." In these comments, Luther several times described music as "the greatest gift of God which has often induced and inspired me to preach." In Luther's view, God gave music to humanity as a way to impress men and women with the glory of divine gifts.[2]

In the preface to a collection of funeral hymns published in 1542, Luther explained that it was important for God's people to sing the very words of Scripture: "We have put this music on the living and holy Word of God in order to sing, praise, and honor it. We want the beautiful art of music to be properly used to serve her dear Creator and his Christians. He is thereby praised and honored and we are made better and stronger in faith when his holy Word is impressed on our hearts by sweet music."[3] Luther had brought with him from the monastery a great love of music used for the liturgical offices. This was one reason he was reluctant to translate the Mass into German, for so much fine music would be eliminated, so Luther set himself to the task of reforming music in the service. First, he changed the method of chanting the Scriptures from monotone to one more nearly like normal speech. Only one note was used for one syllable, and the organ accompaniment was not to obscure the words.[4]

The second musical reform was music for choirs. All of the choral music available was in Latin, but Luther recognized the artistic value of choral music. He promoted trained choirs with the result that choral societies were formed and children were taught music in schools.

The third area of musical reform was the congregational hymn. This is the point at which his doctrine of the priesthood of all believers reached its heights. All the people were once again allowed to sing in church.[5]

---

2. Reed, *Luther and Congregational Singing*. See also Buszin, "Luther on Music," 80–97.

3. Quoted in Noll, "Singing the Word of God," 10.

4. Galli, "Martin Luther's Later Years," 1–9.

5. Noll, "Singing the Word of God," 10–13. See also Grew, "Martin Luther," 67–78.

Luther thought it was biblical to use every form of God-honoring expression to praise the God of grace, just so long as that praise did not violate biblical truth. Lutheran church music, as a result, almost immediately created a rich culture of choir directors, choristers, organists, composers, and performers. In 1538, Luther expressed this theology in yet another preface, this time to a full collection of masses, vespers, antiphons, responsories, and hymns that was published by Georg Rhau, whose career included a stint at the St. Thomas Church in Leipzig where Bach would later serve. At a time when other parts of the Protestant world were narrowing musical expression, Luther boldly defended polyphony and compositional complexity as showing why "next to the Word of God, music deserves the highest praise."

The Zwinglian Reformation

Another center of the Reformation in its early days was eastern Switzerland. Its leader and founder of the Swiss Reformed Churches was Ulrich (or Huldrych) Zwingli (1443–1531). He was an important figure of the Protestant Reformation and a contemporary of Martin Luther. "The starting point for Zwingli's Reformation was different," writes Payne.

> Zwingli was not a monk troubled by the predicament of his own soul. He does not seem to have the same intense soul-searching struggle that Luther had, though he did engage in a battle with his own lusts. He confessed that he had great difficulty in maintaining the requirement of clerical celibacy, but knew he was not alone in his failure.[6]

After graduating from the University of Basel in 1506, he became a parish priest in Glarus. From the beginning, he took his priestly duties seriously. This feeling of responsibility for his congregation motivated Zwingli's increasing interest in the Bible. Zwingli was a humanist and a scholar who lived in an age when priests were often unfamiliar with the Scriptures, so he taught himself Greek and Hebrew to better understand the Scriptures. Zwingli became enamored with the Bible and purchased a copy of Erasmus's New Testament Latin translation and copied by hand the Pauline Epistles from Erasmus's Greek New Testament and then memorized them.[7]

Zwingli rejected the Catholic idea that church tradition was as authoritative as the Scriptures, so he left the Catholic Church in 1522. He rejected the Mass in 1525 and replaced it with the first Reformed communion service

---

6. Payne, "Zwingli and Luther," 4.
7. Payne, "Zwingli and Luther," 5–11.

held in the Zurich Great Minster Church.[8] Since the Roman Catholic Mass was no longer in use, there was the task of explaining the meaning of the Reformed service of worship. Shortly before his death in July 1531, Zwingli wrote his "Exposition of the Christian Faith" addressed to a Christian king and described this new liturgy.[9]

When addressing Zwingli's life, music played an important personal role. He enjoyed music and played several instruments, including the violin, harp, flute. He was so well-known for his music that his enemies mocked him as an evangelical lute player and fifer. "Zwingli—probably the best musician among the major Reformers—had a radically different position from that of Luther," commented Robert Godfrey.

> Zwingli believed that music was too powerful and too emotional to be used in Christian worship. Under the strong influence of Platonic philosophy, he argued that music would too easily move people away from focusing on the Word and its meaning for them. As a result, in Zurich singing was eliminated from worship in Zwingli's day. No musical instruments, no choirs, and no congregational singing were permitted. In the place of singing, Zwingli had the congregation recite Scriptural passages antiphonally.[10]

Samuel Jackson writes that

> The most radical change which Zwingli made in the Church service at Zurich was to do away with both instrumental and vocal music. This action was the more strange since Zwingli himself was a very accomplished musician, being able to play upon ten different instruments and also to sing well; yet in the course of the year 1525 he suspended the choir-singing and on December 9, 1527, had the organ of the Great Minster broken up and insisted that similar action should be taken by the other churches in the city and canton.[11]

Zwingli did not form a church as did Luther and Calvin. The churches that were formed by the reformers in Switzerland were called the Swiss Reformed Church. These were not entirely Calvinist, but more nearly Zwinglian with Calvinist infuence.

---

8. Porter, "What Did Huldrych Zwingli Achieve?," 1–8.
9. Armstrong, "From the Archives." See Appendix I for Zwingli's liturgy.
10. Godfrey, "Reforming the Church's Singing," para. 5.
11. Jackson, *Huldreich Zwingli*, 290.

The Anabaptist Reformation

Another group of the Reformation period is the one called Anabaptist. The exact origins of this group are obscure, for their roots sink back many years before the Reformation began. The term "Anabaptists" was a derisive one applied to those who only baptized persons who became Christians as adults, or who felt that their infant baptism was not valid scripturally. In spite of the label, the Anabaptists did not think they were rebaptizing since they believed those baptized as infants had not received actual baptism.

The first group of Anabaptists arose in Switzerland and at first they were not distinguished from the Zwinglian reformers. The worship practice of the Anabaptists was influenced by Zwingli with whom they broke over questions about believer's baptism, liberty of conscience, and the separation of church and state. Zwingli was willing to compromise convictions to promote his reform movement, so he abandoned the teaching of adult baptism as being impractical.

Anabaptists never had a unified movement, if unified means having a common form of church order and a common leadership. Anabaptist policy of congregational autonomy kept a centralized movement from happening. Fierce persecution made Anabaptists an underground movement, and there were geographical barriers that prevented Anabaptists from becoming a unified group. Therefore, considerable differences existed between the various Anabaptist groups in Bible interpretation, theology and church practice.[12]

The most influential Anabaptist, and one who has been regarded as their founder, was Conrad Grebel. Other early leaders were Felix Manz, who gave the young movement intellectual direction without the loss of evangelistic zeal; Wilhelm Reublin, one of the first Swiss priests to embrace radical reform views; and Balthasar Hubmaier. Hubmaier was the outstanding German Anabaptist, who can be remembered for three outstanding religious principles: (1) the supremacy of the Scriptures; (2) religious liberty; and (3) believers' baptism.

Like many other Christian groups of their time, Anabaptists were pretty certain that all other groups would not inherit the kingdom of God because they were rejecting the truth that they, the Anabaptists, had found. Their conviction that they were the true church was as unpleasant and as unjustified in them as in others. Distinctive beliefs of the Anabaptists, regardless of the country in which they resided, were

- the priesthood of believers;

---

12. Klassen, "A Fire That Spreads."

- the sufficiency of the Scriptures in matters of faith;
- believers' baptism, and thus a regenerated church membership;
- separation of church and state;
- the abolition of force and war;
- the nonparticipation of Christians in politics.

The first two of these beliefs were similar to those of other reformers. Baptism, and the other Anabaptist convictions, however, were points of sharp contention.

Many Catholic practices were changed by Luther and Calvin, but infant baptism had been the accepted mode in the history of the church and was not subject to change. The Anabaptists usually did not immerse, but they did insist upon adult baptism by pouring water over a person's head, as opposed to the firmly established practice of infant baptism of the reform movements. Baptizing only adults—that is, people who chose to be baptized on a profession of faith—was a radical idea that challenged both church and state. To be baptized was a civil issue. Church and State were one, and to refuse baptism ripped a tear in an orderly society as far as civil authorities were concerned. The Anabaptist view of separation exposed them to civil penalties in the courts. However, believers' baptism was just one of many revolutionary ideas typical of the Anabaptists.[13] Because of these beliefs, the Anabaptists were persecuted mercilessly both by the reformers and Catholics.[14]

When Anabaptists started out in the mid-1520s they had a complete ban on singing. The Swiss Anabaptist leader Conrad Grabel joined Zwingli in opposing all church music, including singing in the worship service: "We find nothing taught in the New Testament about singing, no example of it ... Paul very clearly forbids singing in Ephesians 5:19 and Colosians 3:16 ... " This ban did not last long. Felix Manz, an early leader, wrote at least one hymn before his martydom in 1527. Its opening line is "Mit Lust so will ich singen" ("I will sing heartily").[15]

Anabaptist Hymnody

Their doctrines and their martyrdoms are expressed in Anabaptist hymnody. Believers in Switzerland, Holland, Moravia, and Germany all produced a collection of Anabaptist hymns. The first hymnal was *Ausbund* (an

---

13. White, *Protestant Worship*, 81–82.
14. Burrage, *History of the Anabaptists*, ch. 1.
15. Dowley, *Christian Music*, 119. See also Wohlgemuth, "Anabaptist Hymn," 92.

abbreviated title), that was published by the Swiss Anabaptists perhaps in 1564, with a second section added and both published together in 1583. The entire German title is translated as "A selected group of fine Christian songs, composed in the Passau Castle prison by the Swiss brethren, and by other evangelical Christians here and there."

The *Ausbund* deserves our attention, since it is still used by the Amish Mennonites. The second section contains martyr songs by some of the early Anabaptist leaders: Felix Manz, Michael Sattler, Ludwig Hetzer, and Balthasar Hubmaier. A reading of the texts reveals nothing dogmatic, revolutionary or fanatical. Instead, these hymn texts present the moral aspects of the Christian life: faith, love, and steadfastness.

Dr. Rosella Duerksen traces the tunes and texts used in the *Ausbund* and found three main sources of tunes: (1) liturgical hymns; (2) pre-Reformation German sacred songs; and (3) folk songs. Luther adopted many liturgical hymns and these were appropriated by the Anabaptists. Seven tunes in *Ausbund* are from plain song, five from sequences, and four from *Leisen*. Pre-Reformation sacred song was quite vast, and the Swiss brethren dipped into that reservoir for their own use. "In most regions where Anabaptism flourished," writes Rempel, "congregational singing emerged as spontaneously as did prayer and Bible study. It measured the heatbeat of Anabaptist spirituality. Not only were hymns borrowed, great numbers of them were written."[16]

Folk songs were the most popular sources of tunes, since they appealed to the people who knew the tunes and because text writing progressed faster than tune writing. Most of these folk song adaptations were what is known as *contrafacta*, the adapting of a text to a melody already used with another text.

Distinctive Beliefs

Though Anabaptists avoided reciting creeds in worship, they found it necessary to come to a consensus of belief in a document referred to as "The Schleitheim Confession." It is the most representative statement of Anabaptist principles, endorsed unanimously by a meeting of Swiss Anabaptists in 1527 in Schleitheim, Switzerland. The meeting was chaired by Michael Sattler, a former Catholic priest and the leader of the Swiss and southern German Anabaptist movement. The Confession was necessary because

> a very great offense has been introduced by certain false brethren among us, in the way they intend to practice and observe the freedom of the Spirit and of Christ. But such have missed

---

16. Rempel, "Anabaptist Perspective," 36.

the truth, and to their condemnation are given over to the lasciviousness and self-indulgence of the flesh. They think faith and love may do and permit everything, and nothing will harm them nor condemn them, since they are believers.[17]

The Confession has seven main points: Baptism; The Ban [excommunication]; Breaking of Bread; Separation from the Abomination (from the world); Pastors in the Church; The Sword (pacifist statement); and The Oath (before judges or to bind a contract, *etc.*). According to the Confession, the pastor presides over the reading and expounding of Scripture and leads in prayer and also disciplines the congregation.

Water baptism was given to those who have been taught repentance and believed truly that their sins are forgiven, and was simply an outer sign of and inner experience. The mode of baptism was water poured over a person's head, and it was seen as both a crucial seal or commitment to the rest of the Body of Christ and a response of obedience to scriptural command that was not to be ignored or set aside.

Anabaptists understood the Supper to be a memorial or remembrance of Christ's death and sacrifice, a feeding by faith in Christ. In this practice the Anabaptists in Switzerland, Germany, Austria, and the Low Countries followed the path marked out by Ulrich Zwingli. For Anabaptists everywhere, the Lord's Supper was open only to those who had accepted adult baptism and had thus committed themselves to church discipline. A radical economic sharing was expected of all Anabaptist believers as a visible sign of one's commitment to the community, the Body of Christ on earth.

Modern Anabaptists

The Anabaptist tradition is carried on by Mennonites today. Their belief system has not changed and congregational singing is still central in their worship. "Music gives words wings," writes John Rempel.[18] "The musical expression of a truth enlarges it and makes possible a harmony of confession gathered together from different experiences and convictions." Rempel is concerned about present practices of song among Mennonites today. He asks, "What specific lessons can we draw from Mennonite tradition for the practice of church music?"

---

17. The Scheitheim Confession is available online at baptiststudiesonline.com/wp-content/uploads/2007/02/the-scheitheim-confession-2.pdf.
18. Rempel, "Anabaptist Perspective," 34.

> One is that the congregation is the basic actor in worship. This means that hymn singing is the basic carrier of worship. Often this will be brought about by means of previously chosen hymns which carry the movements of worship forward, but where there is a common repository of hymns, spontaneous requests in response to the flow of worship can be meaningful. Vocal and instrumental music can, however, represent the congregation before God just as the preacher does. One of the unique roles of vocal and instrumental music is that they can offer a stylized response to a preceding reading or prayer which expresses the experience of the worshipers but could not have been articulated by them spontaneously with such immediacy.[19]

Gary Harder, a Mennonite pastor, noted that "Anabaptists have stressed that worship involves the whole community."

> The gathered people are not an audience of individuals gathered to be fed or entertained by leaders set apart. Worship gains its Spirit-led power when the people as a whole enter the presence of God . . . coming as a participatory community. This would suggest to me that when it comes to music in worship, the most important music in the church is congregational singing . . . a barometer of the spiritual vitality of the church. It is an indicator of how deeply faith is experienced.[20]

The Calvinist Reformation

Protestant metrical psalmody arose in the rather frivolous and corrupt French court of the Valois. Marguerite, sister of King Francis I and wife of the dispossessed King of Navarre, was a patroness of many of the leading literary figures of the time. Among the recipients of her patronage was the poet Clement Marot, who later became the personal servant of Francis I.

Marot had won fame as a lyricist and satirist, but having come under the influence of the Reformation, he turned his talents toward sacred subjects. His first endeavor was to translate the Psalms into French verse. The first of these translations (Ps 6) was included in a volume of poems dedicated to his patroness in 1533. He went on to translate other psalms as well, these versions being adaptable to current popular tunes. They won acclaim in the court and throughout the countryside. In 1542 Marot published

---

19. Rempel, "Anabaptist Perspective," 43.
20. Harder, "Congregational Singing," 109–10.

thirty of these psalms in a single volume. This incurred the wrath of the church authorities, and he fled to Geneva.

Upon arriving in Geneva, Marot was probably surprised to learn that twelve of his psalms had appeared in the Strassburg psalter of 1539 and the Antwerp psalter of 1541. These two psalters had first been published by John Calvin, aided by a converted Carmelite monk named Alexander.

Two things may have influenced Calvin to introduce singing into his services and to use Marot's settings as a part of the Strassburg psalter. First, Calvin had been exiled in Strassburg from 1538 to 1541 because of his religious teachings in Geneva. In Strassburg he found chorale singing firmly established in the Lutheran churches. Secondly, the popularity and influence of Marot's psalms had spread until Calvin could hardly be unaware of them. This Strassburg psalter was the predecessor of the Genevan psalter and subsequent psalters in every other country where psalm singing developed. Prior to Calvin's arrival in Geneva in 1536, the church was using an order of worship made by Farel, an evangelist from Bern. No singing was included in the services. As noted earlier, in the Zwinglian church in Zurich the worshipers were silent except for a few responses.[21]

Marot left Geneva very suddenly in 1544, barely fifty years old. Calvin was hard pressed to find another lyricist. After nearly five years Theodore Beza filled Marot's position. Beza was well trained in law and theology and eventually succeeded Calvin upon Calvin's death, even writing a short biography of Calvin. Beza remained head of the Genevan church until 1588, but continued to teach until 1597, dying in 1560. It is generally conceded that his poetic work is not of the same quality as Marot's, but his splendid scholarship makes his metrical versions of the psalms creditable in comparison.

Calvin on Worship

John Calvin drew up his *Essentials of a Well-Ordered Church*, in which he held that scriptural worship should include the preaching of the Word, public and solemn prayers, and the administration of the sacraments. He took a serious view of worship and gave no room for any absurdity. For John Calvin, the aim of worship should be the glorification of God, and salvation is connected to worship. The importance and seriousness John Calvin attached to worship comes clear in this statement: "Let us know and be fully persuaded, that wherever the faithful, who worship him purely and in due form, according to the appointment of his word, are assembled together to

---

21. Terry, *Calvin's First Psalter*, vii. See also Terry, "Calvin's First Psalter," 1–21.

engage in the solemn acts of religious worship, he is graciously present, and presides in the midst of them."[22]

John Calvin taught that a church worship service should end with the Lord's Supper. He encouraged weekly participation in the Lord's Supper because he considered the service as a summary of the whole Gospel: while humanity is saved by hearing the Word preached, the Gospel is confirmed by partaking in the Sacraments.[23]

Prominence was given to psalm singing for three reasons: (1) the example of the ancient church and the apostle Paul; (2) the spiritual benefit to prayer; and (3) the pope had deprived the church of the benefit found in the psalms by having them mumbled unintelligibly. Calvin's thought was to begin the training of the children to sing prose psalms to some sober chant; the people listening until they could use their own voices to sing. On his return to Geneva in 1541 Calvin required that the singing of psalms be made a part of the public worship. He was so successful in establishing psalm singing that in 1559 the synod of the Reformed churches of France decreed that every church member should bring his own psalter to worship.

Of Calvin's contemporaries, clearly the most influential on worship was Martin Bucer of Strassburg. Calvin spent his years of exile from Geneva (1538-41) in Strassburg, and Calvin closely followed Bucer's approach to the liturgy. The normal order of Sunday worship would look like this:[24]

ASSEMBLY

    Opening sentence

    Confession of sin

    The Ten Commandments (sung)

    Psalm (sung)

WORD

    Collect for Illumination

    Lesson and Sermon

    Apostles Creed (sung)

MEAL

    The Lord's Supper

---

22. Godfrey, "Calvin and the Worship of God," para. 7. See also Lambert, "In Corde Iubilum," 269–87.

23. Osei-Bonsu, "John Calvin's Perspective," 83–101.

24. See Thompson, *Liturgies of the Western Church*, 159–210 for complete English texts of the Reformed liturgies.

Prayer of Thankslgiving

Psalm (sung) or Canticle of Simeon (sung)

SENDING

Offering for the Poor

Blesssing

Calvin's First Psalter

Calvin opens the Preface to the Genevan Psalter of 1542 with three fundamental things that are to be treated: preaching, prayer, and the Sacraments. First, Calvin emphasizes the importance of observing Sundays and other church days, and secondly, the need for a complete understanding of what the services mean. After discussing these matters, he returns to the subject of prayer by speaking of "the prayers and praises which we use."

> As for public prayers, there are two kinds. The ones with the word alone: the others with singing. And this is not something invented a little time ago. For from the first origin of the Church, this has been so, as appears from the histories. And even St. Paul speaks not only of praying by mouth: but also of singing. And in truth we know by experience that singing has vigor to move and inflame the hearts of men to invoke and praise God with a more vehement and ardent zeal.

In the Preface to the Genevan psalter of 1543 Calvin added an additional passage of 917 words (in the French):

> Now among the other things proper to recreate man and to give him pleasure, music is either the first or one of the principal, and ... we must be the more careful not to abuse it ... to moderate the use of music to make it serve all that is of good repute ... and that it should not become the instrument of lasciviousness or of any shamelessness.[25]

The tunes for Calvin's first psalter cannot be traced to any known source. If the courtiers of Francis I would sing Marot's psalms to popular tunes, so would the Huguenots all over France. It was the ability to adapt the psalms to the popular tunes of the day that created the popularity of Marot's verses. Some of these tunes were adaptations of the Lutheran chorales, some of which were secular songs also. Later English psalm versions labored under

---

25. Garside, "Calvin's Preface," 566-77.

the monotonous "ballad meter," but the early French psalter had many varying meters, providing for variety in musical rhythm.[26]

Calvin wrote, "We shall not find better songs nor songs better suited . . . than the Psalms of David." An acceptable tune should be "moderated in the way . . . that it may have the weight and majesty proper to the subject and may even be suitable for singing in Church."[27] Percy Scholes cites references in Calvin's *Commentaries on Genesis*, *Preface to Liturgy*, and *The Institutes of the Christian Religion*, which show Calvin's approval of music outside the sphere of the church.[28]

Although Calvin was opposed to part singing in church, Bourgeois made some harmonic settings of psalms. Claude Goudimel published three collections of settings of the tunes in the Genevan psalter: one in motet style between 1551 and 1556, and two for four voices in 1564 and 1565. In the Foreword to the harmonized 1565 edition of the Genevan psalter, Goudimel informed his readers that the tunes were adapted to three other parts, "not to induce you to sing them in church, but particularly in your homes."

Between 1541 and 1562 the Genevan psalter grew toward completion. The musical editor of all these smaller editions, except perhaps the first and last, was Louis Bourgeois. At the end of his editorship he had enlarged a psalter of thirty tunes into one containing eighty-three tunes for the psalms and two tunes for the metrical versions of the Ten Commandments and the Nunc Dimittis. Bourgeois had nothing to do with forty of the tunes in the complete edition of 1562.

Both Ulrich Zwingli and John Calvin valued music and shared Luther's belief that a biblical reform of theology required a biblical reform of worship. However, the biblical reform or worship was defined by these Reformed leaders as adhering as closely as possible to specific scriptural guidelines. Since the Bible said nothing specific about polyphonic music (the complex singing of multiple lines of tunes and texts), the use of the organ, or the free composition of new hymns, their churches would use only biblical materials (usually paraphrased Psalms) as their church music.

Conclusions

It might appear there was little that the reformers agreed upon. It is also possible to miss the changes brought about by the reformers, so here are a few things you can know for sure.

26. Truron, "Rhythm of Metrical Psalm-Tunes," 29–33.
27. Strunk, *Source Readings*, 347.
28. Scholes, *Puritans and Music in England*, 341.

What Did the Reformers Reject?

Three issues were at the top of the list that the Reformers protested against. First, the Mass was rejected as a repetition of the sacrifice of Christ. The Mass had ceased being a thanksgiving and had become a means of salvation. People expected all sorts of benefits and advantages from hearing Mass. The Mass had lost the idea of communion—it could be said on the behalf of people in their absence.

Second, the medieval doctrine of transubstantiation was rejected. This is the belief of *opus operate*—the mere performance of the Mass effected the presence of Christ automatically by changing the bread and wine into the essence of the body of Christ. Catholics thought the rite imparted a blessing without the faith of the person, even without bread and wine being given to the congregation.

Third, reformers rejected the idea that the priest was a person who could mediate grace between God and man. Additionally, the idea that salvation could be won by good works was rejected. St. Peter's in Rome was built largely through donations given by people who sought to earn salvation through their giving.

What Was Reformed?

All reformers undertook at least five common religious reforms. However, how those reforms were expressed and carried out was relative to the reformer's concept of congregational song in worship.

- Worship was held in the language of the people.
- The Bible was regarded as the sole authority of faith and its use in worship was restored.
- Congregational singing in worship was restored.
- The priesthood of the believers was emphasized.
- Salvation was by grace through faith in Christ alone.

The Catholic Counter-Reformation

The year 1517 marks the beginning of the Protestant Reformation and the year 1545 marks the beginning of the Counter-Reformation, or the Catholic Reformation. Pope Paul III (1534–49) appointed a commission to examine the state of the church in response to criticisms coming from the Protestant

Reformers as well as some Catholics. The commission issued a report, *Concerning the Reform of the Church*, which contained a list of abuses, such as: popes and cardinals had become too worldly; bribery to gain church office was widespread; monasteries had lost their discipline; and the selling of indulgences was widely abused. Many of the concerns expressed in the report are concerns expressed by the Protestant reformers.

In response to the Commission report, Pope Paul III called for a council to address its findings. After many delays the council first met three and a half years after its opening was announced. The council was named for the city in which it met: Trent, Italy. The Council, made up of four hundred bishops, met in Trent at 9:30 a.m. on December 13, 1545. The purpose of the Council was "concerning the things to be observed and avoided in the celebration of the Mass." The city of Trent hosted the Council in three distinct periods that stretched over eighteen years: 1545 to 1547, 1551 to 1552, and 1562 to 1563. The attendance of two hundred people in the third period was the largest number to participate actively as part of the Council. The third period was also the period in which the issue of music in the church was discussed in the Council.

In the years preceding the Council, many concerns and complaints about worship and song in the church had been discussed in various venues. The pronouncement of the Council on music was a continuation of these earlier meetings where worship and song had been discussed, such as

- The curtailment of liturgical texts in the Mass, the insertion of non-churchly songs in the vernacular, and their unintelligibility.

  In many choral compositions one or more voices would sing the liturgical text and other voices would sing a secular text not connected with the meaning of the Latin text, and perhaps even in conflict with the Latin text. I once studied a motet where one voice exalted the Virgin Mary with a Latin text, a second voice exalted Mary with a different Latin text, and a third voice sang about the lack of virtue in the girls of Paris—with all three texts sung simultaneously.

- Particular abuses of the proper churchly attitude.

  This complaint had to do with the attitude of those leading the Mass. Some things were to be said quietly, other things loudly, with appropriate gestures at specific times. It is not clear what the actual complaint was, but it would seem to be a perceived lack of sensitivity in the celebrant's leadership.

- Worldly and lengthy organ compositions.[29]

This last complaint has been described as "the lack of liturgical sensibility on the part of organists, who played dances, displayed their skill, extended their playing to improper lengths, and so interfered with worship."

The Council did not concern itself with details of musical and stylistic problems, but it did insist upon fundamental attitudes, and thus established directions for further development. "When it came to music and other abuses," writes Monson, "delegates tried to say as little as possible; thus, two lines on music were actually published in the canons and decrees of the twenty-second session of the Council celebrated on September 17, 1562."[30]

After the debates, only some fifteen words remained regarding music as part of that single decree "concerning the things to be observed and avoided in the celebration of the Mass." They translate: "Let them keep away from the churches compositions in which there is an intermingling of the lascivious or impure, whether by instrument or voice."[31] The Committee's recommendations that music must serve to uplift the faithful, that its words must be intelligible, and that secular expression must be avoided were given binding form in the Decrees of the 22nd Session, on September 17, 1562.

The official wording from the twenty-second session placed very little restriction on music. It implicitly permitted the continued use of polyphony and the organ, specifically prohibited secular elements, but made no mention at all of the intelligibility issue. The overall ruling of the Council of Trent emphasized the necessity of church music prioritizing the communication of religious values rather than artistic values, yet it does not specifically ban the two from being combined in some way or another. Much of the council's ruling was taken differently by each church in each nation throughout Europe.

The problem was a conflict between musical elaborateness and musical austerity. The best composers wrote secular music that required a high level of skill in performance and they tended to use the same techniques in composing for the church.[32] This conflict continued to plague the church for

---

29. Fellerer, "Church Music and the Council of Trent," 576–94.
30. Monson, "Council of Trent Revisited," 11.
31. Monson made an exhaustive study of the documents from the Council of Trent, and relates how the Council made its deliberations, and details the many conferences where worship and song were discussed prior to the first meeting of the Council.
32. White, *Roman Catholic Worship*, 19.

several centuries, and various edicts were issued that addressed the issue, and it was partially resolved in Vatican II.[33]

For You to Think about

1. In your church or denominational hymnal, study the index of sources and locate hymns that have their origin in the Reformation.
2. Study Calvin's Geneva service. Is there any simiarity to the worship of your church? Differences? If you organized a Calvinist service for your church, what elements would you add to your church's worship? What would you remove? Give reasons for your choices.
3. In thinking about congregational song, which reformer's ideas about congregational song do you find more nearly your own views? Why is that so? If your ideas are different, why is that so?

---

33. White, *Roman Catholic Worship*, 19–20, 41–43, 65–67, 91–93, 118–19, 135.

7

Congregational Song in the English Tradition

> There is nothing that hath drawne multitudes to be of their
> Sects so much, as the singing of their psalmes.
>
> —Unknown Roman Catholic writer, 1616

In England the reformation took a turn much different from that on the Continent, for there it was initiated by the common people, primarily as a religious protest against abuses and the desire to worship freely. "Peasants took new ideas of freedom into the political realm and demanded rights from their overlords," wrote Jennifer Tait, before adding:

> Priests and nuns married (usually to each other, because no respectable merchant or banker wanted their daughters to marry priests.). Churches looked profoundly different when you entered, because the art that had formerly covered their walls had been forcibly, sometimes violently, removed. Worship services sounded different, and people were asked to behave differently in them (listen to the pastor—save the rosary for your private devotions!). New roles in church (pastor's wife) opened up to Protestant women, while others (nun, abbess, virgin) closed down.[1]

Because the British political scene was more closely related to events in France instead of those in Germany, the influence of Lutheranism on British political and religious life was limited.

---

1. Tait, "Editor's Note," 4.

King Henry VIII (1491–1547)

At first, the pope found in Henry a champion, and Henry's allegiance was expressed in both ink and blood. In 1513, the twenty-two-year-old monarch waged a "holy war" in Europe on behalf of Pope Julius II, who had promised Henry recognition as "Most Christian King" if he would "utterly exterminate the king of France."[2] Eight years later, Henry attacked Martin Luther in a book that defended Catholicism's seven sacraments. For his rhetorical efforts, Rome titled Henry "Defender of the Faith."

Henry was a Renaissance king—he learned to speak Latin, French, and Spanish; and he was an accomplished musician and dabbled in theology and in Renaissance humanism, which was often critical of Catholicism. He approved of a New Testament in Greek and Latin, compiled by his friend, the famous humanist Erasmus—despite the protests of many Catholic clergymen, who believed the distribution of the Scriptures was a great threat to their religious control.

King Henry VIII split with the church in a move of power. Because his first wife was unable to bear him a male heir, because he was infatuated with Anne Boleyn, Henry wanted the pope to annul the marriage. The pope refused. A struggle that involved political and economic factors more than religious ones was brought to a head by Henry's desire for papal approval to end his marriage. This opened a split with the Catholic church that only widened in the 1530s.

The king had long resented the wealth and power of the Roman church and had sought from early in his reign to increase royal power over church affairs. He abolished the monasteries, for example, not as a religious reform, but to suppress them as centers of papal sympathies and to confiscate their wealth. English monasteries of the 1500s were centers of Catholic devotion. They also owned large tracts of land and—in their crosses, vestments, images, and Communion ware—precious metals and jewels. Thus, the monasteries became an obvious target for Henry. One disastrous result was the loss of untold music manuscripts and treatises used by the monks. We know only a little about early English music because there is nothing available for us to study.

"Formally, the dismantling of monasteries in the 1530s had little to do with rising Protestantism," writes Paul Ayris. "The most powerful motive was Henry's need to finance his government, especially his armies. But it

---

2. Alban, "Thomas Cranmer," 16.

was Henry's anti-papal mood—and the acquiescence of the Reformers—that made dissolution possible."[3]

Chantries were also abolished. These were institutions founded for the saying of masses for the dead. Chantries were sources of great income and held large amounts of property. Under an act of Parliament in 1547, chantries were also dissolved. However, the value of possessions seized by the government was less than that taken from the monasteries. The motives for dissolving chantries were mixed: the crown wanted to obtain money for wars against France and Scotland, and praying for the dead was deemed "superstitious."

So, King Henry VIII issued a royal edict stating that he and his successors should be the only accepted heads of The Church of England. No doctrinal changes were made and there were no implications of religious freedom or tolerance. Henry was not a Protestant, even after his break from Rome. He believed in transubstantiation, priestly celibacy, and other Catholic doctrines. He wanted Catholicism without the pope. Thus, he had both Protestants and Roman Catholics executed in his reign—anyone who would not acknowledge him as supreme head of his church.[4]

Though Henry wanted to end papal control of the Church in England, he showed no desire to institute Protestant reforms in doctrine or worship. This allowed him full control of the Church in England. The church had simply exchanged one master for another. Though it was largely because of economic and political reasons, the split still had a profound effect on congregational song of the time. Like Luther, Henry also wanted the laity to be able to understand the music more clearly, but those reforms were carried out very slowly. By the time Henry died, the daily services were still sung in Latin, but steps were being made to change the liturgy to the vernacular.[5]

Thomas Cranmer (1489–1556)

During the course of his struggle with the pope for a divorce, Henry appointed Thomas Cranmer as archbishop of Canterbury. Some have accused Cranmer of making a deal with Henry: if appointed archbishop of Canterbury, he would resolve Henry's need to legally divorce Catherine of Aragon and marry Anne Boleyn. Cranmer believed Henry's divorce was justified and had encouraged Henry to gain wider approval for it long

---

3. Ayris, "Destroying the Monasteries," 1.
4. Galli, "Thomas Cranmer," 2.
5. Blume, *Protestant Church Music*, 694.

before his appointment. Cranmer had earlier suggested that the papal consent for Henry's divorce was not needed.

Cranmer was familiar with Lutheran and Calvinistic reforms on the Continent, and he favored some similar religious reforms in England. Such were not possible, however, as long as Henry lived. Cranmer bided his time, meanwhile instructing Edward, the king's young son, in the tenets of Protestantism.

THE EXHORTATION AND LITANY (1544)

This publication is the first officially recognized service in English and is the foundation upon which all subsequent Anglican services have been built. A litany at this time meant a penitential service in procession used in time of trouble and in a spirit of sorrow. The service was mainly a series of short intercessory phrases said by the priest and a brief response from the choir or congregation. Henry VIII had ordered general processions to be made because of the many troubles the nation was experiencing. Public response was slack because the public did not understand what was being said and sung.

THE BOOK OF COMMON PRAYER (1549)

Cranmer had theological sympathies with John Calvin, but his loyalty to the Romanist liturgical tradition was much stronger than Calvin's. The *Book of Common Prayer*, which Cranmer produced, drew heavily from the Roman breviary, particularly the set prayers and Scripture readings for the canonical hours. He eliminated or modified many anti-Protestant emphases. Cranmer took five medieval liturgical tomes and reduced them into a single volume. Among other things, in line with the teachings of Calvin, Cranmer eliminated most of the medieval hymns, largely leaving only psalms and other biblical hymns to be sung. Original hymns, as sung by Anabaptists and Lutherans, were not permitted. His liturgy, with slight modifications, is still used by the Church of England and the American Episcopal Church today, nearly 450 years later.

THE HOMILIES (1547, 1563)

Sermons could not be preached by every rector or vicar of a parish church in the sixteenth century Church of England; a license was needed. The usual qualification was an MA degree from Oxford or Cambridge. No sermon was scheduled or required at Morning or Evening Prayer, but one was required in the Order for Holy Communion.

The Books of Homilies were authorized sermons issued in two books for use in the Church of England during the reigns of Edward VI and Elizabeth I. They were to provide for the church a new model of simplified topical preaching as well as a theological understanding of the Reformation that had taken place in England. A local vicar or rector could read an authorized homily in services that did not require a sermon.

Thomas Cranmer broached the idea of a Book of Homilies in 1539, but it was not authorized by the church's Convocation until 1542. They were not published, however, until 1547. The first six homilies present distinctive Protestant theology, namely the authority and sufficiency of Scripture, the radical sinfulness of man, justification by faith alone, evangelical faith, and sanctification. The Homilies were revoked under Queen Mary, who wanted to restore Catholicism as the official church, but they were reinstated by Elizabeth I.[6]

The Forty-Two Articles (1553)

Many declarations on faith and discipline were put forward in the sixteenth century by the religious bodies that had thrown off allegiance to the Roman church and its theological and ecclesiastical structure. The various Reformed bodies needed to declare positively what they held in faith, and what ecclesiastical structure they recognized. Not only did every Reformed body put out its own Confession, even clergy who retained their obedience to Rome were required to accept the Creed of Pope Pius IV as formulated by the Council of Trent.

The Church of England may have felt this particularly necessary. When Papal Supremacy was rejected, it was declared that the English church had no intention "to decline or vary from the congregation of Christ's Church in things concerning the Articles of the Catholic faith."[7] Cranmer and his colleagues prepared several statements of faith during the reign of Henry VIII, but it was not until the reign of Edward VI that the ecclesiastical reformers were able to make more thorough changes. Shortly before Edward's death, Cranmer presented the forty-two points. This was the last of his major contributions to the development of Anglicanism.

---

6. Toon, "Whatever are the Anglican Books of Homilies?," 1. See also "The Homilies," The Anglican Library. http://www.anglicanlibrary.org/homilies/.

7. Barry, "History of the Articles," para. 6.

Edward VI (1537–53)

Due to the influence of Cranmer, Edward is the first English monarch to be raised as a Protestant. Since he was only nine years of age when crowned in 1547, the realm was governed by a Regency Council, first led by his uncle Edward Seymour, First Duke of Somerset.

During Edward's reign, the Church of England was transformed into a recognizably Protestant body, because Archbishop Cranmer was able to institute the changes that have prevailed in the Church of England until the present, except for the brief reign of the English (so-called "Bloody") Mary. When Edward VI ascended to the throne, several church choirs began singing parts of the service in English, such as at Westminster Abbey and St. Paul's Cathedral. The use of English in the service officially became codified in 1549 when Parliament ratified the First Act of Uniformity, which stated that the *Book of Common Prayer* be used in place of all Latin service manuals.[8]

Edward made a royal visit to the various English cathedrals to ensure that all elements of Catholic worship had been eliminated. Prescribed to Lincoln Cathedral were these instructions: "[The choir] shall from henceforth sing or say no anthems of our Lady or other saints, but only of our Lord, and them not in Latin; but choosing out the best and most sounding to Christian religion, they shall turn the same into English, setting thereunto a plain and distinct note for every syllable one; they sing them and none other."[9]

The *Book of Common Prayer* was revised in 1592 with a simplified version of the Mass renamed "Holy Communion." The revision was more Protestant, with the deletion of further sections from the Catholic Mass leaving few of the texts composers had formerly set to music until this time. The Latin daily office was rewritten and compressed to create two new English services of matins and evensong.

Mary I (1516–58)

Edward's reign was short-lived, as he died in 1553, and his death led to a bitter struggle for succession to the throne. In his will, Edward stated that neither Elizabeth nor Mary, his half-sisters, were to ascend the throne. Instead, he arranged that the crown would go to Lady Jane Grey, the granddaughter of Henry's younger sister. Lady Jane's accession to the throne was extremely unpopular and deemed unacceptable by most of the populace. It

---

8. Le Huray, *Music and the Reformation in England*, 10–18.
9. Le Huray, *Music and the Reformation in England*, 10.

was also considered illegal, because of the 1544 Act of Parliament restoring Lady Mary and Lady Elizabeth to the line of succession. Lady Jane Grey's accession took place in July 10, 1553 and was revoked on July 19, 1553. Her reign lasted for only nine days.

After Edward's death, Mary challenged and successfully deposed the new queen, Lady Jane Grey. Mary took the throne as the first queen regnant. At first, she acknowledged the religious dualism of her country, but as a staunch Catholic, Mary wanted to undo the church reforms that Edward had overseen. Through a series of legislative acts, she restored the Catholic system of Henry VIII and England's allegiance with Rome. She renewed several laws that included a strict heresy law. The enforcement of this law resulted in the burning of over 300 Protestants as heretics, including Thomas Cranmer. Mary's religious persecutions made her extremely unpopular and earned her the nickname "Bloody Mary."[10]

Not all Protestants conformed to the Catholicism restored by Mary, so many of them fled to Holland and others went underground. After experiencing several years of freedom to worship as they please, some English Protestants continued to worship in secret as early as the 1550s. Since she was childless, she was succeeded by her half-sister Elizabeth.

Elizabeth I (1533–1603)

Elizabeth I preferred the colorful ceremonies of the Catholic Church, but realized that political necessity required her to lean toward Protestantism. Elizabeth issued another revision of the 1552 prayer book and her policies helped to establish a moderately Protestant Church of England. In 1559 Elizabeth replaced the Act of Uniformity of Henry VIII with her own Act of Supremacy. This Act recognized the British sovereign as the head of the Church of England, supplanting the power of the pope in Rome.

That same year, Parliament enacted the Act of Uniformity. This Act made Protestantism the official faith of England and established a form of worship that is still followed in English parish churches today. The Act, which came to be known as the "Elizabethan Settlement," showed that Elizabeth was determined to follow a middle road where religion was concerned. She wanted to create a settlement that both Catholics and Protestants would be happy with, a middle of the road that would allow her subjects to finally live in peace with each other and at the same time allow her to restore Protestantism as the country's faith.

---

10. Loades, "Why Queen Mary Was 'Bloody,'" 38.

From the perspective of congregational song, the Act of Uniformity mandated that all worship services were to follow the service set out in this Act and be in English. The Catholic mass was banned completely. Everyone was to attend church on Sundays and holy days or be fined twelve pence. Clergy who did not stick to the Act and the *Book of Common Prayer* faced civil punishment. In the instructions issued by Elizabeth in 1559, she stated her requirements for Anglican church music:

> a modest distinct song, so used in a parts of the common prayers in the Church, that the same may be plainly understood, as if it were read without singing and yet nevertheless, for the comforting of such as delight in music, it may be permitted that in the beginning, or in the end of common prayers either at morning or evening, there may be sung a Hymn, or such like song . . .[11]

By "hymn," Elizabeth meant a metrical psalm. From the time of the first *Book of Common Prayer* until the English Civil War, psalms in cathedrals and university chapels were sung to harmonized Gregorian chants. This is referred to as English chant and can occasionally be found in British churches today. This was a golden age for English composers, who left us with a rich heritage of choral and instrumental music.[12]

Dissenters

Before 1600 the Elizabethan Settlement had become very unsettled. Whether Catholic or Protestant, those who held to more intense theological views found the Settlement unsatisfactory. Gradually, a distinct party of English churchmen emerged who were not satisfied with what they thought were half-hearted religious changes and were advocating further reforms.

Puritans

The prayer book instructions on vestments to be worn by the clergy caused a long-lasting dispute within the Church of England, and those protesting the wearing of clerical vestments were known derisively as "Puritans." "Puritanism in England was a holiness movement—seeking holiness in church, family, and community, as well as in personal life," writes J. I. Packer. "It

---

11. The full text of the Act of Uniformity 1559 can be read at http://history.hanover.edu/texts/enfgref/er80.html.

12. Dowley, *Christian Music*, 103.

started around 1564 when certain clergy began campaigning for more holiness in the Prayer Book liturgy of the Church of England."

> They complained that the *Book of Common Prayer* still contained "Romish rags" and offensive rituals. Other concerns soon surfaced, and it became clear that Puritanism was at heart a movement to raise standards of Christian life in England, with the conversion of England as the final goal.[13]

All Puritans agreed that four of the ceremonial requirements were unbiblical and revealed lingering Catholic influence:

1. Vestments: Clergy were required to wear vestments during public worship and the Puritans objected that vestments were too associated with the Catholic priesthood in the minds of laypeople. A special uniform implied that the clergy were holier and closer to God than other people, thus denying the priesthood of all believers.

2. Kneeling at the communion table: The Prayer Book required communicants to kneel as they received the bread and wine. But the Puritans argued that this invited people to believe in transubstantiation—the Roman Catholic doctrine that the substance of the bread and wine changed into the body and blood of Christ—and to venerate the elements. The Puritans preferred to sit at a table and pass the bread and wine to each other, as it was done in Reformed churches in other countries.

3. The sign of the cross in baptism: According to Prayer Book specifications, the priest poured water on the head of the child being baptized and then made the sign of the cross on the child's forehead. The Puritans believed that the essence of baptism was the water symbolizing new life in Christ; the sign of the cross was an unbiblical human addition.

4. Wedding rings: In pre-Reformation days, marriage was regarded as a sacrament; the ring given by the bridegroom to the bride was the outward and visible sign of this invisible grace. According to the Anglican Articles, marriage was not a sacrament, but a human partnership blessed by God. A ring, said the Puritans, was thus unnecessary.

The Puritans were divided between those who chose to remain in the Anglican Church and those who withdrew to form separatist churches.

---

13. Packer, "Physicians of the Soul," 10.

Those who separated were called Nonconformists because they refused to conform to the rules of the Anglicans.[14]

The Westminster Assembly

During a violent civil war, an average of seventy ministers regularly met at Westminster Abbey in London from 1643 to 1648. Their purpose: to draft a far reaching and uniformly acceptable ecclesiastical system for the churches of England, Scotland and Ireland. This was a very difficult assignment. The Scots wanted a Presbyterian form of church organization and an ordinance was passed in 1646 to set up a limited Presbyterian system in England in which the church was subordinate to Parliament.

The reforms included a *Directory of Worship* to replace the *Book of Common Prayer,* the Westminster *Confession of Faith,* which set out the creed of the reformed Church of England, complete with scriptural proof of it clauses, two catechisms, and the *Form of Presbyterial Church-Government,* that summarized the principles of the reformed doctrines. The reforms of the Church of England that were implemented by the Westminster Assembly remained in force throughout the Commonwealth period until revoked at the Restoration in 1660. They did remain in force in the Church of Scotland and formed the doctrinal basis of Presbyterian churches established later in the United States.[15]

Puritan Worship

The Puritan critique of the Anglican *Book of Common Prayer* was well established by the time the Westminster Assembly began its deliberations in 1643. When they finally had a chance to reform the Prayer Book, the Puritans crafted a set of guidelines, known as "The Directory for the Publick Worship of God," rather than a set form of service. Although it was never officially approved in England, many Puritan pastors followed its guidelines voluntarily.

The Puritans debated among themselves as much as they did with Anglican authorities about the purpose and nature of worship. In an intensive study of Puritanism, Packer writes that the arguments of their day "remain living issues for us today." Those issues are as follows:

1. In what sense are the Scriptures authoritative for Christian worship?

---

14. Packer, "Physicians of the Soul," 12–14.
15. Murray, "Calling of the Westminster Assembly,"

A church should have worship in accordance with the apostolic principle that all must be done "unto edifying" (1 Cor. 14:26), and that as a means to that end everything must be done "decently and in order" (v. 40). They were all agreed that each church has liberty to arrange its worship in the way best adapted to edify its own worshippers, in the light of their state, background, and needs; so that they all took it for granted that the worship of varied churches in varying pastoral situations would vary in detail.

2. What regulations are proper for Christian worship?

There are three ways to order worship: to have a set liturgy like the *Book of Common Prayer*, to have a manual of general guidance like the Westminster Directory, or to leave it entirely to the minister and congregation to regulate its own worship as they wish. These alternatives are historically associated with Anglicans, Presbyterians, and Independents and Quakers respectively. Which is preferable and why are they preferable?

3. What discipline is proper in connection with worship?

This is the question of sound doctrine. Worship is spoiled when non-biblical elements are introduced. Who ensures that what is said and done in worship is compatible with biblical teaching? What steps are appropriate when error is detected?[16]

Elizabeth I was not sympathetic with the Puritan point of view and tried to enforce conformity by law. Naturally, the bishops were opposed to a change from episcopal to Presbyterian polity and not all bishops welcomed Calvinist doctrines. Many bishops were repelled by the rigidity and narrowness of the Puritan mind and their intolerance. There was also an increasing vocal Puritan movement within the church discouraging the use of the organ and choral music, and stressing the unaccompanied singing of metrical psalms. The general public, the government, and church leaders could not accept the Puritan reforms completely.

Separatists

Since they were unable to purify the Church of England, many clerics determined to separate from the church and form their own independent congregations where they could preach and practice what they considered to be New Testament faith. Some churchmen wanted to stay within the

16. Packer, "Puritan Approach to Worship."

church and to separate temporarily so they could promote reform. Others separated on the basis of principle; they were convinced the church should be free of all government connection. By the 1550s groups of Separatists were visible all over England.

Separatists held a high view of the Bible and were determined to live by it teachings. They believed only the redeemed were proper church members. They rejected an episcopal church polity, favoring more congregational participation. Some Separatist churches had a congregational polity while others had a form of Presbyterian polity. They favored a simple liturgy for worship with little or no required element, written prayers, or other worship helps.

Many Separatist ideas surfaced later among Baptists. However, Baptists parted ways with the Separatists over believer's baptism and the separation of church and state. When the Pilgrims came to the New World there were Baptists with them; because of these two basic principles, Baptists did not fare well with other Separatists or Anglicans.

Baptist Worship

We know a little about how these first Baptists worshipped. McBeth[17] quotes from a letter written from Hughe and Anne Bromhead in 1609 that is the oldest record of a Baptist worship service. The service was lengthy, with the morning session running from 8 a.m. to noon and the afternoon session from 2 p.m. until 5 or 6 p.m. The service began with a prayer, followed by the reading of one or two chapters out of the Bible. Several speakers, including members of the congregation, would expound on the passages read, interspersed with prayer. An offering for the poor and any business of the church were added at the end.[18]

Baptist worship was usually conducted on Sunday and held in homes, a public hall, or outdoors in good weather. Churches did not have their own buildings until nearly 1700. The services were spontaneous and unstructured. Any person could at any time share a psalm or make an exhortation or give a doctrine. Baptist opposition to the *Book of Common Prayer* explains the nature of Baptist worship at this time. The Lord's Supper was an important part of worship, and some churches observed the Supper weekly while others more infrequently. Baptisms were also a part of services and

---

17. McBeth, *Baptist Heritage*, 21–38.
18. McBeth, *Baptist Heritage*, 91–99.

immersions were conducted in lakes or rivers, but some churches prepared indoor "baptistery" or "baptismal cisterns" as they called them.[19]

Baptist Song

Most early Baptist churches and their successors were opposed to music in their worship services. Particular Baptists were less opposed to singing than General Baptists. Their objections were centered mainly around the fear of becoming too formal in worship. Since Helwys and the other early leader had contact with Mennonites and other psalm-singing groups in Amsterdam and Leyden, it is difficult to understand their aversion to singing. By 1671 at least one Baptist church had commenced singing for the Broadmead Church in Bristol had a complaint lodged against them for singing too loudly.[20]

Benjamin Keach introduced the singing of a hymn at the close of the Lord's Supper in the church at Horsley-down in 1673. Those who objected were allowed to leave before the hymn was sung. He is credited with introducing hymn singing to English Baptists and to all English churches.

Thomas Grantham, a Particular Baptist leader, published his objections to congregational singing in 1678:

- Singing should be under the influence of the Spirit upon each individual.
- Instruction is prevented when all sing and none can hear.
- Singing encourages formal prayers.
- Singing encourages instruments in the service and destroys its solemnity.

In 1689 the General Baptist Assembly made a resolution that singing was a dangerous practice that churches should avoid. The churches that had been singing were using one of the psalters of William Barton, author of one of the earliest collections of hymns apart from versions of the psalms. He had published a metrical psalter in 1644.

By 1691 neither party was satisfied, so Benjamin Keach defended his position by writing *The Breach Repaired in God's Worship*, in which he elevated singing to a gospel ordinance and said its neglect was one of the reasons for spiritual dearth among the churches. A proof text was Exodus 32:18: "The noise of them that sing do I hear." Keach argued that one person singing could

---

19. Thomas Crosby, quoted in McBeth, *Baptist Heritage*, 92.
20. Curwen, *Studies in Worship Music*, 92–94.

not have made all that noise, therefore the singing must have been congregational (nor was he deterred by the fact that this singing was to the Golden Calf, as his opponents very gleefully pointed out).

The evolution of the controversy to its ultimate conclusion is illustrated by unhappy members who withdrew from Keach's Horsley-down Church and formed the Maze Pond Church in 1693. This group refused to have fellowship with any of the singing churches. By 1735 the church had tempered its position on singing sufficiently to call Rev. Abraham West as pastor on the condition that a psalm or hymn be sung at the beginning of public worship and after the Lord's Supper. Finally, in 1753, since only two men and two women in the membership opposed singing, the Maze Pond Church voted to make the singing of hymns a regular part of public worship.[21]

In 1691 Benjamin Keach published a hymnal titled *Spiritual Melody* that included three hundred of his own hymns. This is the first English Baptist hymnal and perhaps the first English collection of hymn designed for congregational worship. Keach is an important figure since he was the first to establish the practice of singing hymns, as distinguished from psalms, in the regular worship of any English church. The Baptist experience reflects the struggles that many English churches were having at that time and continued into the early nineteenth century.

From Psalmody to Hymns

Following the victory of the parliamentary forces in the civil war, use of the *Book of Common Prayer* was prohibited and all church music except metrical psalm singing was banned. During the English Republic, a parliamentary ordinance of 1654 called "for the speedy demolishing of all organs" in cathedrals and parish churches.[22] The English monarchy was restored in 1660 and an Act of Uniformity in 1662 reinstated the *Book of Common Prayer* in revised form.

English-speaking believers, both in Anglican and Nonconformist churches, lacked a truly vibrant musical expression as late as 1700. Virtually the only musical texts were wooden renderings of the psalms in verse. As Isaac Watts complained, "To see the dull indifference, the negligent and thoughtless air, that sits upon the faces of the whole assembly while the psalm is on their lips, might tempt even a charitable observer to suspect the fervor of inward

---

21. Curwen, *Studies in Worship Music*, 48–56. See also Hooper, *Church Music in Transition*, 102–34.

22. Dowley, *Christian Music*, 103–4.

religion."[23] However, many people expressed discontent over the state of this singing and were desiring a broadening of what could be sung.

The most common metrical psalter, by Sternhold and Hopkins, was completed in 1562 and held sway over all other psalters for two hundred years. Many voices were raised against this psalter because of its lack of poetic beauty and difficult tunes. Many later psalters were published in England, but the first that seriously rivaled Sternhold and Hopkins for general acceptance was not published until 1696. It was usually known by the names of it authors, Tate and Brady; but its title was *A New Version of the Psalms of David*. This caused the Sternhold and Hopkins to be called the "Old Version" and the Tate and Brady to be called the "New Version."

With some revisions, Tate and Brady continued to be used in the Church of England for a century and a half. Psalters were bound with both Bibles and the *Book of Common Prayer*, which indicates the value people attached to them. Modern English hymnody began in the early eighteenth century, but hymnody did not displace metrical psalmody within Anglicanism until 1820.

Isaac Watts

A leader was needed who could guide the singing of the congregation to a new horizon. The leader was Isaac Watts (1674–1748). Watts was the son of a dissenting schoolmaster who later went into private business. Isaac's early childhood was during the reign of Charles II (1660–85) when Dissenters were penalized. As a result of his nonconformity, Watt's father was placed in prison more than once. Until the nineteenth century, Nonconformists were barred from attending either Oxford or Cambridge University, so Isaac Watts attended a Nonconformist school, received a good education and spent a great deal of his time in literary pursuits.

We might find it difficult to understand how a Dissenter, and a Calvinist who believed in congregational autonomy or "Independence," could be treated with imprisonment. Watts was a loyal British subject, but he and fellow Dissenters accepted many of the principles that had led to the Civil War in England. Anglicans had not forgotten the killing of Charles I and the establishment of the Puritan Commonwealth under Oliver Cromwell.

During the Restoration Period (1660–1700), Calvinist Dissenters were widely regarded as clandestine revolutionaries, eager to upset the peace and return England to its Puritan past. Dissenters were heavily persecuted, subject to fines and imprisonment. Thus, when the Dissenters

---

23. Watts, "Preface," iii–xiv.

sang hymns, those hymns were often associated with Christian extremism and even revolutionary politics.

Watt's greatest literary achievements are his hymn texts. It is said that as a young man of twenty-one he complained about the quality of psalms sung in the worship services. His father informed him that if he could write better ones, he should do it. Taking his father's jest to heart, Watts bent himself to the task and produced the hymn text "Behold the Glories of the Lamb." This met with such great success that the congregation invited him to have a hymn ready each Sunday, which he provided. This was the beginning of a prolific career of hymn writing, for Watts wrote nearly 750 hymns. Watts made an important contribution to worship in three ways:

- He introduced hymn singing into the worship services.
- By precept and example, he gave impetus to others in their hymn writing.
- Watts wrote some hymns that no hymnal of any distinction can omit (e.g., "O God, Our Help in Ages Past").[24]

Two final points. First, Watts' hymns were clearly intended both for congregational and liturgical use. Second, his hymns mark a halfway point between paraphrase and original hymnody.

Watts has been called the "father of English hymnody," but this is a misleading title. Watts was literate enough to recognize the textual inadequacy of the metrical psalms and that people in the pew were demanding better expressions of religious devotion. "Fortunately, Watts set out to solve the problem," writes Kevin Miller.

If he did not exactly create a new genre, he "opened the gate," as Erik Routley put it, for the modern hymn. He gave the church freer, powerful expressions of Christian faith: "Joy to the World," "When I Survey the Wondrous Cross," "Jesus Shall Reign," and many others. Charles Wesley, John Newton, and others soon followed his lead.[25]

Congregational Song of the Methodists

The Methodist Church had its beginning in the lives of two brothers, John (1703–91) and Charles (1707–88) Wesley. These two men were from a very devout family, and while students at Oxford University formed a religious study group. Because of their methodical habits of living and study,

---

24. Hope, *Isaac Watts and His Contribution*.
25. Miller, "From the Editor," 3–4.

they were called "Methodists." John and Charles were ordained into the Anglican Church, and were sent to America to help stabilize the Georgia colonies with religious services.

The turning point in their lives came, perhaps, on the journey across the Atlantic. On board ship, they met a group of Moravians who were enthusiastic hymn singers. During a raging storm, these people maintained their composure and sang hymns for assurance of God's protecting hand. John was so impressed he made a detailed study of their hymnal, *Das Gesang-Buch der Gemeine in Herrnhut*, used in their home church in Herrnhut, Germany. Such hymn singing was practically unknown in the Anglican services, and Wesley promptly set about to introduce some English translations of Moravian hymns into his services in Georgia.

Introducing hymn singing into the services was not as easy as it might seem. In 1737 John Wesley was hauled into court on twelve charges, three of them dealing with his alleged changes in the Anglican liturgy; second, for singing psalms not authorized for the church services; and third, for singing hymns not authorized by the church. These three changes were true. Wesley was using devotional materials prepared by those who refused to answer allegiance to the Crown. He was using the old prayer book of 1549 instead of the authorized prayer book of 1662. Wesley had issued a *Collection of Psalms and Hymns* (1737), printed at Charles Town, South Carolina. Wesley was familiar with the approved psalters, but preferred the psalms of Watts and others that he had included in the *Collection*. Most certainly the church had not approved the hymns of Watts or any of the other authors. The vote of the court was against Wesley, but no sentencing took place.

Since Wesley was not given any kind of sentence or fine, his hymnal was never officially condemned. Perhaps if the trial had taken place in London where the authorities and the Anglican Church were stricter in those matters, he would have been sentenced and his work officially condemned.[26]

The Wesley brothers returned to England and began their work in evangelism and hymnody, which would help to change the religious life of the English-speaking world. They published sixty-three hymnals between 1737 and 1786. Many hymns that were published had their origin in Moravian hymnody and were translated by John. Either Charles or John produced many others. They had discovered that singing was an effective means of spreading the gospel.

The Foundry Collection of 1742 was the first Wesleyan collection to contain tunes only; they came from sources like psalm tunes, the composer

---

26. Ellinwood, "Wesley's First Hymnal," 56–59.

Handel, and German folk tunes. In 1780 the *Sacred Harmony* was published as a harmonized version of the 1761 tune book.

John Wesley realized that no great religious movement could exist without a suitable body of songs and he attempted to supply them. He turned to Moravian tunes, but they were foreign to Englishmen and Americans. In 1753 Thomas Butts, a friend of the Wesleys, published *Harmonia Sacra*, which included decorated melodies. This decoration of melodies was very common among the populace where folk music was popular. Because the singing of psalms had been slowed down, extra notes were added between melody notes the same as was done to secular folk songs. It was not long until John Wesley condemned this type of hymnody.

Over the years, many hymn texts written by Charles were increasing both in number and in complexity of meter. The psalm tunes and simpler folk tunes would not accommodate this change. New tunes were needed to go with the text, so John used newly composed tunes or adapted tunes from sacred and secular and oratorio, and even operatic melodies. The secular music he used was of accepted high standard and almost always from classical rather than popular music.[27]

In 1761, he published *Select Hymns for the Use of Christians*, in which he laid down his directions for singing:

- **Learn these tunes before you learn any others**; afterwards learn as many as you please.

- **Sing them exactly as they are printed here**, without altering or mending them at all; and if you have learned to sing them otherwise, unlearn it as soon as you can.

- **Sing all.** See that you join with the congregation as frequently as you can. Let not a single degree of weakness or weariness hinder you. If it is a cross to you, take it up, and you will find it a blessing.

- **Sing lustily and with good courage.** Beware of singing as if you were half dead, or half asleep; but lift up your voice with strength. Be no more afraid of your voice now, nor more ashamed of its being heard, then when you sang the songs of Satan.

- **Sing modestly.** Do not bawl, so as to be heard above or distinct from the rest of the congregation, that you may not destroy the harmony; but strive to unite your voices together, so as to make one clear melodious sound.

---

27. McIntyre, "Did the Wesleys Really Use Drinking Song Tunes?"

- **Sing in time.** Whatever time is sung be sure to keep with it. Do not run before nor stay behind it; but attend close to the leading voices, and move therewith as exactly as you can; and take care not to sing too slow. This drawling way naturally steals on all who are lazy; and it is high time to drive it out from us, and sing all our tunes just as quick as we did at first.
- **Above all sing spiritually.** Have an eye to God in every word you sing. Aim at pleasing him more than yourself, or any other creature. In order to do this, attend strictly to the sense of what you sing, and see that your heart is not carried away with the sound, but offered to God continually; so shall your singing be such as the Lord will approve here, and reward you when he cometh in the clouds of heaven.

In worship, John Wesley never completely parted with the Anglican service. The background of Methodist worship was the 1662 edition of the *Book of Common Prayer*.[28] He followed the traditional four divisions of the liturgy: Entrance, Proclamation of the Word and Response, Thanksgiving and Communion, and the Sending Forth.

However, by Wesley's day, the observance of the Lord's Table had become very infrequent in the Church of England, and in Roman Catholicism the cup was withheld from the laity. Through a study of Wesley's sermon, notes, letters, theological addresses, and hymn's (by both John and Charles Wesley), McClaren concluded that "the heart of Wesley's theology of worship is the Christ event."[29] Wesley believed that the sacrament of the Lord's Table is the centerpiece for public worship on the Lord's day. McClaren found that "Wesley was very critical of both his church and Roman Catholicism for their practice of the Lord's Table in worship. He believed strongly that the Lord's Table should be celebrated each week in worship and that both the bread and wine should be given to all communicants."[30]

In 1784, Wesley prepared *The Sunday Service of the Methodists for Methodists in America*, patterned after the *Book of Common Prayer*.[31] He felt no qualms in announcing in the preface that he had omitted many psalms as being highly improper for the mouths of a Christian congregation. From this volume he omitted also eight of the Anglican 39 Articles, except that on baptism, which was abridged, and Article 16, whose title was changed from "Of sin after baptism" to "Of sin after justification." He also went on to omit a

28. http://justus.anglican.org/resources/bcp/1662/baskerville.htm.
29. McClaren, "Wesleyan Theology of Worship," 128.
30. McClaren, "Wesleyan Theology of Worship," 59.
31. See a copy at the Princeton Seminary Online Archive: https://archive.org/details/ suervdamoowesl.

further nine. There were twenty-five pruned and revised Articles that Wesley bequeathed to American Methodism that tell us a few things about his theology. He omitted nothing from the Apostles Creed except Christ's conjectural descent into Hell, a point that still distinguishes Methodist usage from that of other churches who use that creed.[32]

Throughout Charles Wesley's life, his Methodist companions sang none of his hymns in Sunday worship. That is because Methodists stayed in the Anglican church which did not use the new hymns in worship. Instead, Wesley's hymns were sung in informal Methodist gatherings during the week.[33]

Isaac Watts had only laid a foundation upon which Charles and John Wesley built. Where Watts had won a place for original hymns in worship alongside psalms, Charles went farther and developed hymns of "human composure." He spent little time on psalm versifications, but engaged himself in hymn production. He is reputed to have written over six thousand hymns but this traditional estimate cannot be verified. By any standard, Charles Wesley was a very prolific hymn writer.[34]

The works of Watts and of Wesley have many contrasts. Watt's hymns tend to be more formal and objective, where Wesley's tend to be more personal and intimate. Both men were alike in the objectives of hymn writing but different in the development of basic materials. The work of each was complementary to that of the other. Even their education and religious persuasions were different. Watts was a Calvinist and worked within the framework of Nonconformity, while Wesley was an Arminian and never really left the Anglican Church.

The *Olney Hymns*

The Church of England did not have the same enthusiasm for hymn singing as did the Wesleyans, but interest grew in the course of the eighteenth century, and several important collections were published. Until this period, original Anglican hymns were intended solely for private devotional use.[35]

In 1779, there appeared in England a collection of hymns that was to play an important part in the development of hymnody and in the evangelical revival. This collection was entitled *Olney Hymns* and was collected by John Newton (1725–1807) and William Cowper (1731–1800). Out of a total of 348 hymns many have had lasting value.

32. Drury, "John Wesley."
33. Townsend, "Golden Age of Hymns."
34. Tripp, "Methodism."
35. Drain, "Study of 'Hymns Ancient and Modern,'" 101.

These hymns are characterized by the simple, personal faith of the compilers. Cowper and Newton both experienced dynamic religious conversions that "saved" them socially as well as spiritually. Newton had been a worker on a slave ship (and had served in a position little better than a slave) in Africa under a slave dealer named Clow. In February 1747 he could leave Clow and start back for England by ship. To pass away the time, Newton began reading *The Imitation of Christ*, which disturbed him. During the night, after he had encountered the writing of Thomas a Kempis, the ship ran into a storm that threatened to destroy all aboard. On that night, March 10, 1748, the turning point came in Newton's life, for he prayed a simple prayer for God's salvation. After an epileptic attack in 1754, Newton decided to enter the ministry, finally taking up residence in Olney in 1764 as curate. His pastorate there was quite successful, lasting for sixteen years, the last thirteen of which were spent in close contact with Cowper.[36]

Cowper was sensitive and delicate in health, suffering from periods of melancholia. Cowper experienced several severe setbacks in his chosen profession as a lawyer and in his personal life that prompted him to attempt suicide: by poison, drowning, stabbing, and finally by hanging. All failed because of intervention or lack of purpose on his part. Finally, he was declared mentally ill and committed to a hospital at St. Albans. He experienced salvation during his confinement by reading the book of Romans, which resulted in a complete reorganization of his life.

Cowper became Newton's lay helper in 1767, doing a great deal of visitation. Cowper had another mental breakdown in 1773. Moving him to the vicarage, Newton encouraged him further to write as a means of regaining his emotional balance. In 1771 Newton had advised Cowper to write, having visualized a compilation of hymns engaging Cowper's collaboration. The final hymnal, in 1799, contained 280 hymns by Newton and 68 by Cowper, who undoubtedly would have written more if it had not been for his emotional troubles.

Newton and Cowper intended for the *Olney Hymns* to be used in prayer meetings held in the Olney vicarage rather than the regular Sunday services of the Olney Parish Church. The first edition contained no music; the hymns were sung to well-known tunes announced by the worship leader. These hymns were printed repeatedly in England and the United States, and were popular on both sides of the Atlantic.[37] The *Olney Hymns* was the last of a group of hymnals that attempted to bring Evangelical

---

36. Armstrong, "Amazingly Graced," 11–19.
37. Johansen, *Olney Hymns*.

hymnody into the church of England without accommodating it to the *Book of Common Prayer*.

Nineteenth-Century Developments

Two characteristic forms of Church of England Christianity were popularly recognized by 1825. One party consisted of orthodox churchmen, "whom their rivals, and not their rivals only, denounced as dry, unspiritual, formal, unevangelical, self-righteous; teachers of mere morality at their best, allies and servants of the world at their worst."

The other party consisted of churchmen who were not inheritors "of Anglican traditions, but of those which had grown up among the zealous clergymen and laymen who had sympathized with the great Methodist revival, and whose theology and life had been profoundly affected by it."[38] The wide scope of social, political, and religious upheavals of the time is better left to other writers. For our purposes, we will limit the discussion to Anglican congregational song, the Oxford Movement, and *Hymns Ancient and Modern*.

Anglican Congregational Song

Among Anglicans, evangelical hymns were first sung in para-liturgical services rather than in Morning or Evening Prayer. The chapels of schools and hospitals were other places where evangelical hymns were sung. Gradually their popularity caused them to be included as part of the regular morning and evening services. While hymn singing was a part of worship, the emphasis upon personal salvation and Christian experience caused considerable alarm among many Anglican leaders whose theology was more sacramentarian than evangelical.

The official adoption of hymns by the Church of England was a late development in the history of English hymnody. Before the Reformation, hymns had their place in the Latin of the English church, but hymns were omitted from the translations of the liturgy which became the *Book of Common Prayer*. The singing of hymns in private devotion or informal church services and the omission of hymns from common worship, is the result of the influence of Calvin upon the English Reformation. That influence was reinforced when some English reformers took refuge in Geneva during the

---

38. Church, *Oxford Movement*, ch. 1, para. 5.

persecutions under Queen Mary. Here, they learned Calvin's prohibition of singing anything but the divinely inspired word of God in the liturgy.

The hymn had no legal status in congregational worship except through the Injunction to the Clergy issued by Queen Elizabeth I in 1559, mentioned previously. Clergy could introduce "in the beginning, or in the end of common prayers either at morning or evening . . . a Hymn, or such like song . . . " Bishops could determine what hymns could be sung or what hymn collections could be used. This allowed considerable variation in the use and type of hymns that were adopted. By 1820 many churches were supplementing their psalters with hymns and using them in worship and even issuing their own collections of hymns.

> This increase in the numbers of hymn books created debate and disagreement among clergy as to the legality of their use since it was evident that the use of hymns in many places exceeded the permission of Queen Elizabeth's Injunction. The legality of singing hymns in public worship was tried in 1819. The eighth edition of Thomas Cotterill's *Selection of Psalms and Hymns for Public and Private Use, Adapted to the Services of the Church of England* was published in 1819. The congregation of Cotterill's church, St. Paul's, Sheffield, refused to use their Vicar's book, protesting that it was unlawful. The Archbishop of York, Vernon Harcourt, called for suppression of the edition. The ninth edition, dedicated to the Archbishop, was duly published in 1820 after Harcourt was able to review and approve each hymn. This is the first authorized Anglican hymn book, and its publication marks the legal beginning of Anglican hymn singing.[39]

The Oxford Movement

In 1833 a reforming government seemed to threaten the disestablishment of the Church of England. The Reform Act of 1832 changed the electoral system by disenfranchising thirty-one to only one MP, and creating sixty-seven new constituencies in so doing, Parliament also eliminated a large number of bishoprics and established some new ones. This, plus earlier legislation, threatened to disestablish the Church of England and to eliminate its financial endowments from the state.

In response, Oxford professor John Keble preached a sermon on July 14, 1833, titled "National Apostasy." The subject matter may seem remote today, for it was a protest against the Reform Act. The theme was crucial: was the

---

39. Drain, "Study of 'Hymns Ancient and Modern,'" 102–3.

Church of England a department of the Hanoverian state, to be governed by the forces of secular politics, or was it an ordinance of God. Were its pastors priests of the Catholic Church (as the Prayer Book insisted) or ministers of a Calvinistic sect? Keble's call for change resonated with three other Oxford professors, John Henry Newman, Hurrell Froude and William Palmer. In September 1833 these men began to publish Tracts which were referred to as The Oxford Tracts giving rise to the later name, "The Oxford Movement."[40]

The Oxford Movement was designed to restore a liturgical connection to the past centuries prior to the Reformation. In order to counter this criticism and to revive the church, the members of the Oxford Movement sought to strengthen the church by emphasizing its apostolic origins as traced through Christian history.

Because of the emphasis upon ancient traditions and liturgies, the High Church Anglican service began to incorporate more and more features of the Catholic Mass, and some outstanding Anglicans left the Church of England and became Roman Catholics. Two of the leaders of the Oxford Movement were John Keble and John Henry Newman. Newman was one who ultimately became a Roman Catholic and was made a Cardinal of that church.

Younger reformers who were influenced by the Oxford Movement became interested in ritual, and began to reintroduce elements of worship from the pre-Reformation church, such as additional vestments, lighted candles on the altar for the celebration of the Eucharist, and church buildings became less plain.

Many of the people associated with the Oxford Movement also wrote new hymn texts as well as translate older ones. Translating hymns and writing new ones were designed to reflect the doctrines and worship of early Christians. Consequently, Greek, Latin, and even German hymns in translation became a part of English hymnody.

Hymns Ancient and Modern

The greatest legacy of the Oxford Movement is the hymnal *Hymns Ancient and Modern* (1859–60), in which many of the texts and tunes we sing today first appeared. Because it provided a wealth of new material for congregational song, this hymnal is one of our most important sources. The main editor of this hymnal was Henry W. Baker and the music editor was William H. Monk. As the title indicates, the text material was drawn from sources representing a wide span of history. John Mason Neale (1818–66) made many translations of

---

40. Phillips, "Oxford Movement."

many ancient hymns from the Greek and Latin. He is also known as a writer of original hymn texts that were inspired by ancient texts.

The result was a book of 271 hymns that concentrated the mind on the words and music, and the biblical text that was quoted at the head of each hymn: it allowed the texts to stand without the problems of religious controversy, combining High Church and Low Church, Tractarian, and Dissenter side by side. The committee refused to be influenced by the suggestion that the book should be confined "without exception to the productions of Churchmen." The hymnal has undergone several revisions and The New Standard Version Full Music edition of this hymnal was published in 1983.

The structure of the book maintained the same balance. It was described on the title page as "Hymns Ancient and Modern, for use in the Services of the Church," and it followed the Prayer Book in beginning with morning and evening prayer, one hymn for each day of the week (except Sunday, which has five) and marking the principal stages of the Church Year: from Advent through to Trinity Sunday, then General Hymns, beginning with Holy Communion, Baptism, Confirmation, Holy Matrimony, special occasions, Saints' days.[41] Medieval texts were translated quite freely and given the meters and rhymes used for Victorian poetry.

The hymn tunes selected were also balanced in source and style. Familiar psalm tunes and folk songs were used and composers were retained to write new tunes. Gregorian chants were used, but since chant has no meter, the tune had to be put into the same meters as those of the text. Most people today would not recognize "O Come, O Come Emmanuel" as a medieval hymn with a chant tune.

For You to Think about

1. Review the various arguments against congregational singing in the churches in this chapter. What would be similar arguments against twenty-first-century contemporary songs in worship? Make the connection by listing and evaluating the eighteenth-century objections in comparison with twenty-first-century objections.

2. Why or why not would John Wesley's directions for singing be effective in an American congregation today?

---

41. Watson, *English Hymn*, 387–421.

8

Congregational Song in Eighteenth- and Nineteenth-Century America

> On Jordan's stormy banks I stand,
> And cast a wishful eye
> To Canaan's fair and happy land,
> Where my possessions lie.
>
> —Camp meeting song

CONGREGATIONAL SONG IN THE United States has been as varied as the people groups who came and settled here. The thirteen colonies in America were divided religiously and continued to worship with the songs they had used in England and elsewhere. In New England congregational churches held sway. The Middle colonies were populated with Baptist, Presbyterian, Anglican, Quaker, Dutch Reformed, and Congregational followers. People in the Southern colonies were mostly members of the Anglican Church, but there were also many Baptists, Presbyterians and Quakers.

Protestant congregational song in twenty-first-century America has emerged from Calvinist psalm-singing. Several different and often overlapping streams of congregational song have flowed from the psalm-singing tradition through the catalyst of the singing school. One is a revivalist stream with its distinctive songs, and the other led to an American body of hymns and more artistic forms of congregational song

Puritan Psalms

Though the Reformation as a movement had ceased, its direct influences were still at work two centuries later, when the American colonies were settled. This was evident particularly in the predominance of Calvinist doctrines among the early settlers and their use of psalters that had originated through the influence of Calvinism. The American psalters were the last vestiges of the European tradition, but these books were not too successful in creating a permanent body of song that would remain within the main stream of Protestantism. Of the major denominations in the United States, the Presbyterians and Reformed churches have been most influenced by the psalter heritage.

The Puritans and Music

The Puritans represent the earliest Calvinist groups in American. Their worship consisted of praise (especially the singing of psalms), prayer (confession, adoration, intercession), preaching, the sacraments ("ordinances"), catechizing, and the exercise of church discipline. The Puritans maintained that in all these activities God comes to meet his people who have met together in his Son's name, but most of all in preaching.[1] The proof of a good ministry was success as a preacher.

It is ironical that the first metrical psalter to be developed, the French Psalter, would be the first to reach the shores of America, being brought over in 1562 by a Huguenot expedition to Florida. They sang French psalms in settlements along the east coast from South Carolina to Massachusetts, but there is no evidence that the French Psalter was ever printed in the American colonies. These same texts are sung today in the Christian Reformed Church, excluding all others. The first English psalms were heard in America in 1579 when Sir Francis Drake landed on the coast of northern California on his trip around the world. He stayed there for five weeks while his men camped ashore.[2]

Today, we find it difficult to understand the narrow attitude toward congregational song in the church held by some of our Puritan forebears. The psalms of David were to be sung, not chanted, and serious questions were raised about the scriptural authority to sing them to man-made tunes. Some people thought the metrical psalms were so sacred that they would not allow them to be practiced outside of church, and the tunes had to be learned by countless repetitions during worship services. Some Puritans considered the tunes themselves sacred, and would doff their hats and make a great show of piety when they heard a metrical psalm tune, even though there was not one word of text.

1. Packer, "Puritan Approach to Worship."
2. Ellinwood, *History of American Church Music*, 10–11. In his book *Protestant Church Music*, Robert Stevenson tells how this psalm-singing affected the Indians and gives examples of the tunes that were sung.

Puritans were not allowed to use musical instruments in church, but could have musical instruments in their homes. The Puritan objection against the use of instruments in church was because it resembled "popery." In spite of this attitude, Farrer reports that

> Devotional singing was permitted and encouraged in colonial New England because like congregational singing, it placed the worshipper on a level that was closer to God and His kingdom . . . Restrictions on personal and private worship were also much more lax—so much so that Puritans were permitted to even write their own songs (assuming, naturally, that they were religiously based) and perform them and various psalms with instrumental accompaniment.[3]

The Ainsworth Psalter

If the Puritans sang psalms, what did they sing from? The psalter brought to Plymouth by the Pilgrims in 1620 was one especially prepared by Henry Ainsworth for the fugitive congregation of "Separatists" in Holland and had been published in 1612. This book was used in Plymouth until the Pilgrim settlement was merged with the Massachusetts Bay Colony in 1692.

From the earliest days of psalmody in England there had existed two opposing tendencies. One was the desire for strict adherence to the literal text of the Scriptures, which usually resulted in awkward English phrasing. The other tendency was the human desire for literary self-expression as exemplified in Bible translations and the *Book of Common Prayer*. The contrast between the beautiful prose that the people heard and the psalms that they had to sing became increasingly evident to worshipers with each successive decade. These two tendencies, together with the idea that other groups were in error and did not adhere closely enough to the Bible, resulted in the Ainsworth Psalter.

However, the Ainsworth Psalter did not exert a permanent influence upon American church music. It came to be overshadowed by the Bay Psalm Book that was published later in Massachusetts. One tune found in the Ainsworth Psalter that is found in hymnals today is the tune "Old Hundredth," the tune to which we sing the "Doxology." The tune is also found in the Sternhold and Hopkins Psalter and is taken from the French setting of Psalm 134. This French setting, in turn, closely resembles a French song of

---

3. Farrer, "'Sing to the Lord a New Song,'" 10–11.

the sixteenth century, "There Is None Here without His Fair One." This tune also resembles an earlier Gregorian chant.[4]

The Bay Psalm Book 1640

The desire for strict adherence to the literal text of the Scriptures and the human desire for literary self-expression also influenced the Puritans. Thus, in 1636 thirty ministers who were "the chief divines of the country" undertook the task of translating and putting into meter the book of Psalms. In 1640 Richard Mather and John Eliot published *The Whole Booke of Psalmes Faithfully Translated into English Metre*, or what is known as "the Bay Psalm Book," the first English book printed in North America. No music was included until the edition published in 1698. A total of 1700 psalm books was printed, and the book was adopted at once by nearly every church in the Colony of Massachusetts Bay, and for that reason became known as the "Bay" psalm book. The last edition, the 27th, was published in 1762.[5]

However, the new psalm book was not widely received at first because it was considered an innovation. This naturally awakened strong feelings of doubt and opposition, and much inquiry, producing the same prejudices and religious scruples as innovations in later days. Part of the problem was that some did not want to give up their Ainsworth psalter. As Gould points out, "Many of the psalms and tunes were so associated with their worship that they were unwilling to relinquish either; so that, when the 'Bay Psalm-book,' so called, was introduced in New England, it met with violent opposition; and the churches in Salem and vicinity did not relinquish Ainsworth till 1667, nor the church in Plymouth, where it was first used, until 1692."[6]

The theology underpinning the Bay Psalm Book was Calvinism as interpreted by John Cotton. One of the reforms that John Calvin insisted upon during the Protestant Reformation involved the role of music in public and private worship. He believed that music was an effective and completely valid way to praise God, but only when God himself divinely inspired the texts for the songs. This rhetoric applied most readily to the singing of psalms.[7] In the Preface, Cotton summarized the problems with congregational song:

> First, what psalms are to be sung in church? Whether David's and other scripture psalms or the psalms invented by godly

4. Smith, *Ainsworth Psalter*, 1938.

5. A facsimile copy of the Bay Psalm Book can be viewed at https://archive.org/details/baypsalmbookbeinooeame.

6. Gould, *Church Music in America*, 32–33.

7. Irwin, "Theology of 'Regular Singing,'" 176–92.

men in every age of the church? Second, if scripture psalms, whether in their own words, or in such meters as English poetry is wont to run in? Thirdly, by whom are they to be sung? Whether by the whole churches together with their voices? Or, by one man singing alone and the rest joining in silence, & in the close saying amen.[8]

Cotton also had firm ideas about what tunes could be used. In "An Admonition to the Reader" he wrote,

> The verses of these psalms may be reduced to six kinds, the first whereof may be sung in very near forty common tunes; as they are collected, out of our chief musicians, by *Tho. Ravenscroft*. The second kind may be sung in three tunes, as Ps. 25, 50, & 67 in our English psalm books. The third may be sung indifferently, as Ps. the 51, 100, & ten commandments as in our English psalm books, which three tunes aforesaid, comprehend almost all this whole book of psalms, as being tunes most familiar to us.[9]

Altogether the fifty tunes referred to in this "Admonition" are either in Ravenscroft's psalter, or in "our English psalm books," meaning editions of Sternhold and Hopkins that included music.[10]

Since notation was lacking and there were too few psalters. Congregations were singing the tunes from memory and gradually congregational song degenerated. In order to have the congregation sing, a deacon would read a line or two of a psalm, give the pitch, and the worshipers would sing after him. Then the next two lines were rendered in the same fashion, and so on, until the entire psalm had been sung. This procedure was known as "lining out" the psalm. The tradition continued through the eighteenth century because of a lack of instrumentalists in Puritan churches.

The fact that the services could be lengthened considerably by singing in this manner can be seen in the diary of a minister who related that, when he had forgotten his sermon one Sunday morning, he had time to walk three-quarters of a mile home to get it and back again before one psalm had been completed. The result was that each congregation had its own version of the original psalm tune. Even individual singers within each congregation would ornament different notes and sing at their own tempo or pitch as they felt moved.

---

8. Cotton, "Preface," 13.
9. Cotton, "Admonition to the Reader," 304.
10. Haraszti, *Enigma of the Psalm Book*.

Help Us Sing!

The first sign of actual music or suggestions for worship practices using the Bay Psalm Book did not appear until nearly sixty years after its first printing. This means that although the psalms had been altered to make their singing easier, congregations still had to rely on the process of lining out the tunes, which did not change the bedlam of voices for the better in any sense. It would seem that during the period between the first version and the version that contained music, Cotton and the other authors were somewhat ambivalent about the musical crisis in the churches. Their purpose in writing the original psalm book was to make it more possible for everyone to participate in musical worship within a church service and enable them to experience God's grace through song.

The Puritans of New England were primarily Congregationalists, which meant that each congregation managed its own affairs without the hierarchical organization structure of churches that included bishops, synods, or presbyteries. They believed that churchgoers should and would be willing to submit to the clergy and other church leaders. This lack of central leadership was evident throughout the entire church service, including the parts that called for congregational song. John Cotton and his contemporaries believed that the psalms should be sung with little accompaniment and little direction so as to diminish opportunities for solo artistry or virtuosic performances. For as long as possible, a "hands-off" approach was taken to control the singing for fear of creating an environment that was governed by rules, orders, and hierarchy, which suggested Catholicism.[11]

The Bay Psalm Book 1698

In an attempt to improve congregational singing the Bay Psalm Book 1698 was created and compiled by three Massachusetts Bay clergy members, Thomas Symmes, Thomas Walter, and Richard Mather, and was the impetus for the movement towards standardizing psalmody, and later congregational singing in general. The authors were educated and well able to study texts such as the Ainsworth psalm book, the Geneva Bible, and the Bible in Hebrew to determine the best translation of every word, line, and phrase. Previous versions had merely paraphrased the psalms from the Geneva Bible, but this new edition appended thirteen Reformation psalm tunes brought over from Europe. These tunes, with a crude notation of circles, squares, and triangles for note heads, were the first music to be printed in America.

---

11. Scholes, *Puritans and Music*.

In the facsimile edition of the original tunes, with transcriptions in modern notation, in addition to tunes, the psalm book has "some few directions for Ordering the Voice," such as how high or low to set the first note of each tune designed so people could sing "without Squeaking above, or Grumbling below."[12] The instructions group the tunes according to how they should be sung and which psalm verses could be sung to a particular tune. Some tunes required a "Cheerful High Pitch," for others "The first note should be 'low'" or "The first note should be 'indifferently high.'"[13]

The Singing School

In spite of this attempt at reform, congregational song continued to deteriorate into the eighteenth century, especially in rural communities. The first wave of immigrants to Massachusetts and Connecticut included people with education and musical background. As new generations succeeded the original settlers, people no longer possessed the skills needed for psalm singing. Many of these later generations could not read, much less read music. This poor singing eventually provoked a reaction known as the Regular Singing movement, which sought to standardize and simplify psalm singing by teaching everyone to read music from tune books according to accepted rules of singing. Gould reported that "when it was made known that some had acquired the art of learning a tune by note, without having before heard it, all were amazed, and still more astonished that all could finish a tune together."[14]

Those favoring regular singing were young, Harvard-educated ministers who actively wrote and spoke in defense of their views. Thomas Symmes was one of the reformers who argued most persuasively in favor of regular singing. His plea appealed to the biblical injunctions pertaining to singing and stated that the establishment of singing schools in the churches enabled obedience to the injunctions of the Bible.

Exact data concerning the first singing schools are scant and almost nonexistent. However, records show that there was a singing school as early as 1730 in Charleston, South Carolina. The singing school existed for many years, and justified its existence as a spiritual music training agency and community social activity. Operation of a singing school was entirely in the

---

12. See Becker, "Ministers vs. Laymen," 81.

13. Appel, *Music of the Bay Psalm Book*, 26. Also see Scholes, *Puritans and Music*, 370–73.

14. Gould, *Church Music in America*, 32–33.

hands of the person who taught it. No available information exists that tells us much about the qualifications of singing-school teachers.

Apparently, there were no female music teachers of singing-schools, though women were encouraged to sing. The teacher was responsible for organizing classes, that usually met at night, teaching them, and collecting fees. Often the fees could be in produce or livestock as well as in cash. Singing school teachers appear to have been avocational rather than vocational. Often a teacher would travel in a circuit, covering one town each day and several towns in one area over a period of several weeks (ten to fourteen evening sessions over a two- to three-week period).

There is little information concerning the actual lesson procedure of the singing school. What information is available enables us to create a hypothetical singing school session. Benches or planks placed between chairs arranged in a large circle served as seats, with the singing master in the center. Each voice part was given a separate book; one each for the treble (or tenor), counter (alto), tenor (or air), and bass. If the session was held at night, pupils furnished their own candles. If in winter, each pupil might be expected to contribute something to the woodbox. The singing master gave the rules for singing and music fundamentals, such as rhythm and the sol–fa syllables. Instruction was given in time beating, and each student was expected to beat his or her own time and follow their voice part. The quality of the school depended entirely upon the quality of the one in charge.[15]

Gates has observed that the time constraints on these early teachers "do not support the assumption that tune-book contents, as presented in print, were learned in singing schools."

> The singing school teacher's function was to reverse thoroughly entrenched and well-loved singing habits that the reformers declared were unacceptable. Given that daunting task, these teachers would have had little choice but to narrow their focus to music-reading instruction and use any motivation techniques that would result in students' progress toward this end.[16]

The tune books that emerged from these first efforts were oblong collections of hymns and psalms with an introductory section that contained information on how to read music.

---

15. Birge, *History of Public School Music*, ch. 1.
16. Gates, "Music Education's Professional Beginnings," 48.

First Instruction Books

Some of the first material for improving singing was provided by the Rev. John Tufts. Between 1714 and 1721, Tufts published a small pamphlet of twenty-three pages and containing thirty-seven tunes titled "An Introduction to the Singing of Psalm-Tunes in a Plain and Easy Method." The tunes were arranged into the various meters that were needed, and Tufts wrote that the tunes "are set down in such a plain and easy Method that a few Rules may suffice for direction in Singing of them." Eleven editions were printed, and the pamphlet was probably bound at the end of psalters so as to be a ready reference. Tuft's book was the first of many such tune books to appear in this country.[17]

In 1721, the Rev. Thomas Walter published "The Grounds and Rules of Musick Explained; or An Introduction to the Art of Singing by Note." The second part of the title indicates one of the terms used by the reformers to define regular singing. The book refers to common singing as a way of singing in the country or a rural folk practice. As Gates has observed, "What seemed to motivate Walter and Tufts to compile tunes with instruction by 1721, however, was not the absence of American instructions for singing; rather, it was the lack of Psalm tune repertoire known by Americans and the low-culture taste reflected in their continual singing of those few tunes they did know."[18]

Most, if not all, of the compilers were active teachers in a singing school. Since there was no widespread commercial source for the production of teaching materials, a singing school teacher had to produce their own. The musical style in most of these tune books by American composers was the fuguing tune, named for its contrapuntal harmonic structure. A fuguing tune starts out with all four voices singing parts in harmonic and rhythmic unity. Later, each voice enters successively and imitatively. The musical theory of the American tune books was an adaptation of English practice and not the product of American composers, so it is probable that all of the early composers were self-taught.

None of the early tune books gave directions for finding the pitch until about 1800, and then the directions were given for a pitchpipe. Some churches used a violin or some "Lord's Fiddle" or other stringed instrument for finding the pitch. These churches were called "catgut churches" by those individuals who did not agree to the use of instruments in the church. The cello or bass

---

17. Tufts, *Introduction to the Singing of Psalm-Tunes*.
18. Gates, "Music Education's Professional Beginnings," 43.

viol that was used for locating pitch was often referred to as "the Lord's fiddle" in contrast to the dancing master's viol or the "devil's fiddle."[19]

Folk Hymns and Hymnals

The tune books used by rural folk in their churches and camp meetings did not use standard music notation, but used what is called shape notes. This is a system that uses a shape for each of the sol–fa syllables, a way of learning to sing that goes back to Guido d'Arezzo.[20] There were several shape systems, but initially, only four syllables were used: fa–sol–la–mi. A scale would be fa–sol–la–fa–sol–la–mi–fa and not the regular doh–re–mi–fa–sol–la–ti–doh. Perhaps the first book to contain shape notes was *The Easy Instructor* (published in 1802 but copyrighted in 1798) by William Little and William Smith. Fa (faw) is a right-angled triangle; sol is a circle; la (law) is a square; and mi is a diamond.

Perhaps the most influential and enduring shape note tune book is *The Sacred Harp*, first published in 1844 in Hamilton, Georgia, and used for congregational singing. *The Sacred Harp* uses the shape note system introduced in Little and Smith's *The Easy Instructor*. *The Sacred Harp* includes many songs from a common repertory shared by other tune books of its era, supplemented by songs composed or arranged by singers from the book's own tradition. The book includes fugues and anthems, camp meeting songs, as well as strophic hymns and secular songs.

The book is representative of a time when tunes and texts were not inextricably linked as they are today. Hymn texts at that time were commonly sung to any of a number of tunes. Thus "tune books"—so named because they included printed tunes—used the names of the tune as the title and might include several tunes for a single text. For example, the text of "Amazing Grace" is listed under more than one tune, one of which is our familiar "New Britain." Of hundreds of books of its kind, *The Sacred Harp* itself has achieved the longest tenure of active use and the widest geographical spread. The most important revisions occurred in 1911, 1936, and 1991.[21]

---

19. Hubbard, *American History and Encyclopedia*, 178.

20. See ch. 5. Guido is also the name of a computer music notation format designed to logically represent all aspects of music in a manner that is both computer readable and easily readable by human beings. It was named after Guido of Arezzo, who pioneered today's conventional musical notation 1,000 years ago.

21. Folksteams (folkstreams.net) has a wide variety of tune book information, recordings, and films.

American Composers and Compilers

The first native American composer of record is James Lyon (1725–94), a native of New Jersey. He received his bachelor of arts degree from the College of New Jersey in 1759. The commencement program included a musical setting of an ode by Lyons that, unfortunately, has not been preserved.[22]

Perhaps the most popular tune composer was William Billings (1746–1800) of Boston, whose popularity came from his fuguing tunes. When singing his tunes, Billings wanted to have as many people singing bass as there were singing the other three parts combined, with a great contrast in volume between the full chorus and the solo parts. By European standards his music was crude, with many "mistakes;" but this is what gave the music its unique character. Billings understood the popular musical craving, and he knew how to produce tunes and texts that would set peope to singing.

Church Choirs and Organs

Apart from learning hymns, another contribution to congregational song made by the singing school is the development of church choirs. As the size and number of singing classes increased, congregational singing was improved. The formation of choirs was the natural result, for the better singers began sitting together. Finally, a special section of seats was assigned in the gallery or balcony. Later, the choir was moved behind the pulpit for evangelistic emphasis.

There was a leader for each choir chosen by the town, church, or by common assent. The leader gave the pitch and established correct tempi. He was also expected to beat time in some conspicuous manner. Since there were no hymn books or instruments in the church, the song leader would select familiar tunes that corresponded to the meter of a hymn text and the starting pitch. In many churches the custom of "lining out" each hymn continued for many years following the organization of singing schools. Often the choir leader and the congregational song leader would disagree about the manner of singing a particular hymn. Records show instances of choirs objecting so violently to singing in the "lining out" fashion that they either refused to sing or would sing a hymn in a different tempo or key. When things went well, the choir usually sounded the first chord before singing and would sing from memory, having learned the music at home or in a singing school.

---

22. Chase, *America's Music*, chs. 3 and 4. Chase gives a very detailed account of the first American composers and examples of their work.

The special music sung by these choirs was a hymn or an American fuguing tune. These tunes afforded choirs and singing school groups an opportunity to display their vocal talents. However, they also threatened to destroy the choir movement in some churches for the music was so complicated and detached from worship that congregations found it difficult to respond to the music. This led many pastors to consider seriously whether or not to retain choirs in worship services. A better quality of choir music was available from England, but with the exception of Episcopalians, there was a prevailing prejudice against any kind of choral music from England. Both this prejudice and a lack of trained choir directors who were able to interpret better choral music kept standards low. By 1800, many music-minded individuals in New England churches, eager to hone their musical skills for their own sake, formed church choirs and usurped congregational song.

The "quartet choir" began to appear in northern city churches late in the nineteenth century. This was a choir composed entirely of a mixed quartet, or often a volunteer choir formed around a mixed quartet. When quartet members were in a choir, they helped lead voice sections and frequently sang solo passages. In wealthier churches a professional, paid quartet provided music for Sunday services, but often the kind of music performed was not always conducive to worship. Sometimes there was rivalry among the quartert members who might even vie with one another over who could sing the loudest.

The struggle to get organs accepted in the service of worship was long and arduous in evangelical churches. The earliest accounts of organs in churches are found among Lutherans and Episcopalians. The first "dissenting" organ in New England was acquired by the First Congregational Church at Providence, Rhode Island, in 1770. After 1800 there was little or no opposition in the seaboard states to the use of organs, but expense was a retardant to widespread use. Because of the large number of foreign musicians living in the United States and the growth of instrumental concerts, the earlier objections to instrumental music had disappeared, except on the frontier.

Sometime in the early nineteenth century a small reed instrument called a melodeon was being made in Europe. It was durable enough to survive both ocean transport and haulage over the mountains. The melodeon made it possible for frontier churches to have an organ-like sound to accompany congregational singing. In 1846 the organ melodeon, an instrument that had two manuals, four sets of reeds, and a pedal board of over one octave, was built. About 1863 the Estey Organ Company in Brattlesboro, Vermont, started building a single-manual reed pump organ that could be used both in homes and in small churches. Before organs became a permanent feature in churches, choir music had no written accompaniment, the instrument simply playing the same notes as sung by the choir. With the development of organs and the music publishing business, choirs were given new importance.

Songs of Revival

By the early 1700s, the European Enlightenment had made its way across the Atlantic Ocean to the America colonies. The Enlightenment, also known as the Age of Reason, was an intellectual and cultural movement in the eighteenth century that emphasized reason over superstition and science over blind faith. Instead of Puritanism, the ideas and theories of the greatest thinkers of the European Enlightenment, from Bacon and Newton to Locke and Rousseau, were celebrated. Much of the literature of this period dealt with the weighty ideals that these figures devoted their writings to. Names like Thomas Jefferson, James Madison, John Adams, and Benjamin Franklin come to mind as some of the Enlightenment thinkers in America.

The religious expression of the Enlightenment was Deism. Deism rejected the idea that church teachings or a direct revelation from God was essential for acquiring spiritual knowledge. In some respects, Deism could be called a rational religion. Rationalism is the idea that humans are capable of using their faculty of reason to gain all knowledge. This was a sharp turn away from the prevailing Puritan idea that people needed to rely on Scripture or church authorities for knowledge.

Some Deists believed in a God, but not a deity who took an interest in the everyday affairs of humans. Their God was one who established order in the universe and kept it running by moral, spiritual, and physical laws. The result of this worldview led to spiritual apathy, and low church attendance became the order of the day.

The First Great Awakening

However, many Christians did not want formal and impersonal worship. They were disillusioned with the wealth and rationalism dominating the culture and began to crave a return to religious piety. They were looking for spiritual renewal and found it in a series of religious revivals called the First Great Awakening.

This Awakening was part of a much broader evangelical upsurge that began with people like the Wesley brothers and George Whitefield in England that crossed over to the American Colonies. These revivals were a reaffirmation that Christian faith meant trusting the heart rather than the head, that religious experience was more feeling than thinking, and biblical revelation was a better source of truth than human reason.[23]

The beginning of the First Great Awakening in America was among the Presbyterians in Pennsylvania and New Jersey. Reverend William Tennent and his four sons, who were also clergymen, initiated religious revivals in those colonies in the 1730s and established a seminary to train clergymen, which is now Princeton University. These men preached that people were sinful and that they needed to be convicted of their sinful state, repent, and find personal salvation through faith in Jesus Christ. This was the message of the Great Awakening, and religious fervor spread quickly from Presbyterians to the Puritans and Baptists in New England.

Unlike the somber, largely Puritan spirituality of the early 1700s, the revivalism ushered in by the Awakening allowed people to express their emotions more overtly in order to feel a greater intimacy with God. Services included emotionally charged sermons delivered extemporaneously that painted vivid pictures of the eternal Hell of the lost. Fervent preaching was accompanied by the fervent singing of hymns taken primarily from the *Olney Hymns* of Newton and Cowper. Because of their popularity the words of individual hymns were taken from the collection and printed over and over.

The Second Great Awakening

The religious fervor of the First Great Awakening had begun to wane following the American Revolution. Baptists and Methodists were making small gains, but a pallor of religious indifference clung to the fledgling nation. Close to a million people had made their way to the area west of the Blue Ridge in Virginia, Kentucky, Tennessee, the Northwest, and in the Indian Territory by 1800. The Louisiana Purchase in 1803 doubled the area of the United States and gave an enormous new impulse to western migration. This would appear to be an opportunity for the spread of the Christian message, but there seemed no way to keep up with the population growth.

However, the situation had begun to change around 1786 with revivals in eastern colleges. These spiritual awakenings were a continuation of earlier great evangelistic movements that had been going on for years. This was the beginning of the Second Great Awakening that took place largely in the Western part of the United States, which in 1820 meant Western New York, Kentucky, and Appalachia. These were places that did not have the strong established churches that you might have found in places like New England.

---

23. Heyrman, "First Great Awakening."

Methodist circuit riders and Baptist preacher-farmers were responsible for most of the religious activity on the frontier, and they started churches that dealt most effectively with frontier needs. These preachers generally lacked a formal education but were thoroughly trained in the doctrines and practices of their denomination. The men were popular because they wore no special garb, their education for the most part was meager, and in all appearances, they were frontiersmen like the rest. However, they were godly men desirous of bringing their neighbors to personal experience with Christ.

Cane Ridge Revival

The most unusual phase of this awakening started in the west around 1800 when the Kentucky Revival broke out. Cane Ridge, Kentucky was the site, in 1801, of a large camp meeting that drew thousands of people. The event was led by as many as eighteen Presbyterian ministers, but numerous Methodist and Baptist preachers also spoke and assisted. Many of the "spiritual exercises" that were exhibited, such as glossolalia and ecstatic attendees, continued into the twentieth century and became more associated with the Pentecostal movements.[24]

Many who came were irreligious, causing drunkenness and immorality to accompany camp meetings. Some came to the camp meetings with the intention of disrupting the services, armed with clubs, knives, and horsewhips. Whiskey salesmen also came, parking their wagons at the edge of the religious settlement.

The emphasis of the early preachers, and following revivalists, was upon regeneration. First, a person felt convicted of sin and guilt; second, he or she had to throw himself upon God's mercy for salvation; and third, he or she might have a great emotional upheaval. The Puritan forefathers had thought salvation and assurance involved a long, arduous process taking many years to complete. The fact that salvation and assurance were now believed to be instantaneous made these revivals a happy thing.

We know very little about the liturgical structure of these meetings, but can gain some insight from diaries and autobiographies of some of the leaders. For example, a James McGready pastored three small congregations at Red River, Gasper River, and Muddy River, all in Logan County, Kentucky. McGready had brought with him from North Carolina a well-deserved reputation for fiery preaching. He was a large, imposing man with piercing eyes and a voice coarse and tremulous. Barton Stone, pastor of

---

24. Foster et al., *Encyclopedia of the Stone-Campbell Movement*, 165–66.

the Cane Ridge Church, said of McGready after hearing him preach, "My mind was chained by him, and followed him closely in his rounds of heaven, earth, and hell with feelings indescribable."[25]

His preaching was so successful that by July 1799, his power over audiences began to be demonstrated visibly. People covered their faces and wept; many fell to the ground, moaning for mercy; others cried out for a release from hell. The winter months suspended operations, but the next summer, in 1800, William Hodges and John Rankin, Presbyterian preachers, and the McGee brothers—John, a Methodist preacher, and Will, a Presbyterian preacher—had joined McGreevy. The result was an even greater manifestation of religious fervor.

News of events during that summer spread to other parts of Kentucky and Tennessee. So great were the crowds that gathered to hear these men and to witness the religious phenomena that food and camping equipment had to be brought along. Some came from as far as one hundred miles. Many came in wagons that were equipped for providing shelter. Others built shelters out of brush. The camp was laid out in a square with the center of the square, with hewn logs arranged in rows around the platform for seats. The wagons were arranged outside the square making a "wagon city."

One Sunday morning sermon evoked groans and cries, and at night, with the pulpit illumined by flaming torches, William McGee exhorted with all the energy and oratory he could muster. "Towards the close of the sermon, the cries of the distressed arose almost as loud as his voice," McGready wrote. "After the congregation was dismissed the solemnity increased . . . No person seemed to wish to go home—hunger and sleep seemed to affect nobody—eternal things were the vast concern."[26]

Camp meeting revivals spread through Kentucky and Tennessee in the succeeding months. Each seemed more dramatic than the last. As 1800 drew to a close, John McGee reported that at Desha's Creek, "Many thousands of people attended. The mighty power and mercy of God was manifested. The people fell before the Word, like corn before a storm of wind, and many rose from the dust with divine glory shining in their countenances." [27]

"The excitement created by these reports," recalled Methodist James B. Finley, "was of the most intense and astonishing character." The movement was marked by "some peculiarities" he admitted, and then added, "The

---

25. Galli, "Revival at Cane Ridge," 45.

26. Galli, "Revival at Cane Ridge," 45. See also Sweet, *Religion in the Development of American Culture*, 147–52.

27. Sweet, *Religion in the Development of American Culture*, 147–52.

nearest approximation to it . . . was the revival on the day of Pentecost." By 1820, Methodists were holding around five hundred camp meetings a year.[28]

Camp Meeting Songs

"The people who gathered in the early camp meetings were a mix of Methodists, Baptists, and Presbyterians . . . and others," wrote Wheeler.

> The singing in these meetings had its own special characteristics, too. From the Methodists came the hymns of Watts and Wesley; from the Presbyterians the heritage of metered psalms. Baptists shared some of this hymnody, particularly the hymns of Isaac Watts.[29]

Generally, the use of this type of material was limited because of illiteracy among the congregations and the lack of hymnbooks. Foot tapping, swaying of the body, hand clapping, and head rolling would accompany the singing. Often the singing would get out of hand, with several songs being sung at one time. Because of the emphasis upon personal faith and experience, the people sang about their own experience.

There was no "song leader" as we think of one today. Usually the evangelist would start a song, or songs would emanate from members of the crowd. Often, the evangelist would sing a part of his sermon with the congregation singing back a response. It appears that at times it was difficult to tell when singing, preaching, praying, and shouting were well defined, as there seems to have been an almost continual commotion. The services consisted primarily of singing until the crowd was ready to hear the sermon.

The people sang freely and with many embellishments. Scoops, slides, and other ornaments were used. Some compilers tried to incorporate these "extra notes" into the printed page, but with little success, as each individual was free to invent his own additions and did, with great liberties taken in making a melody more expressive for the individual.

This freedom is still part of the black church experience today. Your writer taught choral arranging at New Orleans Baptist Seminary, and one of my students was a doctoral candidate who taught choral music at Southern University in New Orleans, a predominately black institution. One week an arrangement of a song was brought to the lesson that had all kinds of extra notes. I said, "Ed, can your choir sing all these extra notes?" Ed replied, "They are going to sing them whether I write them or not."

---

28. Danielson, "From the Archives," 160.
29. Wheeler, "Music of the Early Nineteenth-Century Camp Meeting," 22–23.

Often the hymns of Watts, Wesley, and others were popularized by the insertion of refrains in which all could join. These were set to folk tunes with pulsating rhythm, emotional repetition, and simple refrains that the throngs could catch. At times a "singing ecstasy" would seize the worshipers. At other times it was a chant of mourning, or again of joyous jubilation. Spontaneous song would break forth that would combine both Scriptural phrases and everyday speech, with many hallelujahs and refrains interspersed.[30]

One type of camp meeting song was the call-and-response. This was a pattern of four-phrase verses and repeated choruses. The preacher or other song leader would sing out the verses and the people would enter in on the chorus. An example would be Samuel Stennett's "On Jordan's Stormy Banks."

Verse: On Jordan's stormy banks I stand,
And cast a wishful eye
To Canaan's fair and happy land,
Where my possessions lie.

Chorus: I am bound for the promised land,
I am bound for the promised land;
Oh who will come and go with me?
I am bound for the promised land.

Another camp meeting song was a much-repetition type. These were choruses with substantial repetition:

We'll shout and give Him glory,

We'll shout and give Him glory,

We'll shout and give Him glory,

For His glory is His own.

A type of camp meeting song is still in vogue today in revivalist denominations. This involves taking two lines of a standard hymn that are divided with a repetitive interruption, followed by a simple repetitive chorus. An example is the Wesley hymn "O for a Thousand Tongues":

---

30. Jackson, *White and Negro Spirituals*, 119.

Leader: O for a thousand tongues to sing,

Response: Blessed be the name of the Lord.

Leader: the glories of my God and King,

Response: Blessed be the name of the Lord.

Chorus: Blessed be the name,
Blessed be the name,
Blessed be the name of the Lord.
Blessed be the name,
Blessed be the name,
Blessed be the name of the Lord.[31]

Sunday School Songs

Sunday schools were introduced in Virginia around 1785 and were not, at first, connected to individual churches. The first Sunday school organization in America was probably the *First Day* or *Sunday-School Society*, established in 1791. The idea of having a Sunday School became very popular, and as the nation expanded westward following the Revolutionary War, the number of Sunday schools grew rapidly. The Sunday schools were not limited to Bible teaching. Many frontier towns had no school, so a Sunday school was a place a child could learn to read and write.

The Sunday school movement was an evangelistic force that gained impetus from the Kentucky Revival. The changes that would make the camp meeting obsolete were ripe for the growth and development of the Sunday school. At first, the Sunday school was primarily for children and youth. However, the songs of the camp meeting were found to be inappropriate for children to sing, so a need arose for specific Sunday school song collections for children.

Isaac Watts had published his *Divine and Moral Songs for Children* in 1729. "This book became a very popular children's book throughout England for nearly two hundred years," wrote Kathleen O'Bannon.[32] By the mid-nineteenth century, the book existed in more than a thousand editions. So well known were some of the children's poems that Lewis Carroll parodied them in *Alice in Wonderland* and Charles Dickens referenced them in *David*

---

31. Wheeler, "Music of the Early Nineteenth-Century Camp Meeting," 23.
32. O'Bannon, "Divine and Moral Songs," 1.

Copperfield. Modern hymnologists, however, remember Watts' songbook not so much for its rhymes for children but for its hymns. A look at some of the texts show us why this was not a popular song book for children:

> Let dogs delight to bark and bite,
>
> For God hath made them so;
>
> Let bears and lions growl and fight
>
> For 'tis their nature to.
>
> But, children, you should never let
>
> Such angry passions rise;
>
> Your little hands were never meant
>
> To tear each other's eyes!

There was a reaction against this type of song for children. So, it was not long before the market was flooded with songs for use in Sunday school with cheerful verse and "catchy" music. Many of these songbooks were edited by men associated with early development of the gospel song, like William Bradbury, George F. Root, and Robert Lowry. Their desire was to produce the kind of songs that children could learn and sing very easily.

Professional Revivalism

After the Civil War the frontier religious denominations underwent a big cultural change, and the latter half of the nineteenth century saw an amazing development of various kinds of congregational song in America. An increasing number of colleges and seminaries were established that graduated a more educated clergy. Parishioners, particularly in the North, were better educated, and these changes in education brought a desire for congregational songs that reflected the new era. The rapid growth of cities created new evangelistic opportunities, for camp meeting tactics and songs did not work in a large city.[33]

The Professional Evangelist

The so-called professional evangelist arose out of the need to change the approach to evangelism. An early evangelist was Charles G. Finney

---

33. Lowens, "Our Neglected Musical Heritage," 49–57, and Lovelace, "Early Sacred Folk Music," 11–14, 58–63.

(1792–1875), a brilliant man and exceptional preacher, but possessor of little formal education. He held a middle ground between the well-educated minister and the rough circuit rider. Finney is the so-called father of modern revivalism. Finney selected camp meeting songs he thought would "work" and introduced them into churches to create church "revivals." In doing so, he introduced practices that became a lasting part of American worship practice. In front of the church there were now two places, one for the minister and the other for the song leader.

When Finney accepted the pastorate of a Presbyterian church in New York City in 1832, he brought with him Thomas Hastings, his music director for many of campaigns, to be musical director of the church. Finney had boasted that he helped to bring about the use of choirs in revival services. Well he might have, for Finney himself was a choir director prior to his conversion.

Following Finney's lead as an evangelist, American revival meetings began to use congregational singing to create an emotional atmosphere that would encourage a response to the gospel. Non-church people more readily accepted easily sung tunes with catchy rhythms and simpler theology and texts than the more sophisticated theological themes and music structure of hymns. Many regular church goers repudiated these songs as "vulgar choruses."

Singers in early revivals were primarily soloists. They did not try any "tricks" to induce the crowds or the choirs to sing. The choir was the real leader of congregational singing, with the evangelistic singer directing the choir. A pump organ usually provided accompaniment.

The Professional Song Leader

The forerunner of the modern evangelistic song leader was Charles Alexander. His tactics were an effort to keep the choir and the congregation happy for half an hour or more before the revival speaker appeared. Bouncing upon the platform for a choir rehearsal before the service, whipping off his coat, and jauntily taking the choir through its paces exemplified his personality. Alexander had a winning way: and his selection of popular, singable tunes made it possible for him to develop emotional unity in the group. There was no emphasis on reverence in his part of the service. He used jokes, shouts, wild, vigorous arm motions, and anything that popped into his head. After the crowd was molded a musical selection just prior to the speaker was supposed to set the stage for the rest of the service.[34]

34. Weisberger, *They Gathered at the River*, 236–38. See also Sweet, *Religion in the Development of American Culture*, 147–52.

The Gospel Song

Today, the term "gospel song" is associated with a particular style of black Christian song that combines elements of spirituals and the blues. However, the term originated in 1874 when a man named Philip P. Bliss published a small collection of songs titled "Gospel Songs," and it was not long before the title "gospel songs" was given to this new body of congregational music.

The gospel song proved to be extremely effective in evangelism because of the subjective emphasis of evangelism. Everything is personal—sin, Savior, and commitment—and congregational songs that expressed this personal feeling (set to an easy, singable, rhythmic tune) was popular. Theological topics such as the atonement, incarnation, and resurrection were rarely the substance of gospel song texts. Instead, the texts were very personal and reflected how the individual believer was converted, or how God answers prayer, or the assurance of God's love and grace. There was also an outward appeal to the unconverted with texts about repentance and faith, how to get to heaven and avoid hell, and the blessings of knowing Christ personally. Since evangelism is directed to those who are outside Christianity, gospel songs are directed toward them.

The gospel song gained popularity in the era of the Moody-Sankey English revivals in 1873. Dwight L. Moody was musically ignorant as far as theoretical knowledge is concerned, but he did recognize the value of music in evangelism that resulted in a stirred congregation. Any song that did not produce a response to the gospel was not good music to Moody's way of thinking. Moody also recognized that music for revival campaigns in the new, bustling cities and the well-established churches had to be different from the free-wheeling camp meeting song.

Ira D. Sankey was a prolific writer of gospel song texts and tunes. On the English trip in 1873, Sankey took with him a scrapbook of songs to use in their revival meetings. Sankey's songs were so popular that he published his own songbook, with twenty-three songs from his scrap book, titled *Sacred Songs and Solos, Sung by Ira D. Sankey at the Meetings of Moody of Chicago*. This collection is still in print and used in many churches in England at the time of this writing. The worship practice of many rural churches in middle and southern America today resembles the service structure of these revivals: one or two hymns or songs, followed by a prayer. Then, one or two songs followed by the offering being taken, special music, a Scripture passage, the sermon, and then an appeal for people in the congregation to come forward and confess Christ as Savior.

American Hymns

Distinctive American hymns evolved from the singing school tradition due to the work of Thomas Hastings (1787-1872), Nathaniel Gould (1781-1864) and Lowell Mason (1792-1872). These men, products of the singing school, were influential in establishing a foundation for American hymn writing and singing, the development of music in the public schools, and choirs, organs, and trained leadership music in churches.

Thomas Hastings

Hastings began his career as a choir director in Connecticut and later in New York. He thought congregational song should further the gospel regardless of any artistic merit the music might or might not have. For Hastings, his aim was the greater glory of God through better musical worship; and to this end he was always compiling works, composing music for hymn texts, and training choirs. Tunes and texts by Hastings still appear in hymnals.

Nathaniel Gould

Gould's career was similar to that of Hastings, for he also served as a singing master. Gould composed and adapted many psalm and hymn tunes and compiled several collections of church music and instruction books. In 1853 he published *History of Church Music in America* which proved to be inaccurate in some respects, but it did represent the beginning of scholarly work in this area. Perhaps his greatest contribution was in the area of children's music since he conducted singing schools for children in Boston, Cambridge, and Charleston.[35]

Lowell Mason

Mason has been called "the father of American church music." There is some truth in this label because he was very influential in his day. He and his followers were very critical of church music of his time because it lacked an artistic frame of reference. Today his music does not appear to be on a high artistic plane, but by the standards he set up, it is superior to that which existed at the time.

---

35. A facsimile edition Gould's book can be found at https://archive.org/details/churchmusicinameoogoul/page/n6.

Much of the music Mason compiled came from the work of outstanding musicians, and Mason chose it more for artistic than for religious merit. Any tune that appealed to the public taste, regardless of its origin, was adapted for a hymn. Without the influence of revivalism songs, the artistic movement might have led to a more secularized type of church song. An equal emphasis was given to *how* one sang. Mason trained his church choir at Boston's Bowdoin Street Church to such a high degree of excellence that it was known through the country.

Mason had two cardinal principles for congregational songs. First, the tunes should be written within the average limits of the human vocal range so everyone could sing them. Second, the tunes should be a complement to the text. Mason did make an attempt to compile good music, to see that it contained adequate harmony, and that it was sung properly.

In 1832 Mason established the Boston Academy of Music for the purpose of furthering work with children. The Academy was the first music school in the United States and taught fifteen hundred students—adults and children—the first year. The crowning achievement of Mason's life was action taken by the Boston School Board on August 28, 1838, making music an accepted part of the school curriculum and placing it on an equal par with the other subjects.[36]

Early Hymn Books

Early hymnbooks were printed with only one voice part, which was adequate for the choir as long as the congregation sang only a few tunes. However, as the people learned more tunes, choir members were forced to hold tune books in one hand and hymn books in the other. To facilitate the handling of a tune book with a large number of hymns, some churches built racks in front of the choir members so they could lay their books in front of them. It was around 1860 that hymnals began to be printed in much the same form that they are today.

The Black Experience

On August 20, 1619, a British ship, the *White Lion*, flying a Dutch flag, landed at the British colony at Jamestown, Virginia. The only cargo was a group of twenty African slaves who were traded for food and supplies. This group of Africans is the first on record to be sold as involuntary laborers in the

---

36. Birge, *History of Public School Music*, ch. 1.

British American colonies. Slavery was not an institution at the time in the American colonies and little has been known about the status of these Africans until recently. In an article for the *Washington Post*, Lisa Rein reports that these slaves were part of 350 captured in Angola who were aboard a Portuguese ship, the *San Juan Bautista*, as it headed for Brazil.[37] Two British pirate ships, the *White Lion* and the *Treasurer*, intercepted the Portuguese ship and took twenty to thirty slaves each.

These first Africans were from the kingdoms of Ndongo and Kongo regions of modern-day Angola and coastal regions of the Congo. Both kingdoms were conquered by the Portuguese in the 1500s. The kingdom of Ndongo converted to Christianity in 1490, so these slaves had probably been baptized as Roman Catholics. Many of the slaves were literate, and this background may be one reason some of Virginia's first Africans won their freedom after years as indentured servants. The American slave trade began in earnest in 1636 when the first American slave carrier, "Desire," is built and launched in Massachusetts, which is also the first colony to legalize slavery in 1641. By 1700 slavery was firmly established.

The Angolans, and other slaves, brought with them a rich tradition of song that was adapted to Christian worship. Many of the African songs were typically "call and response," short, with many repetitive sections, and generally based on the pentatonic scale.[38] A leader would improvise a line of text and the group provided a solid refrain in unison. The vocal style contained slides, turns, and challenging rhythms.

Many slaves were allowed to meet for Christian worship in churches or in plantation "praise houses" for singing, but slaveholders did not allow dancing and playing drums as was usual in Africa. At the meetings, participants would sing, chant, dance, and sometimes enter ecstatic trances. One example is the "ring shout," a shuffling circular dance to chanting and hand-clapping that was common among early plantation slaves. A large number of instruments were available to accompany singing and dancing, such as drums, bells, gongs, rattles, string instruments, and flutes.[39]

The slave population was attracted to biblical stories containing parallels to their own lives. They created songs called spirituals that retold the stories of biblical figures like Daniel and Moses. As Christianity became a major influence among the slave population, spirituals served as a way to express the community's new faith, as well as its hopes and sorrows. Spirituals

---

37. Rein, "Mystery of Va.'s First Slaves."

38. A pentatonic scale is five notes that are a part of the eight-note major scale. The black keys on the piano form a pentatonic scale. In C major, notes C, D, E, G, and A would be a pentatonic scale.

39. Marini, *Sacred Song in America*, 109–10.

were typically sung in a call and response form, with a leader improvising a line of text and the congregation providing a solid refrain in unison. The slides, turns, and rhythms in leader's vocal style were challenging for early publishers of spirituals to document accurately. Many spirituals, known as "sorrow songs," are intense, slow, and melancholic. Songs like "Sometimes I feel like a motherless child," and "Nobody knows the trouble I've seen," describe the slaves' struggles and identification with the suffering of Jesus Christ. Other spirituals are more joyful. Known as "jubilees," or "camp meeting songs," they are fast, rhythmic and often syncopated. Examples include "Rock-a-my soul in the bosom of Abraham."

According to Wheeler, one major musicological controversy of the twentieth century stemmed from contrasting claims as to whether the Negro spiritual had its roots in African traditional song or was merely a poor copy or derivative of white hymnody heard by the slaves in plantation churches and camp meetings. "Records of the camp meeting era," writes Wheeler, "make clear that, in this multi-ethnic gathering, each community was exposed to the singing traditions of the other."[40] When characteristics of either whites or blacks served the social and evangelistic purposes of the gathering, they would likely be adopted by members of the other group. The Cane Ridge Revival of 1801 had reached slaves and their heritage and practice of song was modified by the revival music of Evangelical Protestantism. In this way, the hymn texts of Watts and the Wesley's became part of the Black worship song repertory alongside their traditional spirituals.

The End of a Century

The last half of the nineteenth century saw a lot of interesting things happening that go beyond this book. Baptists, Methodists, and Presbyterians split over Civil War issues and those divisions persisted into the next century. Hymnals for congregational song were produced mainly for specific denominations, such as Baptists, Methodists, Presbyterians, and Disciples of Christ. Many Reformed and Lutheran groups also produced hymnals in the native tongue of their membership as well as in English. Because of their worship tradition of psalms and chorales, English hymnal development was slower.

Several new religious groups arose in the late 1800s that are still with us, such as Mormons, Seventh-day Adventists, Jehovah's Witnesses, and holiness groups that arose within Methodism. We shall visit some of them and their congregational song in the next chapter.

---

40. Wheeler, "Music of the Early Nineteenth-Century Camp Meeting," 33–34.

For You to Think About

1. Take a congregational survey of your church's song repertory, what are the top twenty-five titles? What tradition(s) does the list represent? In what does the list reflect the ethnic, cultural, and religious background of the church members? Of the many types of congregational song discussed in this chapter, which are not represented either in the song repertory or the hymnal?

2. How do you account for what you have discovered? Take into consideration the church's history, ethnic background, its social setting, and similar cultural and social factors.

9

Congregational Song in America: 1900–2000

> God, the giver of Song, is present whenever
> his people sing his praises.
>
> —Vatican II

THREE CONGREGATIONAL SONG TRADITIONS were evident at the beginning of the twentieth century, each with its own continuing history, but also with some historical overlapping. I have arbitrarily named these traditions as the liturgical, the Reformed, and revivalist. In many instances we find churches that have undergone revisions in liturgy, worship language, and the type of songs sung, but the historical traditions and liturgies remain. White[1] defines traditions as the "inherited worship practices and beliefs that show continuity from generation to generation."

According to Dyrness, we find that in the twentieth century there was a "convergence, or at least a mutual influence, between and among the forms of Christian worship."[2] One of the things that has brought about this convergence is *The Revised Common Lectionary*, a lectionary of readings from the Bible for use in Christian worship, making provision for the liturgical year with its patterns of festivals and seasons observances. It was published in 1983 as an ecumenical revision of the earlier three-year lectionary produced by the Roman Catholic Church in 1969 following the reforms of the Second Vatican Council. The revised edition of 1983 is the product of both Protestants and Catholics.

---

1. White, *Protestant Worship*, 21.
2. Dyrness, *Primer on Christian Worship*, 42.

I. The Liturgical Tradition

The liturgical tradition includes Episcopal, Catholic, and Lutheran Churches. They have differences in theology, clergy roles, and polity, but have retained much of the historical liturgies and confessions of faith found in the pre-Reformation church. In an article in *Christianity Today*, Mark Galli writes that liturgy is "the prayers, responses, and shape of worship one finds in Anglican, Catholic, and Orthodox services, and to a lesser degree, in Presbyterian, Methodist, Lutheran, and other mainline churches. If you examine the full service of each of these traditions, you'll find a surprisingly common worship order, prayers and responses that are identical in many places."[3]

The Roman Catholic Church

The Catholic world was shocked when Pope John XXIII announced the creation of the Second Vatican Council (also known as Vatican II) in January 1959. An ecumenical council of Roman Catholic religious leaders, meeting to discuss and settle doctrinal issues, had not been held in nearly 100 years. Because papal infallibility had been proclaimed in 1870, most Catholics thought there was no longer a need for councils. Thousands of bishops, observers, auditors, sisters, laymen, and laywomen from 116 countries were called to four sessions at St. Peter's Basilica between 1962 and 1965.

Earlier Reform Efforts

The liturgical reforms of Vatican II grew out of earlier efforts by French and German Benedictine monasteries in the nineteenth century to focus on recovering the original meaning of the liturgy. French Benedictine monks of Solesmes, France attempted to restore Gregorian melodies to their pre-seventeenth-century form and a revised edition of the Antiphonary and Gradual was made in an attempt to conform to the church's ancient traditions. The result of their labor is the *Liber usualis,* a liturgical book containing the most frequently used Gregorian chants, which was published in 1883.[4]

In 1903 St. Pius X promulgated the *motu proprio* "Tra le sollecitudini" that detailed regulations for the performance of music in the Roman Catholic Church.[5] Operatic-style music was prevalent in Italian churches at the

---

3. Galli, "Deeper Relevance," 38.
4. Dowley, *Christian Music,* 61.
5. *Motu proprio* (Latin for: "on his own impulse") refers to a document issued by the

time, and the pope was concerned about the use of music in the liturgy. The pope was motivated by a strong desire to maintain and promote behaviors in the house of God that were socially correct, and his *moto proPrio* detailed regulations for music used in the liturgy.

Another attempt was made by French Jesuit Joseph Gelineau (1920–2008) to breathe new life in singing psalms in the liturgy of the church in the middle of the twentieth century. Gelineau was inspired by the French translation of the then new *Jerusalem Bible* and its more rhythmic translation of the Psalms, and he began setting the newer texts to music. Since the mass had to be sung in Latin, Gelineau's French settings could not be used in worship, but they were readily used in other services. Gelineau later wrote music for the Taizé community, an ecumenical group of Protestant, Roman Catholic, and Orthodox monks in the village of Taizé in eastern France.[6]

Reforms of Vatican II

Sixteen documents called *Constitutions* came out of Vatican II, laying a foundation for the church as we know it today. One theme of the Council, that is reflected in the documents, was reconciliation. The documents gave Catholics permission to pray with other Christian churches, encouraged friendship with non-Christian faiths, and opened the door for languages besides Latin to be used during Mass. In keeping with this theme, an invitation was extended to Protestant and Eastern Orthodox churches to send observers, and as a result, representatives from many of those churches attended. The diversity of national and cultural origins shown among those who attended from all over the world was another obvious feature. Other new developments were concerned with education, the media, and divine revelation.[7]

Changes in the Mass

The first major document that was debated was the "Constitution on the Sacred Liturgy" (*Sacrosanctum Concilium*) and it is arguably the most influential. The Constitution contains seven chapters, 130 articles, and an appendix, and was passed on December 4, 1963 by a vote of 2,147 to 4. New rites were drawn up and implemented within a year, and Pope Paul VI himself celebrated Mass in the revised rite on the very first day it was permitted.

---

pope on his own initiative and personally signed by him. The English title of this *motu proprio* is "Among the Concerns."

6. Dowley, *Christian Music*, 61.
7. Teicher, "Why is Vatican II so Important?"

Dunn believes the *Constitution* set in motion "the most far-reaching liturgical reform in Catholic history."[8]

The form of the Mass had not changed since the Council of Trent in the sixteenth century. "Catholics were accustomed to the chant, incense, and ceremony that took place on Sunday mornings," wrote Bill Huebsch. "They were there, in large numbers, praying their rosaries or missals, while the priest and altar boys prayed the Mass." Huebsch describes how this was changed as a result of Vatican II:

> For Americans, English was heard in all the rites and prayers. The priest turned to face the people. Gregorian chant was replaced with more modern music. Church buildings themselves were soon remodeled to make room for lay ministers and to reflect a theology in which the community itself helped pray the Mass. Rosaries and missals disappeared like sparks into the night. Catholics were invited to pray and sing aloud, to receive Communion from the cup, and to offer their own Prayers of the Faithful. This form of the Mass had not been seen in the church since the third century."[9]

A New Role for the Congregation

As noted in chapter 5, the role of the worship congregation had been reduced to observing the Mass instead of participating in the Mass. "Because of the clerical monopoly on liturgical activity," writes Metzger, "the ministries that had been instituted to foster the participation of the people lost their purpose, and . . . the liturgical ministry was concentrated on the priesthood."[10]

Previously, worship to God could be offered without the people present; worship was offered on behalf of the people and it assured their salvation. Even when the people were present at the mass, they were not able to express themselves consciously in prayer because the liturgy was in Latin. They were obligated to say words they did not understand. In contrast, the following selection of *Constitution* articles (listed by article number) shows the different emphasis given to the role of the people in worship.

- Liturgical services are not private functions, but are celebrations of the church, which is the "sacrament of unity," namely, the holy people united and ordered under their bishops (26).

---

8. Dunn, "On the Occasion," 1. Dunn includes an extensive bibliography of reflections on the *Constitution*.

9. Huebsch, "How Did Vatican II?," 39.

10. Metzger, *History of the Liturgy*, 123.

- To promote active participation, the people should be encouraged to take part by means of acclamations, responses, psalmody, antiphons, and songs, as well as by actions, gestures, and bodily attitudes. And at the proper times all should observe a reverent silence (30).
- Provisions shall also be made . . . for legitimate variations and adaptations to different groups, regions, and peoples . . . provided that the substantial unity of the Roman rite is preserved; and this should be borne in mind when drawing up the rites and devising rubrics (38).
- The church . . . earnestly desires that Christ's faithful, should not be there as strangers or silent spectators; on the contrary . . . they should take part in the sacred action conscious of what they are doing, with devotion and full collaboration. They should be instructed by God's word and be nourished at the table of the Lord's body; they should give thanks . . . by offering the Immaculate Victim, not only through . . . the priest, but also with him, they should learn also to offer themselves; through Christ the Mediator, they should be drawn day by day into ever more perfect union with God and with each other, so that finally God may be all in all (48).

Other reforms that relate to the people include didactic preaching, a greater use of Scripture in the liturgy, worship in the vernacular, an enlarged role for lay people in worship leadership, and adapting the liturgy to the ethnic and cultural setting of the people.

The Role of Music in the Liturgy

Chapter VI of the *Constitution* highlights the ministerial function of sacred music in the service of the Lord and it speaks of music being holy:

> Therefore, sacred music is to be considered the more holy, the more closely connected with the liturgical action, whether making prayer more pleasing, promoting unity of minds, or conferring greater solemnity on the sacred rites. The Church, indeed, approves of all forms of true art which have the requisite qualities, and admits them into divine worship.

It further states that the purpose of sacred music is the "glory of God and the sanctification of the faithful." An appeal is made to the musical tradition of the church as a "treasure of inestimable value, greater even than that of any other art." That pre-eminence is because music "as sacred song united to the words, it forms a necessary or integral part of the solemn liturgy."[11]

The *Constitution* emphasizes that music is always a servant of the liturgy. The meaning of music is derived from the liturgical action taking place, and music selection is based upon that premise. The tradition of Gregorian chant and organ accompaniment to the liturgy is preferred, but there is no limitation on what can be sung or what instruments can be used, so long as they are liturgically appropriate.

Music within the Mass

The traditional music of the church in 1959 was a mixture of Gregorian chant, compositions derived from chant, and Renaissance-style choral music with a Latin text. The lack of music with a vernacular text that fit both the artistic model presented in the *Constitution* and the new role of music in the liturgy posed a problem. Musicians who thought music in the church should only be performed by trained professionals feared the quality of music was deteriorating. Others, who believed music should be participatory for the congregation, thought their day had arrived. To bring order to the situation and to give direction to church musicians, several steps were taken.

First, the Sacred Congregation of Rites issued *Musicam Sacram: Instruction on Music in the Liturgy* on March 5, 1967. The *Musicam* contains a preface, seven chapters, and 69 articles.[12] Five specific ministerial functions of music in the liturgy are given in the *Musicam*. Through music in the liturgy

- prayer is given a more graceful expression;
- the mystery of the liturgy, with its hierarchical and community nature, is more openly shown;
- the unity of hearts is more profoundly achieved by the union of voices;
- minds are more easily raised to heavenly things by the beauty of the liturgy; and
- the whole celebration more clearly prefigures the heavenly liturgy.

Second, Pope John Paul II addressed the Pontifical Institute of Sacred Music in which three pastoral principles for choosing appropriate music are emphasized: (1) music in the liturgy must be holy; (2) the music must serve the spirit and norms of the liturgy; and (3) the music must serve the

---

11. Catholic Truth, *Sacrosanctum,* Article 112.
12. Sacred Congregation of Rites, *Musicam Sacram,* 4–5.

spirit and norms of the faith it expresses. Sacred music is that which, being created for the celebration of divine worship, is endowed with a certain holy sincerity of form. The following come under the title of sacred music: Gregorian chant, sacred polyphony in its various forms both ancient and modern, music for the organ and other approved instruments, and sacred popular music, be it liturgical or simply religious.[13]

At the outset, clergy and composers were at a loss to find music that would meet the new criteria. To fill the gap, publishing companies rushed to produce music for choirs. One choir director I knew at the time was very distressed. Some of the music aimed at Catholic churches did not meet the artistic and musical standards desired. She shared with me some of the new music that had been produced, and it was evident that not only was the music inferior, it seemed to be a way to make money for the publisher rather than providing a service to the church.

A list of primary sources was made available to clergy and composers to help implement music in the liturgy according to the prescriptions of Vatican II.[14] Dunn summarized the situation at that time:

> As the experience of liturgical music continues to develop, it seems that some composers and communities are finding creative ways to integrate the tradition of antiphon singing while maintaining the participation of the assembly. In this regard, the *Constitution* mentions composers as those who meet the needs of the Christian community in its local expressions (VI:121).[15]

Dunn's words have been correct. Catholic congregations now sing many of the same hymns and worship songs as Protestants (including Luther's "A Mighty Fortress is Our God") and many Catholic choirs sing anthems that are also sung by Protestant choirs.

---

13. John Paul II, *Chirograph on Sacred Music*. See also Mason, "Pastoral Implications," 386–413.

14. The following are materials prepared by the Congregation for Divine Worship and Discipline of the Sacraments that clergy and composers could use as guides to implementing music in the: *Instruction on Masses with Special Groups* (1969); *Directory for Masses with Children* (1973); *Lectionary for Mass, Introduction,* 2nd ed. (1981); *General Instruction of the Roman Missal,* 3rd ed. (2010).

15. Dunn, "On the Occasion," 20. Dunn includes an extensive bibliography of reflections on the *Constitution*.

Sing to the Lord

In November 2007 the United States Conference of Catholic Bishops published *Sing to the Lord: Music in Divine Worship*. This is a revision of two earlier church documents, published in 1982, *Music in Catholic Worship* and its companion, *Liturgical Music Today*. *Music in Catholic Worship* was first approved in 1972 and updated in 1983. Parish practices based on directives in *Music in Catholic Worship* have now been redirected to *Sing to the Lord*. This new publication was developed by the Committee on Divine Worship of the United States Conference of Catholic Bishops. The purpose of the publication is to provide guidance to local parish musicians in planning and performing music for Sunday. Technically, *Sing to the Lord* was approved as a set of guidelines, not particular law, for the United States. As the introduction states, "These guidelines are designed to provide direction to those preparing for the celebration of the Sacred Liturgy according to the current liturgical books (in the ordinary form of celebration)."[16] The guidelines are both theoretical and practical; theoretical in interpreting earlier documents from Vatican II and practical in showing how the decisions of Vatican II can be carried out in parish worship. *Sing to the Lord* provides additional guidelines by interpreting the importance of the international directives and adding pastoral suggestions for applying these guidelines to the United States.

A Theology of Liturgical Music

One outcome from the liturgical reform of Vatican II has been an emphasis upon the Paschal Mystery. This is one of the central concepts of Catholic faith relating to salvation history. The word "paschal" is derived from a word in Greek, Hebrew, and Arabic meaning "pass over." The notion of paschal mystery is derived primarily from the writings of the apostle Paul, who uses the term *mystery* (Gk. = mystérion) to refer to the plan of God conceived before creation for the salvation of the world and fully realized in the life and person of Jesus Christ through whom all things are reconciled to God. For Paul, there exists only one mystery, the mystery of Christ, and Paul feels compelled to lead all peoples to grasp this plan hidden for all eternity in God. God's plan of salvation is already fulfilled, the "new creation" is already present, and "the end of the ages" has already come because Christ overcome sin and death. Yet we still live in a world marked by sin and cursed by death. Mankind is living both in the "already" and in the "not yet" of redemption.[17]

---

16. Committee on Congregational Song, *Sing*, 6.
17. See Rom 6:3–5; 1 Cor 12:12–13, 27; Col 1:2–25.

Kathleen Harmon, both a musician and a theologian, explored the theological bases for this concept and developed a theology of liturgical music in her book *The Mystery We Celebrate, the Song We Sing*. Accepting the fact that "singing is not accidental or arbitrary, but a necessary and integral part of the ritual," Harmon raises some basic questions:

> But what, specifically, is the liturgical act that is being done, and why is music the mode of its doing? How is it that music conveys the liturgical mystery to the people who are celebrating it? What exactly is the mystery being conveyed? And what is the essential connection between this mystery and the music the assembly is singing?[18]

When worshipers sing in the liturgy, they encounter and appropriate the paschal mystery. When the Christian community sings,

- it enables the assembled community to become present to God, to themselves, to one another, and to the liturgical action in which they are engaging;
- it opens them to the deepest level of participation in being, that of their identity as the Body of Christ;
- it immerses them in time as a transforming force of Christian existence; and
- it works out within and among them the soteriological-eschatological dialectic of the paschal mystery through the force-resistance dialectic of sound and song.[19]

The full implementation of Vatican II has not taken place, but the changes that have been made to date are significant. Congregational song in American Catholic churches is well established.

The Episcopal Church

The Anglican tradition in America is embodied primarily in the Episcopal Church that traces its heritage to the Church of England. However, a growing number of churches refer to themselves as Anglican and not Episcopal. The Episcopal Church recognizes the Archbishop of Canterbury as its spiritual head, though he has no direct authority over the American church. The Episcopal Church is not a "confessional" church founded on

18. Harmon, *Mystery We Celebrate*, vii.
19. Harmon, *Mystery We Celebrate*, x.

any particular doctrine, such as justification by faith alone, predestination, the necessity to have a "born again" experience, scriptural "inerrancy," "transubstantiation," or the like.

Episcopalians endorse the creeds of the early church—particularly the Apostles' and Nicene creeds—as essential statements of the faith. They also believe in the primacy of the Bible as a definitive account of God's revelation to us. Episcopalians celebrate Holy Communion as the primary Sunday service and they believe in the "real" presence of the Body and Blood of Christ in the bread and wine that is received and all baptized Christians are invited to receive communion. The 1979 Book of Common Prayer is presently the normative guide for worship and contains the texts for most services.[20]

Music in the Episcopal Church can be as diverse as its worship services, though final authority over the music used in an Episcopal service is "the duty of every Minister" (Canon 24, Section 1). In the same way that the *Book of Common Prayer* draws worshipers together in prayer and liturgy, the hymnal draws all Episcopalians together musically. The Hymnal 1982 of the Episcopal Church includes 720 hymns in addition to liturgical chants and responses. While some of the hymns date back to monastic chants, the hymnal offers more modern music as well. The Preface is descriptive of its contents:

> The Hymnal 1982 retains the best of the past and sets forth many riches of our own time. [The Standing Commission on Church Music] looked for theological orthodoxy, poetic beauty, and integrity of meaning. At the same time, the Commission was especially concerned that the hymnody affirms "the participation of all in the Body of Christ the Church, while recognizing our diverse natures of children of God." . . . Texts and music which reflect the pluralistic nature of The Hymnal 1982 retains the best of the past and sets forth many riches of our own time. [The Standing Commission on Church Music] looked for theological Texts and music which reflect the pluralistic nature of the Church have been included, affording the use of Native American, Afro-American, Hispanic, and Asian material.[21]

Though other liturgies of Episcopal Church are included in the *Book of Common Prayer*, newer liturgies are also included, such as blessings for same-sex weddings and rites for departed pets. These have been and are developed and reviewed by the Episcopal Church's Standing Commission for Music and Liturgy on a continuing basis. The Episcopal General Convention

---

20. Information prepared by St. Ann's Episcopal Church, Nashville, Tennessee.
21. *The Hymnal 1982*, "Preface," para. 3.

of 2015 adopted Resolution A169 directing the Standing Commission on Liturgy and Music (SCLM) to prepare a plan for the comprehensive revision of the 1979 Book of Common Prayer and The Hymnal 1982 to be presented to the next Genera Convention in 2018.

The Commission responded and presented four possible paths the church might follow for the revision, but no one path was favored. Since then, discussion has been lively with all kinds of opinions being expressed and no one path or combination of paths seemed to garner approval. To help clarify the issues, two prominent Episcopal liturgical theologians from the Church Divinity School of the Pacific, Ruth A. Meyers and Louis Weil, were asked to offer their views on the question of revision.[22] They raised a host of very pertinent questions and concluded that more church-wide discussion was necessary before the church could come to any final decision.

The Hymnal 1982 revision has also come under criticism. "As conflicts between clergy and choirmasters across the church suggest," comments Cones, "the relationship between music and liturgy, and ultimately which one is at the service of the other, is not a question upon which there is wide consensus, at least in mixed company of liturgists and musicians." He asks a question that is valid for any hymnal revision: "At heart is what kind of song the assembly needs to celebrate its liturgy, and whether historic forms, mostly derived in the European and even more specifically English contexts, are still suitable . . ."[23]

The Episcopal Church has had problems with the incorporation of contemporary songs into the worship service. The proliferation of contemporary songs makes it difficult to maintain a relevant hymnal, and in many parishes, worshipers prefer to sing from slides rather than from the hymnal. Other voices have been raised about including instruments in worship as an alternative to an organ. Supporters are arrayed on both sides of these arguments, and the conclusions of Meyers and Weil are instructive for the discussion.

Evangelical Lutheran Church in America

More than forty different Lutheran denominations currently exist in North America. However, most North American Lutherans belong to one of the three largest denominations, namely, the Evangelical Lutheran Church in America, the Lutheran Church—Missouri Synod, or the Wisconsin Evangelical Lutheran Synod.

22. MacDougal, et al., "Revising," 501.
23. Cones, "78th General Convention," 691–92.

The Divine Service

Historically, the phrase used to describe Lutheran worship is the Divine Service. The two main parts of the Divine Service are (1) the proclamation of the word of God, and (2) the celebration of the Lord's Supper. Other orders of service used in the Lutheran church feature a more extended service of the Word as well as times of prayer, such as the services of Matins and Vespers, Morning and Evening Prayer, Compline, and the Litany. Lutheran worship puts the focus squarely on Jesus Christ, who is present "for us and with us through His Word and Sacraments."

In Lutheran services, pastors and congregations sing or speak the liturgy back and forth or together. Congregational singing of hymns has always been a hallmark of Lutheran worship. The Lutheran church in its worship embraces the best of musical traditions, both ancient and modern, with an emphasis on congregational singing, reinforced by the choir.[24]

However, Lutherans have been engaged in their own distinctive "worship wars." Rolf Preus describes it like this:

> . . . now you go to church and everything is different. You go expecting to find something that is no longer there. Perhaps it's the singing of the Kyrie. Or maybe the Creed is replaced by a homemade version of it that isn't really very good. Instead of a sermon, there is a kind of chancel drama. The familiar canticles are gone. The Lutheran chorales have given way to shallow and repetitious "praise" songs. The Benediction is replaced by a rather lengthy exhortation to be whatever kind of Christian is in vogue for the season. You don't want to criticize. You wonder if your expectations were a bit unreasonable . . . you have the definite sense that something important is gone and you want it back. Church is no longer home.[25]

Preus prefers the historic Divine Service, but concludes by saying, "We need to respect the conscience of our brothers and sisters in Christ, even if we don't quite understand why they think as they do."[26]

---

24. Barry, *What About Lutheran Worship?*

25. Preus, "Lutheran Worship Wars," para. 4.

26. Preus, "Lutheran Worship Wars," para. 57. See also Churchmouse Campanologist, "Changes in Lutheran Liturgy."

Impetus for Change

Lutheran liturgy had changed little over the years, but it began to change in the 1950s when the Lutheran Churches of North America embarked on a program of liturgical restoration and organized a Joint Commission on the Liturgy and the Hymnal. A new worship book, *The Service Book and Hymnal*, was introduced in 1958 and it includes prayers and hymns from the broader Western church that are outside the Lutheran tradition.

In 1966, an Inter-Lutheran Commission on Worship convened to discuss how church services could be made more relevant to contemporary society. The Commission's work culminated with the 1979 *Lutheran Book of Worship*, approved by the church groups involved except for the Lutheran Church—Missouri Synod. However, many Missouri Synod congregations bought copies for their churches. The *Lutheran Book of Worship* was influenced by ecumenism, reiterated the importance of Holy Communion as the main Sunday service, and borrowed texts from the Episcopal Church's 1979 *Book of Common Prayer*. A broad campaign of workshops in churches across North America ensured its acceptance.

The Lutheran World Federation created a document in 1996 called the "Nairobi Statement on Worship and Culture." The importance of worship and song is evident in the Introduction: "To consider worship is to consider music, art, and architecture, as well as liturgy and preaching." The Nairobi Statement frames worship's relationship with culture in four ways:

> *Worship is transcultural*, meaning there are basic theological beliefs that are accepted by everyone.
>
> *Worship is contextual*, for Jesus was born in the context of a particular culture at a particular time, and if a different culture is consonant with the values of the Gospel, worship elements from one worship culture can be incorporated into another worship culture.
>
> *Worship is counter-cultural*, recognizes that the task of the Church is to transform culture without being itself transformed by culture. However, Christian worship may also include the deliberate maintenance or recovery of patterns of action which differ intentionally from prevailing cultural models.
>
> *Worship is cross-cultural*, is the recognition that music, art, architecture, gestures and postures, and other elements of different cultures can be assimilated in worship. When worship elements from a different culture are used by churches elsewhere

in the world, care should be taken that they are understood and respected.[27]

The Process for Change

The Evangelical Lutheran Church in America has perhaps addressed liturgical change more than any other Protestant church or denomination to date. It began as a series of consultations in 2001 under the theme, "Renewing Worship." The church used the four statements from the Nairobi Statement as "lenses" to guide conversations about worship in terms of what worship looks like, what worship sounds like, and how worship engages body, mind and spirit. More than one hundred people, representing the breadth of the church, met in a series of consultations that led to the publication of *Principles for Worship* in 2002.

The consultations developed principles and supporting materials that address four dimensions of the church's worship: language, music, preaching, and worship space. For example, in asking what worship sounds like, it is noted that "although sacred Scripture and other texts in worship are transcultural, there is no single or preferred sacred language. Preaching is by its very nature a contextual act. Likewise, there is no single musical expression that works equally well in all places."[28]

Principles for Worship is the first in a series of semiannual publications "to assist the renewal of corporate worship in a variety of settings, especially among Lutheran churches, in anticipation of the next generation of primary worship resources."[29] Addressed to churches as "assemblies," *Principles for Worship* addresses four areas as an affirmation of the Nairobi Statement: language, music, preaching, and worship space.

The material in *Principles for Worship* are presented in three categories: principles, applications, and backgrounds. Principles are brief statements that articulate a central understanding. Each principle has a number of background statements and practical applications. The principle is stated, then enlarged upon. Below is an example of how the *Principles for Worship* is organized:

Part 1: The Nature of Music

---

27. For the full text of the "Nairobi Statement," see https://worship.calvin.edu/resources/resource-library/nairobi-statement-on-worship-and-culture-full-text.
28. Evangelical Lutheran Church in *America, Principles for Worship*, 17.
29. Evangelical Lutheran Church in *America, Principles for Worship*, iv..

> *Basic Principle*: The voice is the primary instrument in worship.
>
> In the church, the primary instrument is the voice given by God to sing and proclaim the word of God.
>
> *Background*: Scripture speaks of Jesus Christ as the incarnate Word of God. "In the beginning was the Word, and the Word was with God, and the Word was God" (John 1:1). "Let the word of Christ dwell in you richly . . . and with gratitude in your hearts sing psalms, hymns, and spiritual songs to God" (Col 3:16).
>
> *Application:* Regardless of musical style or instrumentation, leadership confidently supports and enables the voice of the congregation. Likewise, the voice of a soloist, cantor, assisting minister, or presiding minister is most effective when it does not overwhelm or dominate the congregation's voice.[30]

This effort by the Evangelical Lutheran Church in America is impressive. Other churches and denominations would benefit from reading *Principles for Worship*.

II. The Reformed Tradition

Presbyterians and various Reformed churches evolved from the Reformation. Presbyterianism developed in Scotland while the Reformed churches were formed on the Continent. Reformed churches can be divided according to their nomenclature. Some churches call themselves Presbyterian while others call themselves Reformed. At least two denominations refer to themselves as Reformed Presbyterians.

Reformed churches in America were founded by the Germans, Dutch, and Scots who immigrated to the United States and brought their church with them. The word "Reformed" refers to the church's adherence to the biblical principles set down by the Protestant Reformation of the sixteenth century. Historically, Reformed churches are connected by a similar Calvinist system of doctrine as it is expressed in various confessions, and a Presbyterian church government. Some of these churches will have a worship directory that has both prescribed features and other features that are left to a local pastor and congregation.

The Westminster Confession (1648) is still widely used among Reformed churches as well as a number of other confessions. Different denominations

---

30. Evangelical Lutheran Church in America, *Principles for Worship*, 26–27.

use different confessions, usually based on historical reasons. The largest Presbyterian denomination in the United States, the Presbyterian Church (USA) has adopted a Book of Confessions, which incorporates versions of both Continental and Presbyterian Reformed confessions of faith.

Many of these churches generally follow the Revised Common Lectionary (1983), a lectionary of readings from the Bible for use in Christian Worship, making provision for the liturgical year with its pattern of observances of festivals and seasons. Reformed churches generally have a liturgy that includes historical elements that the early church had agreed should be said in each Sunday service, as well as other elements that are appropriate for the local church. The pastor and the church's governing body determine the order of a Sunday worship service. Prayer, music, Bible reading and a sermon based upon Scripture are usually included, along with the Sacraments, a time of personal response/offering, and a sharing of community concerns. The frequency of communion varies widely from church to church.

The Reformed Church in America

The Reformed Church in America was established in 1867 and was originally a Dutch Reformed denomination. The church has a Presbyterian polity where authority is divided among representative bodies: consistories, classes, regional synods, and the General Synod. The General Synod meets annually and is the representative body of the entire church, establishing its policies, programs, and agenda. Measures passed at General Synod are executed and overseen by the General Synod Council. Council members are also appointed by the General Synod. The authority in local churches is the consistory.

The RCA has a fixed Liturgy, particularly in connection with the sacraments. However, there is also flexibility for local consistories to guide the worship of their congregations. A distinction is made between Liturgy and liturgy. The Liturgy declares what the early church has agreed to say in the same way each Sunday as it gathers to worship in local congregations. The Liturgy also includes various rites, and the words to perform those rites, that have been proposed to the General Synod and ultimately approved by the General Synod. Both The Liturgy and Directory for Worship are part of the constitution of the RCA, and the Directory for Worship functions as an instructional appendix to the Liturgy.

In addition, the church has a number of liturgies that are not part of the Constitution, but are recommended for use throughout the church. The use of these liturgies is not required by the church, but they are held in high esteem and used as exemplars of the Reformed liturgical tradition.

Liturgical Reform

Official liturgical reform came slowly for the Reformed Church in America. Early Dutch settlers brought an approved Liturgy to America in 1628. The first revision was in 1793 and the next major revision was in 1906. The 1906 liturgy was the officially sanctioned liturgy until 1968. A single normative Order for the Lord's Day was published in 1987, the hymnal *Rejoice in the Lord* and the 1989 volume, *Worship the Lord* (the Liturgy of the Reformed Church in America), brought Word and Sacrament together for the first time since Calvin and was updated in 2015.

The Directory for Worship starts with a definition of worship as "the action of acknowledging God's worth!" Everything that may and should happen in worship points to this central meaning. Consequently,

> Our worship from votum to benediction is both a dialogue between minister and congregation and between God and people. It is the sung, verbal, and acted expressions of adoration, confession, forgiveness; the receptance of grace in Word and Sacrament; and response in acknowledging God's worth.
>
> The source of worship is the God who has revealed himself in the history of Israel and in Jesus Christ, and this revelation is found authoritatively in the Scriptures as the Holy Spirit opens our hearts in the experience of God's worth. We acknowledge God's worth in worship through congregational actions; faith is articulated and acted out in word, song, and gesture.[31]

The structure of corporate worship, or the Order of Worship for the Lord's Day, is organized under three headings: Approach to God, Word in Proclamation and Sacrament, and Response to God. Numerous items fall under each heading, and music and Scripture are given a prominent place.

The importance of choirs in worship is addressed in Section 4. Skilled persons of "articulate voice and accurate note" should be in the choir. The choir assists the congregation in the singing of its hymns, reciting its responses, and helps set the tone of worship as desired by minister and choral director. An anthem should be part of the ongoing flow of worship and not inserted as a piece of special music. The choir and organ should be placed

---

31. Reformed Church in America, "Directory," 229.

in such a way as to give maximum support for congregational singing and minimizing any visual distraction from the service.

Theology and Music

A separate paper has been produced with the title "The Theology and Place of Music in Worship." This is a very thoughtful document and has value for anyone involved with worship and song in the church. The purpose of the paper is "to further dialogue in the RCA about music and worship, and to encourage healthy and vibrant congregational singing as a vital part of ministry." The paper closes with some excellent guidelines for evaluating and selecting music for the congregation's worship. Reflections on theology and the place of music in Christian worship are given, with additional discussion added under each heading. Only the seven headings are given below:

1. Music is a gift of God and part of the created order.
2. Of all the musical instruments that may be employed in the praise of God, the human voice has priority.
3. Singing is a ministry that belongs to *all* the people of God.
4. Of all the art forms that may be employed in worship, singing is especially corporate.
5. The church's ministry of song is for the glory of God.
6. The church's ministry of song is for the edification of God's people.
7. The emotional power of music, rightly employed, is a vital and moving aid to worship.

The *Book of Church Order* specifies that "the hymns used in public worship shall be in harmony with the *Standards* of the Reformed Church in America" and assigns this responsibility to the consistory.[32] Under the heading," Suggested Guidelines for Evaluating and Nurturing Congregational Singing," ten major questions are listed, with a series of related questions listed below each. A church that used all of these questions in their context would certainly gain an understanding of worship and song in that particular body of believers. Here is the complete question 1:

1. What theology is expressed in our congregational singing?

    Is it biblical? Is it consistent with Reformed theology? Is the range of what we sing representative of the "whole counsel of God"? What do

---

32. *Book of Church Order*, Part I, Article 2, Section 11d.

our songs and hymns say or imply about the sovereignty and grace of God? About the life, death, resurrection, and ascension of Jesus Christ? About the work of the Holy Spirit, the nature and mission of the church, the sacraments, and the Christian life?

The other nine questions are as follows:

2. Is there sufficient pastoral breadth in our music ministry?
3. Is there sufficient liturgical breadth?
4. Is there sufficient historical, cultural, and generational breadth?
5. Is the language of our hymns inclusive?
6. Are we providing our congregation with a sufficient vocabulary of praise?
7. Does the music serve the text?
8. Does our music encourage corporate worship?
9. Is the music appropriate to the ability of the congregation?
10. Do the hymns and choruses we sing assume and encourage growth in discipleship?

The final paragraph is an excellent summary of everything the Reformed Church in America has achieved in liturgical renewal: "Learning more difficult music and coming to understand and appreciate richer theology may be difficult work, but it can also be a source of spiritual renewal and growth."[33]

Presbyterian Church (USA)

American Presbyterians, along with Reformed churches, have inherited the singing tradition of John Calvin. The largest Presbyterian denomination in the United States, the Presbyterian Church (USA), is known for its progressive stance on doctrinal, environmental, and economic issues in comparison to other Presbyterians groups, though its members are also divided on these issues. Consequently, this church has made the more comprehensive study of worship and song and is less wed to traditional Calvinist views of worship. The constitution of the church consists of the *Book of Confessions* (Part I) and the *Book of Order* (Part II). The *Book of Order* has four parts:

---

33. Commission on Worship, "Theology and Place of Music in Worship," Suggested Guidelines, No. 10.

The Foundations of Presbyterian Polity, Form of Government, Directory for Worship, and Rules of Discipline.

The 222nd General Assembly approved a *Revised Directory for Worship* in 2016, and it "reflects the conviction that the faith, life, and worship of the Church are inseparable."[34] The *Directory* describes "the theology that underlies our worship, outlines appropriate forms for worship, and highlights connections between worship and Christian life, witness, and service."[35] This theological base is quite broad and inclusive. In a section titled "Time, Space, and Matter," it states that "Through Christian worship—at certain times, in particular places, and with material gifts—we participate in God's plan for the redemption of time, space, and matter for the glory of God."[36] Music is one of the material things that we offer to God in our worship.

> The Church acknowledges that psalm singing is an important part of the Reformed heritage, but to the psalms "the Church has added other hymns, canticles, and spiritual songs. has developed many other forms of congregational song, accompanied by a great array of instruments . . . In worship, music is not to be for entertainment or artistic display. Care should be taken that it not be used merely as a cover for silence."[37]
>
> Psalms, canticles, anthems, alleluias, songs of praise, or other musical responses may accompany the reading of the Word. A psalm may be sung in response to the first reading, giving the congregation an opportunity to reflect on and pray from that text.[38]

The Order of Worship

The order of a Sunday worship service in a Presbyterian (USA) church generally includes prayer, music, Bible reading, and a sermon based upon Scripture. The constitution of the PC(USA) suggests that worship be ordered in terms of five major actions centered in the word of God (gathering around the word, proclaiming the word, responding to the word, the sealing of the word, and bearing and following the word into the world), but recognizes

---

34. Presbyterian Mission Agency, "Revised Directory for Worship," para. 1.
35. Presbyterian Mission Agency, "Revised Directory for Worship," para. 2.
36. Presbyterian Mission Agency, "Revised Directory for Worship," W-1.0201, line 2.
37. Presbyterian Mission Agency, "Revised Directory for Worship," W-3.0203, line 4.
38. Presbyterian Mission Agency, "Revised Directory for Worship," W-3.0304.

that "other orders of worship may also serve the needs of a particular church and be orderly, faithful to Scripture, and true to historic principles."[39]

The Style of Worship

The Presbyterian Mission Agency of the PC(USA) has a worship resource section on its website titled "Presbyterian USA Planning and Leadership."[40] The material is organized around two basic questions: who is responsible for planning worship, and should Presbyterian worship be traditional, contemporary, or blended?

WHO IS RESPONSIBLE FOR PLANNING WORSHIP?

The order of worship is determined by the pastor and the Session, the church's governing body. In addition to the normal leading in prayer, reading Scripture, and preaching, the pastor is responsible for the music to be sung; and the use of drama, dance and other art forms. The pastor may confer with a worship committee in planning particular services of worship. If a church has a minister of music, the pastor consults with him or her in the selection of Sunday music. The selection of hymnals, song books, service books, Bibles, and other materials for use of the congregation in public worship is the responsibility of the session with the concurrence of the pastor and in consultation with musicians and educators available to the session.

SHOULD PRESBYTERIAN WORSHIP BE TRADITIONAL, CONTEMPORARY, OR BLENDED?

This is a question that has been problematic for many churches and denominations, but the PC(USA) has opted for all three:

> *Traditional*: worship is grounded in scripture, established on the practices of the ancient and ecumenical church and guided by the principles of our theological ancestors in the Reformation.
>
> *Contemporary*: worship is attentive to the present concerns of the church, community and world, voiced in the common language of the people of God and responsive to the leading of God's Word and Spirit in this age.

---

39. Directory for Worship, "W-3.0103," para. 2.
40. Presbyterian Church, "Who is Responsible?," paras. 1–7.

> *Blended*: in the profound unity and rich diversity of the body of Christ, with myriad languages, customs and styles, we join our voices with the saints of every time and place to praise and glorify God.

The church has recognized there are some significant questions to be raised about the meaning and implications of these brief statements about worship style:

> From these assumptions, a more meaningful set of questions emerges: Which traditions and to what ends? Is a particular habit or practice rooted in the heart of Christian tradition or steeped in sentimentality? Does it lead us to fresh revelation or deadening repetition? How can we renew an ancient and valuable pattern of worship? Do some of our traditions exclude the outsider, oppress the powerless and obscure the faith? How do we engage our contemporary culture(s) in ways that are faithful and responsive to the gospel? Are the trends of contemporary culture consonant with Christ's realm? What are we communicating about the church, and what is being lost in translation? When are we following the Spirit, and when are we chasing after worldly success? What blending of ancient and modern is most appropriate for a particular worshipping community? How do we evoke the fullness of Christian tradition and meaning in different cultural contexts? In a particular worshipping community, whose voices are lifted up most often, and whose are often silenced?[41]

Glory to God: The Presbyterian Hymnal

A new hymnal, titled "Glory to God: The Presbyterian Hymnal," was released by Westminster John Knox Press, the publishing arm of the PC(USA), in 2012. Its contents are an excellent provision of congregational hymns and songs that meet the criteria of the three worship styles listed above. However, the hymnal has been the subject of theological controversy over the exclusion of the popular contemporary hymn, "In Christ Alone."

The Presbyterian Committee on Congregational Song of the Presbyterian Church (USA) wanted to add the song to their new hymnal. In doing so, the committee requested permission from the song's writers, Stuart Townend and Keith Getty, to print a previously published version of "In Christ Alone" that altered a line in the second stanza from "the wrath of

---

41. Presbyterian Mission Agency, "Planning and Leadership," para. 7.

God was satisfied" to "the love of God was magnified." Unfortunately, the copyright holders declined this request. After discussion and deliberation, the Committee voted and failed to reach the two-thirds majority that is the threshold for inclusion of a song in the final list of contents.

The altered version had been published without permission of the writers. The Committee did not know this and assumed permission would be forthcoming. The PC(USA) was tried in the media and accused of holding a defective theology or unwillingness to reckon with the judgment of God. The Committee Chair, Mary Louise Bringle, gave a nuanced response to these charges, and the church issued a news release on August 9, 2013 that said in part, "Scripture speaks in a variety of ways about what happened in Christ's death, and a model of atonement that understands the cross as satisfying God's wrath and saving us through the blood of Christ is already richly presented in this collection."[42]

The desire to change the wording of a hymn text is nothing new. Historically, that has been done when there were theological concerns with a given phrase or archaic words or phrases have been used. Unfortunately, this has often been done without proper permission and serious ethical and legal issues were ignored.

III. The Revivalist Tradition

The evangelistic services of the 1800s centered around four theological ideas: lives need to be changed through repentance and faith in the Christ; an emphasis on the sacrifice of Christ on the cross to make salvation possible; a high regard for the authority of the Bible in matters of faith and practice; and sharing the gospel with others. These services had no fixed liturgy of any kind and the services consisted of three parts: singing songs to prepare people for the sermon, preaching, and concluding with an appeal to receive Christ. Scripture readings were usually connected to the sermon.

This worship structure continued throughout the nineteenth and twentieth centuries, and continues today in many evangelical churches, such as Assembly of God, Baptists, Church of Christ, Nazarenes, some Methodist and Disciples of Christ churches, and many others. A typical worship order developed from the revival service would include a prelude, call to worship, hymns and songs, offertory, special music, sermon, invitation to Christian discipleship and postlude. The Lord's Supper would be added to this basic order and its frequency would depend upon each individual church.

---

42. Van Marter, "Presbyterian Hymnal Producers," para. 10.

The United Methodist Church

Methodists are difficult to classify, for they have roots both in the liturgical tradition of the Anglican Church and in the revivalism of the camp meeting. As noted earlier, Methodist circuit riders and Baptist preacher-farmers were responsible for most of the religious activity on the American frontier in the early 1800s.

The United Methodist Church, created by the merger of the Methodist Church and the Evangelical United Brethren Church in 1968, experienced a liturgical renewal in the latter half of the twentieth century. The original worship order of Wesley's *Sunday Service* gained new importance and provided the framework for this renewal. There was a desire to have the service in contemporary English and to include ecumenical rites reflective of early church practices. There was also a desire to have an expression of contemporary Neo-orthodox theology rather than the liberal theology that had been prevalent in the early twentieth century. Pastors also wanted maximum pastoral flexibility in the selection and use of liturgical materials.

The Book of Worship

The 1965 *Book of Worship* reflected this renewal effort that had led to a new emphasis upon confession and creeds. The current edition of *The United Methodist Book of Worship* was published in 1992. The publication of the *Common Lectionary* and its adoption by Methodists created a new emphasis upon expository preaching and the events celebrated in the Church Year.

In 1995 the United Methodists published a three-page paper titled "The Basic Pattern of Worship." Its purpose is to "guide those who plan worship and to help congregations understand the basic structure and content of our worship. Though it is not an order of worship, a variety of orders of worship may be based upon it."[43] The Basic Pattern answers the question of what order things should be said and done and is the same as the one given in Wesley's *Sunday Service for the Methodists of North America*:

- Entrance
- Proclamation and Response
- Thanksgiving and Communion
- Sending Forth

---

43. United Methodist Discipleship Ministries, *Basic Pattern of Worship*, 1.

To implement the Basic Pattern of Worship given on pages 3–5 of the United Methodist Hymnal, "An Order of Sunday Worship" was published to show "some of the variety that is possible within the Basic Pattern of Worship."[44] This document gives detailed background notes on each element, copies of prayers and responses, and suggestions for sermons and songs.

Congregational Song

Liturgical renewal reached a high point with the publication of the United Methodist Hymnal in 1989. The hymnal was designed as a complete resource for planning a service by placing prayers and other non-musical texts with hymns that were related by liturgical season or content.[45]

In addition to the Hymnal 1989, two other collections of congregational songs are available. One is titled *Worship & Song*, and is a distinctive collection of 190 songs comprising a broad variety of genres collected from all over the globe, including new hymns in traditional style, plus older traditional hymns no longer found in modern hymnals, contemporary songs, global songs, and USA ethnic (Spirituals, Black Gospel, Asian, and more) songs.

The second collection is *The Faith We Sing*, a distinctive collection of 190 songs comprising a broad variety of genres collected from all over the globe, including new hymns in traditional style, plus older traditional hymns no longer found in modern hymnals, contemporary songs, global songs, and USA ethnic songs.

In 2007 the Boards of Directors of Discipleship Ministries and The United Methodist Publishing House (UMPH) proposed legislation to the 2008 General Conference to develop a new hymnal for the USA. During the months leading up to the General Conference, Discipleship Ministries conducted a series of six online research surveys designed to provide information regarding the opinions of United Methodists—pastors, musicians, worship leaders, and laity—on a variety of subjects related to United Methodist worship, congregational singing, and *The United Methodist Hymnal* (1989) and *The Faith We Sing* (2000).

The surveys drew 19,091 responses. Some surveys were open to all United Methodists, while others were open only to pastors and chief musicians of the congregation because of the specialized nature of the information requested. For most of the surveys, respondents were asked to identify themselves as clergy or laity, their role or position in the local church, and in some cases, their age (under 30, 30–50, 50–70, over 70), and their zip

---

44. Discipleship Ministries, *Order of Sunday Worship*, 1.
45. Tanton, "Ten Years Later."

code. Some surveys required a simple mouse click to respond while others required fill-in-the-blank or short answers. However, because of the current (2019) unrest over the future direction of the denomination, work on a new hymnal has been deferred until a later time.

Contemporary Worship

Many Methodist churches are offering contemporary worship services in addition to the more traditional service. Consequently, the Discipleship Ministries of The United Methodist Church is providing a variety of materials and other helps for these services. These include texts and music for contemporary hymns that can be downloaded and reproduced at the local church. A list of music recommendations for worship services based upon the Common Lectionary is available and the list ranges from Negro spirituals through traditional and contemporary hymns to praise songs.

A Methodist Vetting Team analyzed the Top 100 Christian Copyright Licensing International Songs for 2015–2016 to select those that adhered to Wesleyan theology, appropriate use of language for God and humanity, and singability. CCLI is the major provider of licensing services for churches that reproduce song texts on screen or in print for congregational singing. Each year CCLI publishes the 100 top songs that subscribing churches are using the most. There is no information provided about the theological or musical quality of the songs.

The majority of the contemporary worship songs reflected in the CCLI Top 100 list reflect charismatic, Pentecostal, Calvinist, or neo-Calvinist theology. Some of these songs would have texts at odds with Methodist Wesleyan theology, so the Vetting Team selected those songs they thought United Methodists could and should sing, and that adhered to Wesleyan theology.[46]

Pentecostalism

In 1900 there were no Pentecostals, but today the number of Christians associated with Pentecostal movements make up about twenty-five percent of the world's Christian population.[47] The Pentecostal movement, which itself emerged from the Methodist Holiness movement of the nineteenth century, began in the early 1900s. Midwestern Methodists and other Christians

---

46. United Methodist Discipleship Ministries, "CCLI Top 100."
47. Caldwell, "Assemblies of God."

associated with the Holiness movement had become obsessed with divine healing and the possibility of speaking in tongues—doctrines and practices that most Christian scholars argued had ended with the apostolic age.

One of these Holiness Christians was an eighteen-year-old Kansas collegian named Charles Fox Parham. He believed that sanctification was a second work of grace, separate from salvation. But he also adopted the more radical Holiness belief in a third experience—the "baptism with the Holy Ghost and fire." As early as 1891, Midwesterners heard young Parham claim that speaking in unknown or foreign tongues should accompany this baptism in the Holy Spirit. A handful of his listeners accepted him as a latter-day Elijah, ushering in Christ's return. To perpetuate his views, Parham opened a Bible school in 1900 in a Topeka mansion. Parham believed God would supernaturally give known, earthly languages to baptized believers so they could quickly evangelize the world.

Parham took a group of his followers to Texas in 1905, where he was successful in winning converts and setting up a non-credit Bible school. One of the students attracted to Parham was William J. Seymore, a former black waiter and southern Holiness preacher. Seymore was invited to pastor a small Los Angeles Baptist church that had been expelled from its association for preaching Holiness doctrine. His teaching about speaking in tongues was not readily received, so he and a small group began meeting in the home of Edward Lee. On April 9, 1906, Edward Lee asked Seymore to pray for him that he would be given the gift of tongues. As Seymore prayed, Lee spoke in tongues, which was fulfilling a vision he said he had received in which the apostles taught him how to speak in tongues.

Soon, the Lee home was too small to accommodate the crowds attending, so they moved to the home of Richard and Ruth Asberry for prayer and Bible study, though the Asberrys disagreed with what Seymore was teaching. Soon, both black and white faces were in the crowd meeting in the Asberry home, and on April 12, 1906, the first white man began to speak in tongues.

Azusa Street Revival

When the front porch of the Lee home collapsed under the weight of the crowds, the group negotiated a lease for the former Stevens Methodist Episcopal Church at 312 Azusa Street. In less than four months after arriving in Los Angeles, Seymour was preaching to crowds in Azusa Street that numbered anywhere from three to fifteen hundred. The meetings were loud and boisterous. Though there were periods of silence in the meetings, most of the meetings were loud and unlike the services of established churches. The meetings began at 10 a.m. and continued for at least twelve hours, often lasting until two or three the following morning. There were reports of healings, speaking in tongues, along with shouting and spontaneous preaching by those who felt led of the Spirit to speak.

There was no order of service, no liturgy; worship was spontaneous. There were no hymn books, and usually there were no musical instruments. Participants jumped and shouted, danced and sang. Sometimes people sang together, but with completely different syllables, rhythms, and tunes. The leaders were sure that this was evidence of revival and even a new Pentecost.

Marini[48] cites the experience of a black woman, Jennie Moore, who is the first to receive Spirit-baptism exhibited in speaking in tongues at the Azusa revival. She testified that she spoke in a language God had given her. The Spirit directed her to the piano, where she played and sang in many languages, though she had never learned to play the piano. Others had similar experiences, and "tongue songs" were common.

Evolution of Pentecostalism

During the first half of the twentieth century Pentecostalism remained a sub-movement within American fundamentalism and revivalism, and numerous new denominations were developed as the movement grew, including most notably the Assemblies of God. Consequently, the basic theology of these groups reflects the orthodox Christian views of conservative, evangelical Protestants in the pietist-revivalist tradition.[49]

Soon, some features of Pentecostalism made their way into mainline Protestant and evangelical churches as well as Roman Catholic churches.[50] Many Christians believe in and practice supernatural gifts of tongues speaking and prophecy, though they may not believe speaking in tongues is the initial, physical evidence of the infilling of the Holy Spirit. For example, in 1960, in Van Nuys, California, there was an outburst of tongues speaking in St. Mark's Episcopal Church. This event was so significant that both Time and Newsweek covered the story. Then, the Holy Spirit came upon a group of middle-class Catholics at Duquesne University in 1966 and at Notre Dame University in 1967.[51] Since that time, the various gifts of the Spirit—speaking in tongues, prophecies, interpretations, and healing—have

---

48. Marini, *Sacred Song in America*, 113.
49. Zeller, "Brief History of Pentecostalism."
50. O'Connor, *Pentecostal Movement*.
51. Olson, "What Is Pentecostalism?"

been manifested to countless Roman Catholics. Generally, these believers are referred to as "Charismatics" rather than Pentecostals.

Pentecostal theology teaches that the Christian life consists of two primary turning points: justification and sanctification. Justification describes how a person is made right with God through Christ's death and resurrection. Sanctification describes how believers becomes more Christlike in every area of their lives through the practice of spiritual disciplines.

To the Pentecostal, both of these happen at different times in the life of the believer. A person must have another encounter with the Spirit after salvation; otherwise, he or she will not progress into holiness or the "deeper" things of God. Without moving forward into the deeper things, it is possible a person could lose their salvation. In Pentecostal terminology, the second encounter with the Spirit, is called "entire sanctification," "the second blessing, or "the second touch."

The concept of a "second blessing" is rooted in the Pentecostal doctrine of the baptism in the Holy Spirit. This is described variously as the crucial blessing to be sought, the ultimate experience to strive for, and the greatest achievement of the Christian. According to Pentecostals, the initial evidence of the baptism in the Holy Spirit is speaking in other tongues as the Spirit gives utterance. The means of achieving this second work of grace is conceived of as an act of faith akin to the act of faith involved in justification.[52]

We must note that Pentecostals do not have complete unity on the doctrine of tongues and second blessings. You will find some variations, such as an emphasis on a third experience of grace where a person becomes free from sin in this life, sometimes called "entire sanctification" or "sinless perfection," and emphasis upon "Jesus only" to the exclusion of the Trinity.[53]

Pentecostal Worship

Historically, Pentecostals rejected much worship that had a formal or structural overtone to it. They reject the liturgy of the mainline churches in favor of a non-liturgical style that was both spirited and spontaneous with the Spirit guiding the worship with his own pace, direction, and with his own inclusions. Pentecostals have favored testimonies, choruses and prayers over intellectual or critical reflection about worship and congregational song. A review of the many Pentecostal services available on YouTube indicate that standard hymns, folk songs, choruses, and gospel

52. Archer, "Pentecostal Way," 301–4. See also: Gilley, "Pentecostalism."
53. Olson, "What is Pentecostalism?"

songs are all genres of music that Pentecostals use in worship. According to Mosher, Pentecostal worship has

> strongly rhythmic music; the use of a wide variety of instruments . . . highly emotional singing and displays of devotion, including the exhibition of unrestrained physical movement such as ecstatic dance . . . spontaneous and seemingly undirected congregational singing, sometimes called "singing in the Spirit"; the interpolation of testimony into any part of the worship service, including the singing; improvisation; and vocal techniques such as melisma (several or an elaborate series of notes improvised on a word or syllable in a song lyric), interjected calls and moans, and singer/choir or singer/congregation call and response.[54]

Using 1 Corinthians 14:26 as the biblical base, some Pentecostals refer to a threefold biblical pattern for worship: worship of God, the word of God (Scripture and preaching), and the gifts of the Spirit. While most of us are familiar with the emphasis upon speaking in tongues as a spiritual gift, Pentecostals do not limit spiritual gifts to that alone. Any gift listed in the New Testament is available to worshipers, especially the gifts of prophecy and divine healing.

Recent years have seen a development of serious theological study of Pentecostal beliefs and practices, including music. In one study, Griggs has pointed out that since congregational music consumes "a significant portion of Pentecostal liturgy and practice, musical worship deserves substantial theological inquiry." Griggs argues for a Pentecostal sacramentalism that parallels Pentecostal/Charismatic musical worship with sacraments:

> The interplay of sacramentality and musical worship shows that beyond cognitive and symbolic representation, these practices allow Pentecostals to abide with Jesus in a tangible, perceived reality. Both functionally and semiotically capable of fulfilling a sacramental role in Pentecostal spirituality, music is a sign of God's presence within us, a dynamic context for transformation, and a vehicle of Spirit-empowered unification.[55]

At present, there seems to be little or no organizational structure among Pentecostal groups that can implement what Griggs, and others, are writing about. We will need to visit Pentecostals in the future to see how this interplay of music and theology develops.

---

54. Mosher, "Ecstatic Sounds," 96.
55. Griggs, "Musical Worship," 8, 54–55.

For You to Think About

1. List some outcomes of Vatican II that could be useful to your church in planning for congregational song in worship and explain why you think so? If you believe nothing is useful for your church, then list those outcomes you think would not be useful and tell why you think so.

2. Compare the three-fold pattern of Pentecostal worship with the renewed liturgies of the Reformed Church in America and the Evangelical Lutheran Church in America. What are some similarities? Differences? Do you think congegational song could be a uniting factor between these three Christian groups? If so, how? If not, why not?

10

Congregational Song in Contemporary America

> Christian song is never static, never quite the same from one generation to another. When viewed from two or three decades the changes appear rather small... Differences become more sharply defined over a passing century.[1]

ANYONE WHO HAS BEEN involved with worship leadership over the past twenty-five years knows how the landscape has shifted. Musicians have taken center stage in worship and the influence of popular music has permeated the worship of over fifty percent of the churches in the United States.[2] That popular music would influence worship song is not unique to the latter half of the twentieth century. This has happened often throughout the history of the Christian church, most notably in the late nineteenth century when gospel music was influenced by the popular music of the day.

Congregational song has also been greatly influenced by the many churches and parachurch groups that originated in the twentieth century that have had little or no connection with the worship hymns and songs of previous generations. This influence has been both positive and negative, and that is what this chapter is about.

Seeking a Definition

In today's world, many people will define worship primarily in terms of what kind of music is used and not in terms of a liturgy or a particular order of worship. This is an oversimplification, but this is how the average worshiper probably defines his or her worship service. Some parishioners

---

1. Reynolds, *Survey of Christian Hymnody*, 124.
2. LaRue, "Worship Music Trends," 4.

might even include the style of preaching in addition to the music. Any liturgy or order of service could be contemporary, traditional, or blended if the worship is defined in terms of the music used. Church size, cultural and theological orientation, local social and religious values, the human and financial resources that are available, and the location of the church influence the type of worship a church has.

Contemporary Worship

The word "contemporary" means what is happening right now. Given that definition, all worship today is contemporary. However, there are definite styles of worship in the twenty-first century that are much different than the worship of 100 years ago. Worship styles can affect everything from the choice of songs, as well as how and what instruments will be used for accompaniment. Worship styles are also affected by how the preacher, pastor, or minister presents his or her sermon. In addition to the traditional worship styles discussed in the last chapter, we have two variants: contemporary worship style and blended worship style.

The things that define contemporary worship varies from congregation to congregation, but Womack includes these elements in contemporary worship:

1. Only upbeat popular-style songs are sung, and there are extended times of uninterrupted congregational singing. The aim is to have people hear music in church like they hear at home.

2. So people can hear language they hear and use every day, contemporary English is used. Churches have worship centers rather than sanctuaries and stages rather than chancels. They have opening prayers rather than invocations and talks rather than sermons.

3. Contemporary worship is highly dependent upon electronic technology, such as PowerPoint presentations, videos, and electronic instruments. Organs, Bibles, and hymnals are rarely used.

4. Anything done in "traditional worship," such as hymns, prayers, confessions of faith and passing the peace of Christ, are avoided—though an offering usually is taken. Dress is informal and physical expressiveness is encouraged.

5. Musicians are central in contemporary worship. Often, contemporary worship means "do your own thing"—whatever that may be—with no

guidelines or standards. Traditional liturgies are excluded and worship structure is whatever the worship leaders feels like doing at the time.[3]

It is possible that a church could retain the same liturgy and merely replace hymns with praise songs. This would not be contemporary worship as understood by many people.

Blended Worship

In order to minimize controversy, many churches have started blended worship services. This is basically a traditional service that has "contemporary" instruments and praise songs in addition to choir, organ, and hymns. A church has blended worship if

1. both hymns and contemporary worship songs are sung;
2. words are projected on a screen but a hymnbook is also used;
3. accompaniment is by an orchestra of strings, woodwinds, and brass, drum kit, electric guitars, piano and pipe organ;
4. the leader of worship is a worship pastor or a minister of music and style and dress are a mixture of formal and informal.

Cherry sees this approach as a matter of fulfilling a certain quota of musical styles; a matter of compromise in order to keep people happy.[4] This is a valid concern if the church in question only has one worship service.

Contemporary Worship Music

The term "contemporary worship music" is also problematic. I define "worship music" as music that is appropriate for Christian worship. Contemporary worship music, then, could mean all forms of music that are appropriate for use in Christian churches at the present and would include anthems for choirs, hymnals, cantatas, organ and piano music, choruses, and praise songs. Contemporary worship music could also include concert music with a Christian text. Seldom are these forms of music in mind, however, when people use the term "contemporary worship music." They are thinking mainly of choruses and praise songs, which is not far off the mark since contemporary worship music is the term used to describe the

---

3. Womack, "What Does 'Contemporary Worship' Really Mean?" See also Lim and Ruth, *Lovin' On Jesus*, 2–3.

4. Cherry, "Blended Worship," 6–8.

broad and diverse world of rock and pop music used in worship services around the country. This wedding of popular music and religion is nothing new. The Wesleys, William Booth, and Ira Sankey, for example, all appropriated secular tunes and styles.

Contemporary worship songs tend to use simple, repetitive lyrics, and chords. Contemporary rhythms are syncopated and the strong syllables of text do not always occur on strong beats. Worship songs do not adhere to any particular poetic structure or meter. The musical style of worship songs runs the gamut of popular music styles, everything from rap to bluegrass. "When the semantic dust settles," notes Greg Scheer, "contemporary worship music has come to mean a musical style that originates in contemporary popular culture rather than in church culture." He then adds:

> Critics often focus on the simple or repetitive lyrical structure of contemporary worship songs. Others are critical of what they see as a simplistic theology in some contemporary worship songs. Many have criticized the repetitive rhythms and up-tempo beats, but those who favor this kind of music enjoy its simplicity and its rhythms. They have the perception that this music allows both the congregation and musicians the flexibility to improvise.[5]

In a 1990 church survey, John C. LaRue Jr. discovered that traditional music was the primary style of music in half of American church worship. By 1996 a major shift had occurred with traditional music giving way to contemporary music and blended worship. Nearly half (49 percent) of the churches surveyed chose a traditional style and only 13 percent used a contemporary style; the rest used a blended style. A similar study by LaRue in 2004 showed a surge in the use of contemporary music with a corresponding drop in traditional. In 2004, churches were evenly grouped in each category: 37 percent blended, 32 percent contemporary, and 31 percent traditional.[6]

A Look at the Beginning

As we have seen, the church throughout history has had to contend with new elements being introduced into an existing tradition. The problem has always been the introduction of so-called secular elements into worship, particularly into congregational singing. As Lim and Ruth have observed, "The history of music in contemporary worship is not only about a shift in

---

5. Scheer, *Art of Worship*, 12.
6. LaRue, "Worship Music Trends," 4.

the role and function of music in worship. It is also about the rise of new styles of worship music drawn from popular music."[7]

The desire to have a more popular style of congregational song is due, in part, to a reaction to what is seen as pomp and formality in worship. In previous centuries there was a well-defined distinction between sacred and secular, so the secular arts could be subjected to moral, theological, and intellectual standards to determine their usefulness in worship. We no longer have that ability. Doukhan has defined our modern problem as "the changes that have transformed the modern world in regard to its understanding of the sacred and the secular. Here lies the principal difficulty in adopting secular elements for worship. Today's society is characterized by a great rift between the secular and the sacred. Daily life is no more permeated by the sacred; there are no more laws, no more taboos, no more direction."[8]

Wen Reagan[9] argues that three main motivations fed the rise of contemporary worship music in America: the desire to reach the *lost*, to commune in emotional *intimacy* with God, and to *grow* the flock. These three motivations evolved among different actors and movements at different times, such as

1. the Jesus People movement, anchored in Southern California, adapting the music of the counterculture to attract hippies to church in the 1970s;
2. the Vineyard Fellowship combining rock music forms with lyrics that spoke of God in the second person in order to facilitate intimate worship with the divine in the early 1980s;
3. the church growth movement embracing contemporary worship music as a tool to attract disaffected baby boomers back to church in the late 1980s.

By the 1990s, these three motivations had begun to energize an entire industry built around the merger between secular, popular music and worship.

Gospel Music

The nineteenth-century gospel song was discussed in chapter 8. There, we saw the gospel song had texts that were very personal and reflected how the

---

7. Lim and Ruth, *Lovin' on Jesus*, 59.
8. Doukhan, "Historical Perspectives," 5.
9. Reagan, "Beautiful Noise," 348–57.

individual believer was converted, or how God answered prayer, or the assurance of God's love and grace. There was also an outward appeal to the unconverted, with texts about repentance and faith, how to get to heaven and avoid hell, and the blessings of knowing Christ personally. Twentieth- and twenty-first-century gospel songs have the same textual emphases.

Black Gospel Music

The roots of Black Gospel music are not well documented. However, we know something about the Black experience in the Kentucky Great Awakening and how elements of the camp meeting style of singing and repertoire were absorbed by the indigenous African music of the slaves. These experiences grew and became the norm for worship in the south as Black churches and denominations were developed after the Civil War.

We know that in the Azusa Street Revival, the singing was exuberant and accompanied by hand clapping, foot tapping, or other rhythmic devices such as spoons, drums, and wash boards. The congregation was the choir and it was common to sing with neither instrumental accompaniment nor hymn books. Singers would improvise extra notes as they were "moved by the Spirit." The preaching was dialogical, conducted as a conversation between preacher and congregation. At times it would be difficult to tell the difference between singing and speaking the sermon.[10]

The modern music of jazz and rhythm and blues had a significant influence on the musical form of Black gospel music; they developed together. The form of many early black gospel spirituals is identical to the twelve-bar blues chord progression made popular in secular jazz and rhythm and blues music. Reagan[11] described it as "the fusion of slave spirituals and white Protestant hymnody, combined with the emotional angst of the blues and the syncopated rhythms of jazz." This emerged in the urban storefront Afro-Pentecostal churches in early twentieth-century America.

As Afro-Pentecostals brought the sounds of ragtime, blues, and jazz into the church, they also often brought the accompanying instruments, such as drums, tambourine, triangle, guitar, upright bass, saxophone, trumpet, and trombones. Organs and pianos were not shunned in the Black churches, but they were expensive instruments that were not affordable by storefront congregations. When money was scarce and instruments could not be purchased, folk churches simply sang without accompaniment.[12]

10. Robeck, "Azusa Street Mission," 31.
11. Reagan, "Beautiful Noise," 28.
12. Reagan, "Beautiful Noise," 35.

At first, Black Gospel was not met with enthusiasm in the mainline Black churches. In the 1930s Afro-Pentecostal artists like Arizona Dranes and Sallie Martin and black Baptist artists like Thomas Dorsey and Mahalia Jackson pioneered what we know as Black Gospel music, both in established black denominations and the Afro-Pentecostal and Holiness churches. As black churches came to embrace gospel music, an industry emerged, complete with its own artists, songwriters, record labels, and publishers. Black gospel's birth and development served as a starter for contemporary worship music that influences white Christians in America. Black gospel has made its way into white church hymnals with songs like, "Go Tell It on the Mountain," "Just a Closer Walk with Thee," "Precious Lord, Take My Hand," "To God Be the Glory," and "Children of God, We Are Marching to Zion."

Southern Gospel Music

The development of southern gospel music can be traced to the southeastern region of the United States and is an outgrowth of the singing school movement of the early to mid-1800s. In its modern professional form, southern gospel music comes from a broad-based, post-Civil War culture built around singing schools and community sings that were popular among poor and working-class whites throughout the South and Midwest. The term "southern gospel" was not used to describe this music until the 1970s and it did not gain widespread use until the 1980s. Before then, the music was simply known to its practitioners and fans as gospel music.

Today's southern gospel includes a variety of musical expressions constituting the Protestant evangelical musical universe of the South. Harrison writes that southern gospel music falls into four general types:

> There are songs of celebration . . . as well as more commonplace toe-tappers and other upbeat feel-good songs meant to entertain within the Christian context of praise to God; patriotic and political songs; songs of supplication (any invocation of God's power, help, comfort, or forgiveness); and songs of surrender, which espouse lyrical statements of unworthiness, unmerited favor, or resolutions to abandon the self to God's mercy and direction.[13]

The male quartet with piano accompaniment is probably the most familiar image of southern gospel music. Male quartets traveled a performance

---

13. Harrison, *Then Sings My Soul*, 6. For an analysis of the interaction of lyrics, music, and religious experience in southern gospel music, see Harrison, "Why Southern Gospel Music Matters."

circuit, primarily in the South, promoting songbooks, garden seed, or any other commodity. These quartets are still with us, but their accompaniments may include drums and guitars in addition to piano.

Elvis Presley had a Pentecostal southern gospel upbringing and this is reflected both in his style of singing and the songs he sang. Early in his career he traveled with a southern gospel quartet and featured southern gospel songs in his concerts. Bill and Gloria Gaither's television programs that feature southern gospel singers are still shown weekly on Public Broadcasting System. Some southern gospel songs have made their way into church hymnals, such as "I'll Fly Away," "Victory in Jesus," and "Have a Little Talk with Jesus." Some hymnals are available that contain, with a few exceptions, nothing but southern gospel songs for worship.

The Youth Culture

The years following World War II saw the rise of youth as a distinct category set apart from older generations. A notable component of the youth experience was music, and the advent of the seven-inch 45 rpm single compact disc in 1952 made music easily accessible. These discs were almost indestructible, and easily carried from place to place. The major types of recordings on the market in 1952 were classical, movie theme music, big band, and show tunes distributed by large companies. Production and distribution costs were low for these new 45 singles, and this made it possible for smaller companies to compete and have hit records. The new single discs also made it easier a for small company to start up and for lesser-known soloists and groups to gain recognition for their music. This also made it possible for new forms of Christian songs to be widely distributed.

Choruses

Choruses and chorus singing became popular as a result of a variety of youth camping experiences and youth rallies such as Youth for Christ. I remember going with my friends to Youth for Christ rallies in my teenage years. We sang choruses on Saturday night and hymns and gospel songs on Sunday morning. We never sensed any conflict between the various types of music we were singing. Choruses were already a part of gospel hymnody, so it seemed natural to sing the chorus without the verse.

Individual denominations also had their own retreat centers where youth gathered during the summer: Lake Junaluska, North Carolina (Methodist); Massanetta Springs, Virginia (Presbyterians); Glorieta, New Mexico

(Baptists); and Ridgecrest, North Carolina (Baptist). At these and other similar gatherings, choruses would be borrowed from a variety of sources and then were taken back home by the youth to be sung in their home churches. Publishers picked up on the popularity of the choruses and by 1970 began publishing small paperback collections.

Among the earliest chorus providers was Dave and Dale Garrett, a husband-and-wife duo in New Zealand whose Scripture-based praise choruses made their way into independent charismatic churches in the United States in the late 1960s by way of their first album in 1968, "Scripture in Song." In 1969 they organized "Scripture and Song Music," a company that was devoted to collecting and publishing Scriptural settings for congregational worship. Their roster of songs included Nadia Hern's "Jesus, Name Above All Names," Bob Cull's "Open Our Eyes, Lord," and Laurie Klein's "I Love You, Lord."

Music publishers, including denominational publishers, noted the popularity of choruses and began publishing small paperback collections of these songs. Soon, denominational publishers both in England and the United States began issuing hymnal supplements of choruses to augment congregational singing. From there they made their way into mainline hymnals which were published in the mid and late 1970s. Two examples of choruses included in some hymnals is "Seek Ye First the Kingdom of God" and "Majesty."

The Folk Revival

There was a revival of American folk music in the United States in the 1950s to mid-1960s. The revival included music brought forward from earlier times as well as newly written songs in folk music style. Folk music style contributed to the development of country and western, jazz, rock and roll music, and contemporary Christian music. Folk music was extremely popular in the early to mid-1960s, and the revival included music brought forward from earlier times as well as newly written songs in folk music style.

The "youth musical" became another important influence on the growth in popularity of worship choruses. These productions were used primarily by youth and music leaders as a way to involve the young people in the life of the church. Patterned after current Broadway musicals, the youth musical had a dramatic theme—usually evangelistic—brief bits of dialogue to carry the drama, and songs that gave feeling to the dialogue. The song styles were patterned after the songs of current folk groups such as Peter, Paul, and Mary or The New Christy Minstrels, with occasional excursions into a soft rock style. Many of the songs from youth musicals became standard for congregational song.

Similar changes were occurring in liturgical churches. One of the earliest influences on contemporary Christian music was the work of Geoffrey Beaumont and the "20th Century Light Music Group" in the Anglican Church. In 1956 Beaumont composed an innovative and controversial setting of the Mass in the style of the big Broadway musical of 1950s titled "The 20th Century Folk Mass." Beaumont also set a number of traditional hymn texts to tunes reminiscent of the popular ballads of the1950s.

As we saw in the last chapter, Vatican II had decreed that the congregation should worship through song, and that music other than Gregorian chant and instruments other than the organ could be utilized in the mass. As a result, Catholics embraced the folk Mass as a way to increase lay participation in church services and to create an environment that Catholic youth saw as relevant and authentic to their lives. Inspired by the secular folk song renewal, Catholic musicians rose to the challenge by writing new congregational songs in the folksong revival style of Pete Seeger and others.

These masses still contained many of the traditional elements—prayers, creeds, and communion—but the folk music and guitars became prominent. The folk mass also included priests in casual dress, informal seating and spaces, drumming, and interpretive dance. The songs were primarily original tunes and texts, but could also include new words sung to folk songs or even secular hits.

Reagan[14] tells how this all started with one man named Ray Repp. As a high school student planning on entering the priesthood, Repp listened to folk music like that of the Kingston Trio. He finally bought a Gibson guitar and learned to play, and at the same he discovered the beauty of the psalms and began to compose songs. In 1965 Repp was a volunteer attending orientation for a Catholic society's lay volunteer program in Chicago and was invited to lead worship for four hundred college-age volunteers with his guitar.

The positive response was immediate; the students had never heard this kind of music in a Mass and Repp was surprised by such enthusiasm. The summer program for volunteers held daily Mass, and Repp was busy composing new music constantly. Out of these songs his "Mass for Young Americans" began. At the end of the orientation program, Repp gave each participant copies of his folk tunes as a souvenir. His songs were then transmitted person-to-person by way of paper and mouth around the country.

---

14. Reagan, "Beautiful Noise," 90–95. Reagan's dissertation is an excellent source of information for further study of the history of contemporary worship music, especially in connection with Catholic churches and the personal details of many of the people involved in the development of contemporary worship music.

As Reagan tells it, Repp's "keepsake became a seed carried out by four hundred winds in forty-eight continental states."[15] Over ninety of Repp's songs are still available from Oregon Catholic Press.

Folk music style contributed to the development of country and western, jazz, rock and roll music and contemporary Christian music. It was early 1970 when Protestant "Jesus Music" evolved from popular folk music.

Jesus Music

The year of the Summer of Love and the hippy movement was in full swing in 1967. President Kennedy had been assassinated four years earlier. Protests and demonstrations against the Vietnam War made daily newspaper headlines. The Beatles had released *Sgt. Pepper's Lonely Hearts Club Band* and the garish artwork on the album cover was a snapshot of the social upheaval of the era. In the thick of this, the seed of the Jesus People Movement was beginning to germinate on the West Coast. Many hippies heard Jesus' invitation to live a new kind of life and embraced the gospel message. Within four years "The Jesus Revolution" would be *Time* magazine's front cover.

"From the beginnings of the Jesus People Movement, music was an integral part of its very soul," writes Larry Eskridge.

> Indeed, it is hard to imagine there having been a "Jesus Movement" had there not been "Jesus Music." Whether a home Bible study, a worship gathering of a commune or local "fellowship," the Friday night program at a coffeehouse, or an outdoor festival attracting thousands, "Jesus Music" was a prominent—and frequently the central activity.[16]

"A paradigmatic image of the Jesus Movement was a group of young people sitting in a circle, playing guitars, and singing new devotional songs termed 'Jesus music,'" wrote Ingalls. "Music with Christian lyrics that was set to popular music styles of the day."[17]

A major reason for this influence is that many of the early Jesus Music musicians became followers of Christ as a result of this spiritual awakening. Many of these new converts had been secular musicians and saw no reason to stop playing the music they had always played. At the same time, thousands of young people who had recently become Christ followers found a "sanctified" version of their preferred musical style. Another

---

15. Reagan, "Beautiful Noise," 94.
16. Eskridge, *God's Forever Family*, 254.
17. Ingalls, "Style Matters," 9.

factor is that the Jesus People believed music had no inherent morality; thus, they could readily appropriate the popular music style of Jesus Music with no theological qualms.

Charismatic Renewal

Charismatic renewal began in the 1970s and refers to a new emphasis upon the work of the Holy Spirit in the life of a Christian. The Charismatic Renewal is thought to be God's way of renewing the church, a renewal rooted in the early twentieth-century Pentecostal movement with its emphasis upon manifestations of the Spirit in worship. The beliefs of Charismatic Christians vary widely, so it is difficult to say "all" charismatics believe thus and so. The term "charismatic" comes from the Greek words *charis*, which is the English transliteration of the Greek word for "grace," and *mata*, which is the Greek word meaning "gifts." *Charismata*, then, means "grace gifts." These gifts are also known as biblical "charisms," or special spiritual gifts that supposedly give a person influence or authority over large numbers of people. The prominent gifts among these "charisms" are speaking in tongues and prophesying. Charismatics hold that the manifestations of the Holy Spirit given to the first-century church may still be experienced and practiced today. Listings of spiritual gifts are found in Romans 12, 1 Corinthians 12–14, and Ephesians 4.[18]

Virtually all Christians believe that the presence of God can be experienced in a supernatural way by believers, usually during times of intense spiritual reflection during a worship service, a small group meeting, or personal prayer. The effects of singing songs on this experience is also an important element in this belief.

There are two primary beliefs that define charismatic beliefs from those of other Christians. One is the belief that the "charismatic gifts" of the Holy Spirit, such as tongues, prophecy, and miraculous healing, are still in effect today. Many Charismatics also believe that Bible passages are sometimes misinterpreted in order to declare that charismatic gifts are not valid for today's believers.

The second is the belief that the Baptism of the Holy Spirit is separate from both salvation and water baptism. These primary beliefs are characteristic of the Pentecostal movement as well, but are less dogmatically held by Charismatics. Many Charismatics may experience "speaking in tongues," but not view this as being the Pentecostal phenomenon of Spirit Baptism. Charismatic-like experiences that are thought to be manifestations of the Holy Spirit

18. Boyd and Eddy, *Across the Spectrum*, 212–24, 237–40.

include speaking in tongues, dancing, euphoria, being slain in the spirit, healing power, prophecy, and singing in the Spirit.

For many Charismatics, a liturgy or order of worship, hymns, Scripture readings, organ, choir, and even a sermon, are distractions and barriers to the immediate reception of the Spirit. Therefore, worship is simple and is primarily singing. On the other hand, many people have found a new meaning in the traditional liturgies through their charismatic experiences. This has been the testimony of many Catholics and Anglicans.

Calvary Chapel

The Calvary Chapel church movement was born out of Costa Mesa, California, in the early 1960s. In 1965, the church hired Chuck Smith as its pastor, and under his leadership, the church grew into a fellowship of over 1300 churches. Calvary Chapel presents itself as a "fellowship of churches," in contrast to a denomination, and includes more than one thousand congregations worldwide.[19]

Early in Calvary Chapel's ministry, the church began reaching out to the hippie culture that was so prevalent on California beaches. These hippies were welcomed into Calvary Chapel, and the church began to grow exponentially. The church was among the first to emphasize contemporary worship and a welcoming atmosphere for non-Christians, while at the same time not neglecting the proclamation of the truth of God's word. Worship is charismatic, and this fit the lifestyle of the Jesus People beautifully.

Love Song

Chuck Girard and three of his buddies walked into Calvary Chapel in Costa Mesa, California to play some songs for pastor Chuck Smith at the suggestion of a young hippie preacher named Lonnie Frisbee. These men had been on a two-year spiritual journey, trying various eastern religions and even moving to Hawaii to meditate. Nothing was satisfying spiritually until they came to Calvary Chapel.

They were hippies who had turned their lives over to the Lord only days before, yet they had a few songs they had written before becoming Christians that were about God and Jesus. The pastor thought the songs were of God, and invited them to play at one of the weekly Bible studies.

---

19. More detailed information is available on the Calvary Chapel website: calvarycca.org., including the free document, "The Reproducers," that gives more information on the organization's history.

Within six months the church attendance ballooned from 150–200 people to more than 2000, the media got involved, and the Jesus Movement was off and running.

Chuck Girard and his friends were just writing the same kind of songs they would write if they weren't Christians, but now had Jesus to sing about. The music was called "Jesus Music" and it was a mixture of folk, rock, pop, and country music. It was simple, direct, and anything but subtle in its message of the love of Jesus. They called themselves "Love Song" because they didn't want a religious sounding name, but they were the first Christian rock band to become popular in the United States.

Love Song was named before they ever did Christian music. In an interview, Girard remembered how it happened:

> There was a fella named Jack Schaeffer that came up with the name. He was never in the band but he said, 'I've got a great name for a band!' I think he called it 'The Love Song'. We left the 'The' off. When we got born again a few years later we thought about different names, changing our name. We didn't want to do anything gospelly-sounding or religious-sounding. We thought, well you know, we've got a pretty good name because now our music is about God's love. So we just stuck with the name and just figured we'd tell people, anybody that remembered us from before, we'd say, 'Well the band got born again.'[20]

Love Song was the first Christian rock band to become popular in the United States.

Maranatha! Music

The contemporary Christian music movement was helped immensely by Calvary Chapel. There were several music groups at Calvary, and Chuck Smith was amazed at how this new music had impacted his ministry. Smith privately funded a compilation of the best Calvary Chapel bands. Love Song, Country Faith, and four other groups recorded the album *The Everlasting Living Jesus Music Concert*. The album was an instant success, and in 1971, to "handle the runaway record sales, concert bookings, voluminous follow-up mail and Bible correspondence courses, Calvary formed a subsidiary nonprofit organization called Maranatha Music/Publishing."[21]

---

20. Girard, "Church Girard Remembers," para. 7.
21. Smith and Steven, *Reproducers*, 80–81.

The Vineyard Movement

The Vineyard Movement is an expression of Pentecostal Christianity in the evangelical Protestant tradition. It is known by many Christians today partly through the well-known worship songs that the Movement has produced. The Vineyard network originally developed as a subset of Calvary Chapel churches that emphasized a more "intimate" setting in corporate worship, where intimacy implied folk simplicity in the music, lyrics of adoration expressed in the second person, and emotional expression of the body in worship. The two men primarily responsible for the birth of the Vineyard Movement are Kenn Gulliksen and John Wimber, whose ministries merged in the early 1980s.[22]

A Short History

In 1974 Calvary Chapel sent Ken Gulliksen, the founder of popular Bible studies in Southern California, to West Los Angeles to start a new church. This would be known as the first Vineyard church. From Gulliksen's church, the first Vineyards were planted in 1975. Believing that God had instructed him to do so, Kenn officially gave the name "Vineyard" to this association of churches, and led them for about five years. By 1982, there were at least seven "Vineyards" in a loose-knit fellowship of churches.

From 1950 to 1962, John Wimber had been a professional musician, a songwriter and band member of the famous Righteous Brothers musical group. Wimber had "made it" in the music industry by the early 1960s with two albums in the *Billboard* Top Ten. However, his pursuit of musical success, combined with his hectic schedule, led to the deterioration of his marriage and family life and an impending divorce. He and his wife Carol were able to reconcile and started attending a Friends (Quaker) Bible study where they had a dramatic conversion in 1963 that included convulsing and sobbing on the floor. This resonated with the traditional Quaker concept of "quaking," where the individual, filled with the Holy Spirit, shook with involuntary bodily movements.

From his conversion in 1963 to 1970, Wimber served as a prolific evangelist for his Quaker congregation, the Yorba Linda Friends Church in Yorba Linda, California. In 1970, Wimber joined the church staff as co-pastor and Carol followed him into Quaker leadership as a church elder. Eventually, John Wimber became a pastor in the Calvary Chapel network before doctrinal disagreements caused a separation. In 1982 Wimber's church joined

---

22. Reagan, "Beautiful Noise," 223.

the Vineyard network of churches and Gulliksen anointed him as leader of the movement. In a move from which Wimber would later regress, the Vineyard movement associated with churches that emphasized the practice of modern-day prophecy. But after several failed prophecies, Wimber redirected Vineyard churches to concentrate on church planting.[23]

Church Beliefs

The Vineyard Church did not originally have an official "statement of beliefs" (or an official creed) like other denominations had, but this does not mean beliefs and doctrine are unimportant to the church or its members. Those who were involved in establishing Vineyard churches believed that doctrine kept people from coming to church and feeling a sense of belonging. So, theological dogma has been in the background, instead of the foreground, of the ministry of Vineyard churches. Over time, however, many in the Vineyard body thought it would be wise to clarify and articulate what Vineyard churches believe in order to find unity among like-minded Christians and also to shield themselves from false teachings.

As stated in their *Core Values and Beliefs,* Vineyard churches have been evangelical in belief and practice throughout their history: "As evangelicals, the Bible is our final authority for faith and practice. Therefore, the statements that follow reflect our best attempt to understand and live out biblical precepts . . . the Association of Vineyard Churches Board of Directors has formally adopted . . . our official statement of faith as of the Board meeting of November 1994."[24] At the same time, the church believes that all spiritual gifts mentioned in the New Testament are still available to individual believers, particularly the gifts of healing and prophecy.

Worship Style

Wimber believed that worship drew the heart of God to his people. As worship ascends, God comes down and is experienced as immanent. God was expected to release prophetic words and visions during worship.[25]

---

23. For an excellent discussion of John Wimber's conversion and early years as a pastor, see Reagan, "Beautiful Noise," 223–25. In addition, the official website of Vineyard churches has a page devoted to Wimber, his life, teachings, and legacy. Go to https://vineyardusa.org/about/john-wimber/.

24. Vineyard USA, *Core Values and Beliefs*, 17–20.

25. Basden, *Exploring the Worship Spectrum*, 143. For further information, see *What is Worship?*, a free resource published by Vineyard Resources.

Thus worship has a two-fold aspect: communication with God through the basic means of singing and praying, and communication from God through teaching and preaching the word, prophecy, exhortation, etc. We lift Him up and exalt Him, and as a result are drawn into His presence where He speaks to us.

Using Psalm 95 as a basis, Wimber developed a five-phase model for worship with the goal of "intimacy with God."[26] This involves long, uninterrupted sections of worship to allow people time to offer their whole selves (mind, emotion, and will) to the Lord. Sustained sections of congregational singing require more planning, more skill, and more insight by worship leaders in order to carry them out. Wimber's five-phase model includes

> **Invitation**—like a call to worship. It accepts people where they are and begins to draw them into worship. The feeling of it may be celebratory, upbeat, and praise oriented. The lyric is directed to the people, not to God, and it tells them what they are about to do.
>
> **Engagement**—the people begin to draw near to God, and the lyric is now addressed to God, not one another. Songs are more attentive and serious.
>
> **Exaltation**—the people sing out to the Lord with power, giving meaningful expression to words of transcendence, like *great, majestic, worthy*, etc.
>
> **Adoration**—the dynamic level and the melody range are reduced and lyrics express the closeness of God and some key words may be *you, Jesus*.
>
> **Intimacy**—the quietest time. God is addressed as *Abba* or *Daddy* and lyrics are very personal.

The five phases may end with a closeout chorus or hymn that leads out of intimacy and helps the people to adjust to the next event in the worship service, the time of teaching.

Worship Music

"Both Calvary Chapel and the early Vineyard shared a musical culture rooted in the songs of Maranatha! Music," wrote Reagan.

---

26. John Wimber, quoted in Park et al., *Worshiping with the Anaheim Vineyard*, 117.

Congregational Song in Contemporary America

Both Gulliksen's early Vineyard congregations and Wimber's CCYL shared the same worship music repertoire as Calvary Chapel because they all drew from Maranatha's catalogue. The early Vineyard relied heavily on this shared repertoire of Maranatha songs and helped spread Maranatha's music across the country as new Vineyard churches were planted. Eventually this shared repertoire gave way as John Wimber, Andy Park, Carl Tuttle, Eddie Espinosa and other Vineyard worship leaders began publishing new worship songs for the Vineyard in the mid-1980s. Yet musically, Maranatha's sound continued to shape the sound of Vineyard music.[27]

Each phase of worship would include a set of songs appropriate for that worship event. The idea was to take a musical journey into the presence of God with a seamless, coherent flow of events: the right act of worship at the right place at the right time. Song sets were organized around key relationships, tempo, rhythm, and mood. No song set would include songs with the same tempo, same key, same rhythmic accompaniment, and same mood. To help plan worship music more efficiently, the song repertoire of the congregation was listed alphabetically and organized according to key, tempo, and theme.

Hillsong Church

Hillsong Church, in Sydney, Australia, is an international Pentecostal megachurch affiliated with the Australian Christian churches (formerly known as Assemblies of God in Australia). The church was planted in 1983 as the Hills Christian Life Center by Brian and Bobbie Houston with a congregation of forty-five people. According to the 2014 Annual Report of Hillsong Church, some thirty-four thousand people can be found worshipping at a Hillsong campus each week. Much of the success of the church is due to Hillsong's media arm, of which Hillsong music is the most well known.[28] According to *Christianity Today*, the church now has "over 30 worship services in Australia, plus extension services in multiple languages, including Mandarin, Cantonese, and Spanish. They also have more than ten other independent sites in London, Kiev/Moscow, South Africa, New York City, Paris, Stockholm, Germany, Amsterdam, Copenhagen, Barcelona, and Los Angeles."[29] They have

---

27. Reagan, "Beautiful Noise," 237–38.
28. Hawn, "Congregational Singing from Down Under," 23.
29. Stetzer, "Hillsong Church at a Glance," para. 19.

an estimated one hundred thousand people attending these churches every weekend and more than ten million followers on social media.

Hillsong is a seeker-sensitive church with the goal of reaching those without Christ. As part of the neo-Pentecostal movement, the church espouses a three-part theological position upon which the Hillsong church, its music industry, and its network of churches are built: (1) the prosperity gospel, (2) an emphasis on gifts of the Holy Spirit, and (3) a doctrine of end times that promotes the idea that the coming Kingdom is here and now, not just in the future.

Hillsong Church is unique in that it has used the marketing and branding techniques of business to create an identifiable brand of congregational song in a media-saturated consumer culture. Having a brand is the method of organizing, patterning, and communicating information to consumers about a desirable product. The Hillsong target consumer is the person who wants a deeper spiritual experience of God. In terms of the church's website, if you have found Jesus, have a desire for authentic worship, and are passionate to see God's kingdom established across the earth, we have songs (and other materials) that can help you achieve your siritual objective.

Hillsong's main songwriters are full-time worship pastors who draw a salary from the church and have the time and support to devote to writing songs for services. They are also part of Hillsong's inner circle and are more familiar with the church's vision at any given time. "A strong brand is fluid, changing concomitantly with an organization as it evolves," writes Wagner, "and therefore its music needs to reflect that. From a branding perspective, then, it benefits Hillsong to maintain a core of songwriters who are deeply involved in the 'life of the church.'"[30] The worship songs created by the church revolutionized the church's music ministry to such an extent that the name of the church was changed to Hillsong in 1999. Since that time, Hillsong has been known for the creation of its own brand of worship songs and the development of a distinctive worship style.

Indeed, it is song that best represents the spirit of Hillsong, for its message is inseparable from its song texts and music. There is a continuous outpouring of new song material directed toward believers, for song is the delivery system for Hillsong's authentic worship that leads to a passion for God's Kingdom on earth. Hillsong worship services provide a safe cultural environment where people can seek a deeper experience with God that they can express in tongues speaking and various kinds of physical responses.

In Wagner's study of Hillsong, music is featured in all worship services and the worship is staged like a rock concert with the full complement of

---

30. Wagner, "Hearing the Hillsong Sound," 127.

singers and musicians and sometimes with smoke machines to give additional stage effects. So important is music that there is an almost continuous flow of music throughout the service, even during the prayer time and announcements. At worship the music is loud and worship leaders encourage the congregation to lift up their hands, sway and move with the rhythmic tunes. Hillsong's objectification of the body and the senses is integral to the place given to music at the worship service. Music is almost treated as another sacrament of the church, on a par with communion and baptism. The worship leaders and pastors are seen to be the embodiment of God himself as Hillsong's goal seems to be to translate the infinite God into a tangible entity. This theological idea underpins much of the Hillsong philosophy of ministry and the construction of its worship services.[31] Every service at Hillsong is planned and orchestrated with precision. "The worship leaders who lead worship are given the status of pastors," writes James, "but they appear more as entertainers and performers, using song, television, and media technology in their delivery of the Christian message."[32]

The Hillsong sound is promoted by three bands that tour and feature Hillsong songs and through recordings produced by Hillsong and distributed through commercial recording outlets. Hillsong United is a worship band that originated as a part of Hillsong Church. Formed in 1998 as part of Hillsong's youth ministry, the band consists of several rotating worship leaders from the church. The band tours constantly with a repertoire of primarily Hillsong songs. Their purpose is a commitment "to creating a musical expression that is almost uncomfortable in its uniqueness . . . to write songs that awaken churches and individuals to the fact that we are redeemed and called into the story of God."

There is also Hillsong Worship, a touring band that features Hillsong songs. The difference between Hillsong United and Hillsong Worship is their purpose. The purpose of Hillsong Worship is a commitment "to building the local church . . . to champion passionate and genuine worship of our Lord Jesus Christ in local churches right across the globe . . . to do our part in resourcing local church worship teams across the many denominational faces of The Church."

A third Hillsong touring and recording band is called Hillsong Young and Free. The group was formed in 2012 in Sydney, where they are located at Hillsong Church and whose members are worship leaders in the Hillsong Church. The original Hillsong group began when the members were all relatively young, because it was started as part of the youth ministry at

---

31. Wagner, "Hearing the Hillsong Sound," 142–44.
32. James, "Hillsong Church," 4.

Hillsong Church. As they began having families of their own and take on adulthood, many people at the church felt there was a need for a new group that would aim its message at younger people with a stimulating new sound; Young and Free is the result.[33]

Hillsong music has influenced churches all around the world, including the UK and Europe. A quick look at the CCLI Top 100 for 2019 confirms that worshipers in churches all over the world encounter Hillsong's music every Sunday. In 2018, Hillsong Worship was honored with a number of awards, including a Grammy award for Contemporary Christian Music Performance; a Grammy award for the Top Christian Song; a Dove award for the Worship Recorded song of the year; a Dove award for the Long Form Video of the Year; and a Billboard Music Award. These honors demonstrate the impact Hillsong has on millions of people. In addition, the Billboard listing of the top fifty Christian songs for the week of June 22, 2019 features ten Hillsong songs. All of this is accompanied by various apparel and mementos appropriate for each group.[34]

Contemporary Christian Music

The term "contemporary Christian music," as opposed to "contemporary worship music," is typically used to refer to the Nashville-based pop, rock, and worship Christian music industry. Contemporary Christian music is popular music that is composed and performed by professional bands whose work is not centered primarily in a church and with no intent for their songs to be used primarily for worship. Unlike most other popular music styles, Contemporary Christian music is identified with Christianity lyrically, not musically, and the music style is as varied as is popular music.

In an interview on National Public Radio, Jay Swartzendruber, managing editor of *Contemporary Christian Music Magazine*, commented that contemporary Christian music is "the only genre of music that's defined by its lyrics. I would say it's kind of a manmade box. The purist in me would say that Christian music is actually any music that's created from a Christian perspective . . . But the industry has . . . taken the definition and based it on the lyrics and who distributes the album."[35]

---

33. Readers must visit the church's website to get a better understanding of all that Hillsong is and does. Information about the three Hillsong groups and other information is available on the Hillsong website: https://hillsong.com/music/.

34. National Public Radio, "Contemporary Christian Music." The program can be heard online at https://www.npr.org/templates/story/story.php?storyId=1921620.

35. National Public Radio, "Contemporary Christian Music."

The contemporary Christian music (CCM) industry was started in the early 1970s by evangelicals as an alternative to the secular entertainment business. The goal was to evangelize unchurched youth. Unfortunately, these concerts and recordings attracted youth who were already evangelized. One problem was the quality of early recordings and songs did not equal the quality of popular music recordings. According to Powell, "The scene was once the haunt of radicals ... antiestablishment Jesus freaks whose passionate piety sometimes covered a multitude of theological and musical sins. In the 1980s, it became an industry, and in the 1990s, an empire. In 2001, music categorized as CCM accounted for more than $1 billion in sales, up 12 percent in a year when the recording industry as a whole took a downturn."[36]

Contemporary Christian music exploded in the 1980s with successful crossover recording artists like Amy Grant and Michael W. Smith. Soon, major record labels took notice and began buying out independent Christian labels and transforming them into their own subsidiaries. "At one time, the Christian rock scene was a cultural ghetto," writes Powell, "frequently ridiculed and easily avoided. But now Christian rock is big and loud; it'll shake your windows and rattle your walls."[37] Rabey has observed that "praise and worship music, launched with guitar and tambourine ... has evolved into a multimillion-dollar industry offering a wide array of recordings, videos, publications, and Internet Web services. The industry has transformed the way music is produced and disseminated, and in the process, it has changed the way the church sings."[38]

But is the music any good? More specifically, how does contemporary Christian music hold up artistically as music, and theologically as a reflection of the Christian faith? Artists in the Christian music scene have a tendency to copy the styles of successful mainstream performers in order to provide godly alternatives to whatever is popular at the time. Consequently, value judgments need to be made about a specific group, perhaps, rather than the industry as a whole.

Some bands, whose members are Christians, and Christian solo performers often focus their lyrics on matters concerned with the concept of the Christian faith. The extent to which their lyrics are explicitly Christian varies between bands. Other Christian bands perform music influenced by their faith or containing Christian imagery, but see their audience as the general public and not Christians. They may avoid specific mention of God

---

36. Powell, "Jesus Climbs the Charts," 20.
37. Powell, "Jesus Climbs the Charts," 22.
38. Rabey, "Profits of Praise," 32–33.

or Jesus, or they may write more personal, cryptic, or humorous lyrics concerning their faith rather than direct praise songs.

Christian bands almost never deny their conviction, but typically avoid preaching since they want their music to be entertaining while still containing their message. Some Christian bands do not declare their conviction at all and only concentrate on the entertainment aspect of music. Mark Allan Powell has noted that

> a genre distinction is usually drawn between 'contemporary Christian music' (CCM for short) and 'modern worship music.' The great majority of CCM artists do not envision their music being used in church . . . They expect it to be played in homes and automobiles just like regular pop music. One Christian rock star told me, 'I'm not trying to change what goes on in church. I think it would be a bad idea to make worship more entertaining. I just want to make entertainment more worshipful.'[39]

Jim Bryson, former keyboardist/leader of the band MercyMe, commented in an interview on *Talk of the Nation* that "we write about life experiences and what matters to us . . . We are totally consumed by Christ. And so not every song necessarily is blatant and, you know, uses the word 'Jesus' and 'Christ' in every other sentence, but they're along the same theme. And, you know, whether it's from our perspective or from maybe a non-Christian's perspective, but we try to incorporate everything that we believe in."[40]

Though the professional concert performer does not intend for his or her music to be worship music in churches, contemporary Christian music has made a huge impact on contemporary worship music. People hear songs produced on recordings or heard at concerts, learn to sing them, and then want to experience them in the worship setting of their church. Some contemporary Christian songs are within the performance ability of local congregations, but many of the songs are not appropriate because rhythmic patterns and/or vocal range make it too difficult to sing.

Profit is a primary motive, and commercial interests can influence the criteria for the selection of Christian music. The record companies, publishing companies, various Christian performing groups, and soloists too often determine indirectly what music a church will use because their followers want to sing the same songs in church. This influence can take the form of companies promoting certain recordings and getting Christian radio stations to play them.

---

39. Powell, "Jesus Climbs the Charts," 24.
40. National Public Radio, "Contemporary Christian Music."

This arrangement is advantageous for Christian performers, who want to be heard, but they can find the industry problematic, for if enough records are not sold, or attendance at concerts lags, they could very well be dropped from a recording company's roster. Or, if their lyrics are not sufficiently Christian they will be dropped from Christian radio stations and many people will refuse to buy recordings or concert tickets.[41]

In the same interview on NPR, Jim Bryson described the pressure put upon MercyMe to have a second "hit" song: "When you come out and have a song of the year in the Christian market and sell X-amount of albums and whatever, it's kind of hard to follow that up. And so there was some pressure on us and pressure on the record label, and just everybody in the industry was really going to watch what was happening."[42]

Contemporary Christian music is big business. Jay Swartzendruber reported that in 2003, Christian market albums accounted for seven percent of all album sales. It's almost a $1 billion industry in the US alone. That came about with 47.1 million albums being sold just in 2003. More contemporary Christian music was sold than soundtracks, Latin music, jazz, and classical music combined.[43]

Contemporary Christian Music has had a tremendous impact upon contemporary worship music. After a thorough study of contemporary Christian worship tunes and texts, Margaret Brady identified five styles of contemporary worship music that were the same styles found both in popular rock music and contemporary Christian music. This was based on a study of the 77 most frequently sung worship tunes in the United States between 1989 and 2005. The 77 songs were selected from the Top 25 lists for each of those years published by Christian Copyright Licensing International. Songs with high levels of activity give an idea of the values, priorities and beliefs of worshipping Christians. "Praise and worship music," Steve Rabey writes, "has evolved into a multimillion dollar industry offering a wide array of recordings, videos, publications, and Internet Web services. The industry has transformed the way music is produced and disseminated, and in the process, it has changed the way the church sings."[44]

In reviewing both popular music and the seventy-seven songs by each decade, Brady discovered many similarities between current popular music and the seventy-seven songs as well as many differences. Contemporary Christian music was quick to follow popular music models but

---

41. See Romanowski, "Evangelicals and Popular Music," 103–22.
42. National Public Radio, "Contemporary Christian Music."
43. National Public Radio, "Contemporary Christian Music."
44. Rabey, "Profits of Praise," 32.

it took longer for contemporary worship music to adopt contemporary Christian music styles.[45]

However, there are some signs that the contemporary Christian music industry may be in decline. McCullen wrote that

> CCM is not the cutting-edge genre that it used to be. It has become another corporate (even if certain aspects of it are non-profit) genre of mass appeal music. Too many of its songs sound like your typical love songs in popular culture and lack the theological meat and potatoes. It also lacks the need for critical thinking which has been lost in church worship in recent years. You think hymnody sounds all the same? So does the contemporary worship groups and the churches that back them . . . if not worse.[46]

Vieth gives examples of a lessening interest in contemporary Christian music and concludes, "The descent of CCM is a reflection of America's waning interest in Christianity as a whole. The precipitous dropoff in CCM sales has left Christian labels and artists staring into the void alongside their pastors, scratching their heads, wondering where they went wrong."[47] Godwin comments on Vieth's comments and adds her own thoughts about the decline. She concludes with a very valid question: "Should there even be a Christian worship music industry . . . ?"[48] We will need to wait for the end of this story.

Contemporary Hymns

We have contemporary worship music, but we still have hymns being written and choral material for choirs being published. A study of hymns and choral materials is beyond our scope here, but you need to know that there are things being written, performed, and sung besides contemporary worship songs.

There has been a resurgence of hymns, and this helps bridge the gap between traditional and contemporary worship. As Challies has noted, "There are two different kinds of contemporary hymn. In the first place, we have artists writing new hymns that come complete with new tunes. Alongside that we have artists who are finding old hymns and setting them to new

---

45. Brady, "When I Survey," 154–68.
46. McCullen, "We Must Weaken the Contemporary Music Industry," para. 7.
47. Vieth, "Is Contemporary Christian Music Dead?," para. 7.
48. Godwin, "Is the Contemporary Music Industry Really Dead?," para. 18.

music—either completely new melodies or contemporary adaptations of the traditional ones."[49] Challies mentions Keith Getty and Stuart Townend as examples of writers who produce new hymn tunes and texts. We could add Chris Tomlin, Keith and Kristin Getty, Matt Redman, and others who are writing new hymns in a contemporary style. They, and others, are arranging traditional hymn texts and tunes, but set them to a more contemporary style of accompaniment using keyboard, guitar, bass guitar, and sometimes drums. Three volumes of materials titled "Traditional Hymns for Blended and Contemporary Worship" published by The United Methodist Church is an example of this practice.

Often, traditional texts are retained, but tunes will have a change in the time signature. For example, "Amazing Grace" will be sung in four beats per measure instead of the traditional three beats. In addition to changing meter, hymns that have no chorus will have one added. Chris Tomlin's "My Chains Fell Off" is an example. The original hymn is intact, but there is a chorus or refrain added after stanza two that is a text from a line in Charles Wesley's hymn "And Can It Be," for which Tomlin has composed a new tune. "Thankfully, there are . . . ways to approach our inherited hymnody," comments Parrett. "Many artists are using their creative gifts to write new tunes or arrangements for rich but forgotten texts of old. Others are writing theologically and spiritually weighty choruses and hymns that complement them."[50]

Modern popular culture has become less literary and more visual. Relatively few people in modern culture know about or can relate to classical music. Traditional worship services with hymns and organ accompaniment are equivalent to that which is literary and classical. As minister and contemporary hymn writer Brian Wren points out, classical music and traditional organ/hymn worship services are like a foreign language to most baby boomers, those born after 1946. Consequently, this does not allow anyone who has not studied and/or experienced classical music to worship through traditional church music and to express the joy that comes from that experience.[51]

Contemporary worship music will not go away, so Wren gives us some suggestions about using it in worship. He contends that having separate services for traditional and contemporary worship is divisive. There is always one group that is trying to be "the correct one" and vying with the other. Separate services also go against the Christian concept of inclusiveness.

49. Challies, "Contemporary Hymns," para. 2.
50. Parrett, "Raising Ebenezer," 62.
51. Brady, "When I Survey," 152–66.

We end our journey by giving you these thoughts from Wren that are pertinent for congregational song of any generation, not only the contemporary era: "For congregational music, in any idiom, the test of a song is if an instrumentalist can play it, and a congregation sing it, when the composer is silent or absent. Because congregational song is indispensable, any style of contemporary music needs to be, or become, congregational."[52]

For You to Think about

1. Do you think the Christian publishing/recording industry influences what people want in worship music? Is this a good influence? Explain why you think so.

2. Do you think the quality of contemporary Christian music can be determined primarily in terms of commercial return? What are the reasons for your answer? What other way(s) could quality be determined?

3. How much should churches depend upon the contemporary music industry for sources of song material? Why do you think so?

4. Take the worship order of your church and remold it in two other different styles. For example, if you have contemporary worship, remold your worship order into both traditional and blended styles. What additional and/or different human and music resources would be needed for each? What elements of your present service would need to be eliminated or reworked? What barriers would you need to overcome in order to have these different worship styles in your church?

---

52. Wren, *Praying Twice*, 166.

POSTLUDE
What Have We Learned?

At the beginning of our study I wrote a prelude as a guide for our journey together. As a postlude, let us see what we know for sure about congregational song in the church.

We have discovered that singing has been an integral part of worship. Even in those years when people could not sing in church services, there was religious congregational song outside the church. We have discovered that changes in both theological thinking and the way music is written and performed have impacted congregational song in various ways. We have discovered that congregational song in the twenty-first century, regardless of its form and style, has roots in what has come before, and we have begun to understand those roots and respect them for what they are.

Several questions were raised in the prelude, so a short review of a few of them is in order.

How Does Worship Take Place?

From what little we know at present, people have always worshipped a god or gods. We have visited people who have worshipped in several different ways at various times in history. We have discovered that some ritual activities are both effective and affective and have endured and are used today.

How is Song Used in Worship?

The people of God have worshipped him from ancient times until the present, and the human voice has been the primary instrument used in worship. In our study, the interest has been directed toward how song has been used to worship as a ritual activity. Granted, people can worship without singing, and people can sing without recognizable words, but for the majority of worshipers it is song that is their primary worship involvement.

What Songs are Appropriate for Worship?

In order to worship, the things to be sung must be appropriate. What is appropriate for worship has been the subject of heated debate and denominational division for centuries. At every stop on our historical road, questions are asked about what is appropriate to act, to say, and to sing in the worship of God. In trying to find appropriateness, appeals have been made to the Bible, papal decrees, and church traditions. Councils, synods, and committees have been called to settle the issue, but a final answer is elusive.

We have discovered quite a variety of songs sung by congregations. How and what a congregation sings and has been revised in an attempt to reach a post-Christian world. In many instances, we have found that song has been a driving force behind many changes in worship structure and content.

How is Worship Structured By Song?

On our journey we have discovered that song occurs in some orderly manner, but the structure of the worship service has been determined by a liturgy. Things began to change in the early twentieth century, and currently some worship services are structured around almost continuous congregational song.

What is the Biblical and Theological Context of Worship?

Biblical and theological understandings and cultural settings provide the content of worship, so congregational song as a ritual action differs from one group of believers to another. We have discovered also that worship has a theological basis. What we believe about God, Jesus Messiah, the church, salvation, baptism, the Lord's Supper, and other issues, defines who we are, how we worship, and what we sing.

We discovered that serious differences in theological understandings brought about some major changes and differences in the practice of congregational song. This has not changed today.

I trust you have enjoyed the journey!

APPENDIX I

Zwingli's Zurich Liturgy

IN THE CATHOLIC CHURCH instructions for conducting Mass are called "rubrics" and the same words are said by the priest at each Mass. Members of the congregation may also have their copy of the rubrics for the day and follow everything the priestg is reading. Depending upon the events in the Liturgical Year, there is some variation in the rubrics for the Proper of the Mass. Instructions for both the Ordinary and Proper of the Mass are collected in a book called a "Missal."

In the letter to the King, Zwingli described his new liturgy and included the directions for how the minister should conduct the service. This would be in keeping with Zwingli's previous experience as a Catholic priest. Luther and Calvin would also perceive their liturgies in the same structured way. Notice that the congregation does not sing, but recites.

I have rearranged Zwingli's letter so that the structure of the liturgy is clear. The italics are Zwingli's explanations; the rubrics are not italicized.[1]

Here Follows Substantially the Order of Service We Use at Zurich, Berne, Basel, and the Other Cities of the Christian Alliance:

First, in a sermon of appropriate length is preached the goodness of God which He has shown us through His Son, and the people are directed to the knowledge of this and thanksgiving for it. When this is finished a table is placed in front of the choir, so-called, before the steps; this is covered with a cloth the unleavened bread is placed upon it, and the wine poured into cups.

Then the pastor comes forward with two assistants, and they all turn towards the people, so that the pastor or bishop stands between the others, having on only the usual garb worn by men of

---

1. See **Armstrong**, "From the Archives," 1–2.

standing and ministers of the Church. Then the pastor begins in a loud voice, not in the Latin tongue, but in the vernacular, so that all shall understand what is going on.

Pastor: Let us pray.

Now the church kneels.

Pastor: In the name of the Father, and of the Son, and of the Holy Ghost.

The assistants respond in the name of the whole church, "Amen."

Almighty and everlasting God, whom all creatures rightly worship, adore, and praise, as their Maker, Creator, and Father, grant unto us miserable sinners that we may in sincere faith render that praise and thanksgiving which Thy only begotten Son, our Lord, Jesus Christ, instructed us to do, through that same Jesus Christ, Thy Son, our Lord who liveth and reigneth with Thee, God, in the unity of the Holy Spirit world without end. Amen."

Then the assistant who stands on the left reads, "What is now read is written in the first Epistle of Paul to the Corinthians, eleventh chapter: 'When ye come together therefore into one place, this is not to eat the Lord's Supper,'" (v. 20), and the rest as far as, "not discerning the Lord's body" (v. 29).

Assistants and the Church: Praise be to God.

Pastor: Glory to God in the highest.

Deacon: And on earth peace.

Sub-deacon: To men a sound and tranquil mind.

Deacon: We praise Thee, we bless Thee,

and the rest to the end of this hymn, the assistants reciting it alternately, verse by verse, the Church understanding the whole and admonished at the beginning that each man is to say over in his heart and consider in the sight of God and the Church the things that are said.

Deacon: The Lord be with you.

Assistants: And with Thy spirit.

Deacon: What is now read is written in the Gospel of John, the sixth chapter.

Church: Glory be to Thee, O Lord.

Deacon: Thus spake Jesus, "Verily, verily I say unto you, he that believeth on me hath everlasting life. I am the bread of life. Your fathers did eat manna," etc., to the words, "the words that I speak unto you, they are spirit, and they are life."

Pastor: Glory to God who deigns to forgive all our sins according to His word.

Assistants: Amen.

Pastor: I believe in one God . . .

Deacon: . . . the Father Almighty, Creator of heaven and earth.

Sub-deacon: . . . and in Jesus Christ, His only begotten Son, our Lord . . .

and the rest to the end of the Apostles' Creed, so-called, the ministers repeating it alternately in loud voice just as they did before the hymn, "Glory in the highest."

Pastor: (*Invitation to the worthy celebration of the Supper*): We now desire, dear brethren, in accordance with the custom instituted by our Lord Jesus Christ, to eat this bread and drink this cup, as He commanded should be done in commemoration, praise, and thanksgiving, because He suffered death for us, and poured out His blood to wash away our sins. Therefore, let every man examine and question himself, as Paul suggests, as to how sure a trust he puts in our Lord Jesus Christ, that no one may behave like a believer who yet hath not faith, and so become guilty of the Lord's death, and sin against the whole Church (which is His body) by thus showing contempt for it. Accordingly fall upon your knees and pray, "Our Father which art in heaven," etc., to the end.

*And when the ministers have responded "Amen,"
let the pastor again pray.*

Prayer: Lord, God Almighty, who by Thy spirit hast united us into Thy one body in the unity of the faith, and hast commanded Thy body to give praise and thanks unto Thee for that bounty and kindness with which Thou hast delivered Thy only begotten Son, our Lord Jesus Christ unto death for our sins, grant that we may fulfill this command in such faith that we may not by any false pretenses offend or provoke Thee who art the infallible truth. Grant also that we may live purely as becometh Thy body, Thy sons and Thy family, that even the unbelieving may learn to recognize Thy name and Thy glory. Keep us, Lord, lest Thy name and glory come into ill repute through the depravity of our lives. We always pray, "Lord, increase our faith," that is, our trust in Thee, who livest and reignest, God, world without end.

Church: Amen.

Pastor: (*Then the pastor speaks the sacred words with the following actions*):

The Lord Jesus the same night in which He was betrayed to death took bread

(*Here the pastor takes the unleavened bread into his hands*)

and when he had given thanks, he brake it, and said, "Take, eat: this is my body, which is broken for you; this do in remembrance of me."

(*Here the pastor hands the bread to the ministers who are standing about the table, and they immediately take it with reverence, divide it between them, and eat. Meanwhile the pastor continues*)

After the same manner also he took the cup, when he had supped

(*Here the pastor takes the cup into his hands*)

gave thanks and said, "Drink ye all of it. This cup is the new testament in my blood; this do ye, as oft as ye drink it, in remembrance of me. For as often as ye eat this bread, and drink this cup, ye do shew the Lord's death," (ye praise Him and thank Him) "till he come."

After this the assistants carry round the unleavened bread, and each person takes a piece of the bread with his own hand, and then passes the rest to his neighbor. If any one does not wish to handle the bread with his own hand, the minister carrying it round hands it to him. Then the assistants follow with the cups and hand one another the Lord's cup. Let not Your Majesty shrink from this custom of offering and receiving the elements, for it has often been found that men who had accidentally taken seats next each other when they yet felt enmity and hatred towards each other, have laid aside their angry feelings through this participation in the bread or wine.

> *Another assistant reads again from the pulpit out of the Gospel of John, while the congregation is eating and drinking the sacrament of the Lord's body and blood; beginning at the thirteenth chapter. When all the cups have been brought back, the pastor begins,*

Pastor: Fall upon your knees for we eat and drink the Sacrament of the Supper sitting and silently listening to the word of the Lord

> *and when all kneel, the pastor begins,*

Pastor: Praise, O ye servants, the Lord, praise the name of the Lord.

Deacon: Blessed by the name of the Lord from this time forth and for evermore (Psalm 113:2ff).

Sub-deacon: From the rising of the sun unto the going down, etc.,"

> *and so again the assistants go through alternately this psalm which the Hebrews say used to be said by their ancestors after eating. After this the pastor exhorts the Church in these words:*

Pastor: Be mindful, dearly beloved brethren, of what we have now done together by Christ's command. We have borne witness by this giving of thanks, which we have done in faith, that we are indeed miserable sinners, but have been purified by the body and the blood of Christ which He delivered up and poured out for us, and have been redeemed from everlasting death. We have borne witness that we are brethren. Let us, therefore, confirm this by love, faith, and mutual service. Let us, therefore, pray the Lord that we may keep His bitter death deep in our hearts so that though we daily die to our sins we may be so sustained and increased in all virtues by the grace and bounty of His Spirit that the name of the Lord shall be sanctified in us, and our neighbor be loved and helped. The Lord have mercy upon us and bless us! The Lord cause His face to shine upon us and be gracious unto us! Amen."

Pastor: We give thanks unto Thee, O Lord, for all Thy gifts and benefits, who livest and reignest God world without end. Amen.

Pastor: Go in peace. Amen.

> *Then the church separates.*

APPENDIX II

Presbyterian Church (U.S.A.) Order of Worship

Enter

To Greet One Another in Love

To Be Still and Know that God is God / Prelude

Entrance in Light (*In some churches, acolytes process up the aisle to light the candles on the table.*)

Call to Worship

Hymn(s) of Praise

Confession of Sin and Response

Call to Confession

Confession of Sin

Assurance of Pardon

Response (*Do this in song that comes bursting forth with full-throated praise or reflective wonder.*)

Passing of the Peace

To Hear a Word from the Lord

Prayer for Illumination (*This is a prayer for the Spirit to open our lives to hear God's Word.*)

Scripture

Anthem (*God speaks through many means, including music.*)

Sermon

To Respond in Joyful Service

Affirmation of Faith

Hymn

Reception of New Members

Minute for Mission

Prayer of Intercession

Offering

Doxology/Song of Praise

Prayer of Thanksgiving

The Lord's Prayer

To Go Forth to Serve

Hymn

Charge (*We are charged to be faithful ministers of Christ in the world we're going back into.*)

Benediction

Postlude (*We exit through the curtain of music in which we came.*)

Bibliography

Alban, Don, Jr. "Thomas Cranmer and the English Reformation: A Gallery – Reform from on High." *Christian History Magazine* 48 (1995) 16–17.
Apel, Willi. *Gregorian Chant*. 1698. Reprint ed. Bloomington: Indiana University Press, 1990.
Appel, Richard G., ed. *The Music of the Bay Psalm Book*. 9th ed. Brooklyn: Institute for Studies in American Music, Brooklyn College of the City University of New York, 1969.
Archer, Kenneth J. "A Pentecostal Way of Doing Theology: Method and Manner." *International Journal of Systematic Theology* 9 (2007) 301–14.
Armstrong, Chris R. "The Amazingly Graced Life of John Newton." *Christian History Magazine* 81 (2004) 11–19.
———. "From the Archives: Replacing the Mass with a New Order of Worship." *Christian History Magazine* 4 (1985) 1–2.
Armstrong, Karen. *A Short History of Myth*. New York: CanonGate, 2005.
Ayris, Paul. "Destroying the Monasteries." *Christian History Magazine* 48 (1995) 1–17.
Bainton, Roland. *Here I Stand*. New York: Abingdon, 1950.
Barry, A. L. *What About Lutheran Worship?* Burns, WY: Steadfast Lutherans, 2000.
Barry, Alfred. "A History of the Articles." *Anglican Way Magazine,* February 22, 2014. https://anglicanway.org/2014/02/22/a-history-of-the-thirty-nine-articles/.
Barton, George A. "Ashtoreth and Her Influence in the Old Testament." *Journal of Biblical Literature* 10 (1891) 73–91.
———. "A Liturgy for the Celebration of the Spring Festival at Jerusalem in the Age of Abraham and Melchizedek." *Journal of Biblical Literature* 53 (1934) 61–78.
Basden, Paul. *Exploring the Worship Spectrum: Six Views*. Grand Rapids: Zondervan, 2004.
Becker, Laura A. "Ministers vs. Laymen: The Singing Controversy in Puritan New England, 1720–1740." *The New England Quarterly* 55 (1982) 79–96.
Beckwith, R. T. "The Jewish Background to Christian Worship." In *The Study of Liturgy*, edited by Cheslyn Jones et al., 68–79. Rev. ed. London: SPCK, 1992.
———. "Thomas Cranmer and the Prayer Book." In *The Study of Liturgy*, edited by Cheslyn Jones et al., 101–5. Rev. ed. London: SPCK, 1992.
Birge, Edward B. *History of Public School Music in the United States*. New York: Harper & Row, 1955.
Black, Cristopher F., and Pamela Gravestock, eds. *Early Modern Confraternities in Europe and the Americas*. Aldershot, UK: Ashgate, 2006.

Block, Daniel I. *For the Glory of God: Recovering a Biblical Theology of Worship*. Grand Rapids: Baker Academic, 2014.

Bloesch, Donald G. "Whatever Happened to God?" *Christianity Today* 45.2 (February 5, 2001) 54–55.

Blume, Friedrich. *Protestant Church Music*. New York: Norton, 1974.

Boonstra, Harry. "Old-Fashioned Innovations: There's More than One Way to Celebrate the Lord's Supper." *Reformed Worship* 22 (December 1991). https://www.reformedworship.org/article/december-1991/old-fashioned-innovations-theres-more-one-way-celebrate-lords-supper.

Boyd, Gregory A., and Paul R. Eddy. *Across the Spectrum: Understanding Issues in Evangelical Theology*. Grand Rapids: Baker Academic, 2002.

Bradshaw, Paul F. *The Search for the Origins of Christian Worship*. London: SPCK, 1992.

Brady, Margaret. "When I Survey the Wondrous Cross." In *The Message in the Music*, edited by Robert Woods and Brian Walrath, 154–68. Nashville: Abingdon, 2007.

Bringle, Mary Louise. "Debating Hymns." *The Christian Century* 130.9 (May 1, 2013) https://www.christiancentury.org/article/2013-04/debating-hymns.

———. "Singing from One Book: Why Hymnals Matter." *The Christian Century* 130.9 (May 1, 2013) https://www.christiancentury.org/article/2013-04/singing-one-book.

Bruce, F. F. "Colossian Problems, Pt. 2: The 'Christ Hymn' of Colossians 1:15–20." *Bibliotheca Sacra* 141 (1984) 99–111.

Brueggemann, Walter. *Worship in Ancient Israel: An Essential Guide*. Nashville: Abingdon, 2005.

Burge, Gary M. *John*. NIV Application Commentary. Grand Rapids: Zondervan, 2000.

Burgh, Theodore W. "Music and Musical Instruments in the Hebrew Bible and Ancient Israel/Palestine." http://www.bibleinterp.com/commentary/comment_BiblicalInterpretation.htm.

Burrage, Henry S. *A History of the Anabaptists in Switzerland*. Philadelphia: American Baptist Publication Society, 1882.

Buszin, Walter E. "Luther on Music." *Musical Quarterly* 32 (1946) 80–97.

Campbell, Donna R. "A Compendium of Musical Instruments and Instrumental Terminology in the Bible." *Theological Librarianship* 3 (2010) 48–50.

———. "Critical Review." Review of *A Compendium of Musical Instruments and Instrumental Terminology in the Bible* by Yelena Kolyada. *Theological Librarianship* 3.2 (2010) 48–51.

Challies, Tim. "Contemporary Hymns." https://www.challies.com/resources/contemporary-hymns/.

Charlemagne. "Admonitio Generalis." https://barbarian_europe.enacademic.com/2/Admonitio_Generalis.

Chase, Gilbert. *America's Music, from the Pilgrims to the Present*. Rev. ed. Urbana: University of Illinois Press, 1992.

Cherry, Constance. "Blended Worship: What It Is, What It Isn't." *Reformed Worship* 55 (March 2000) 6–8.

Church, R. W. *The Oxford Movement: Twelve Years, 1833–1845*. London: Macmillan, 1900.

Churchmouse Campanologist. "Changes in Lutheran Liturgy from the 1950s to the Present." https://churchmousec.wordpress.com/2015/03/11/changes-in-lutheran-liturgy-from-the-1950s-to-the-present/.

Colson, Charles, with Anne Morse. "Soothing Ourselves to Death." *Christianity Today* (April 1, 2006) 116.
Committee on Congregational Song. *Glory to God: the Presbyterian Hymnal*. Louisville: Westminster John Knox, 2012.
Commission on Worship, "The Theology and Place of Worship." https://www.rca.org/resources/theology-and-place-music-worship.
Cones, Bryan. "The 78th General Convention of the Episcopal Church and the Liturgy: New Wine in Old Wineskins?" *Anglican Theological Review* 98.4 (Fall 2016) 681–701.
Contzius, Erik. "Why Do We Sing?" https://contzius.com/why-do-we-sing/.
Coogan, Michael David. *The Old Testament: A Historical and Literary Introduction to the Hebrew Scriptures*. 3rd ed. Oxford: Oxford University Press, 2014.
———, ed. and trans. *Stories from Ancient Canaan*. Philadelphia: Westminster 1978.
Cotton, John. "An Admonition to the Reader." In *The Digital Bay Psalm Book: A Virtual Reconstruction of the New World's First English–Language Book*, edited by Ian Christie-Miller et al., 304. Tuscaloosa: University of Alabama Press, 2010.
———. "Preface." In *The Digital Bay Psalm Book: A Virtual Reconstruction of the New World's First English–Language Book*, edited by Ian Christie-Miller et al., 13–25. Tuscaloosa: University of Alabama Press, 2010.
Curry, Andrew. "Gobekli Tepe: The World's First Temple?" *Smithsonian*, November 2008. https://www.smithsonianmag.com/history/gobekli-tepe-the-worlds-first-temple-83613665/.
Curwen, Spencer. *Studies in Worship Music: Chiefly as Regards Congregational Singing*. London: Curwen, 1880.
Danielson, Robert A. "From the Archives: Methodist Camp Meetings and Revival." *The Asbury Journal* 68 (2013) 160–64.
David, Rosalie. *The Ancient Egyptians: Beliefs and Practices*. 2nd ed. Eastbourne, UK: Sussex Academic, 1998.
Day, John, ed. *Temple and Worship in Biblical Israel*. London: T. & T. Clark, 2007.
Dever, William. "Archaeology of the Hebrew Bible." *Nova*, November 17, 2008. https://www.pbs.org/wgbh/nova/article/archeology-hebrew-bible/.
Dilley, Paul. "Jesus as Lord of the Dance: From Early Christianity to Medieval Nubia." *Bible History Daily* (blog), August 8, 2014. https://www.biblicalarchaeology.org/daily/people-cultures-in-the-bible/jesus-historical-jesus/jesus-as-lord-of-the-dance/.
Doukhan, Lilianne. "Historical Perspectives on Change in Worship Music." *Ministry* (September 1996) 7–10.
———. "Music in the Bible." *Shabbat Shalom* 49.2 (Autumn 2002) 18–25.
Dowley, Tim. *Christian Music: A Global History*. Minneapolis: Fortress, 2011.
———, ed. *Introduction to the History of Christianity*. 2nd ed. Minneapolis: Fortress, 2013.
Drain, Susan Carolyn Mary. "A Study of 'Hymns Ancient and Modern,' 1860–1875." PhD diss., Kings College London University, 1985.
Drury, John. "John Wesley and the Shaping of Liturgical Time." http://www.drurywriting.com/john/Wesley%20and%20Time.htm.
Duggan, Stephen. *The History of Education*. New York: Scribner's, 1948.
Dunn, Brian J. *On the Occasion of the 50th Anniversary of the Constitution on the Sacred Liturgy*. Latham, NY: Roman Catholic Diocese of Albany, 2013.

Dyrness, William A. *A Primer on Christian Worship: Where We've Been, Where We Are, Where We Can Go*. Grand Rapids: Eerdmans, 2009.

Easton, Burton Scott, trans. *The Apostolic Tradition of Hippolytus*. Cambridge: Cambridge University Press, 2014.

Eisenberg-Degen, Davida. "Archaeological Views: The Archaeology of Scribbles." *Biblical Archaeology Review* 38 (2012) 24, 61–62.

Ellinwood, Leonard. *The History of American Church Music*. New York: Morehouse-Gorham, 1953.

———. "Wesley's First Hymnal was Never Officially Condemned." *The Hymn* 12.2 (April 1961) 56–59.

Elliott, Ralph H. *The Message of Genesis*. Nashville: Broadman, 1961.

Eskridge, Larry. *God's Forever Family*. New York: Oxford University Press, 2013.

Etherington, Charles L. *Protestant Worship Music: Its History and Practice*. 1962. Reprint, Westport, CT: Greenwood, 1978.

Evangelical Lutheran Church of America. *Principles for Worship*. Chicago: Evangelical Lutheran Church of America, 2002.

Farrer, Katie. "'Sing to the Lord a New Song': The Regular Singing Movement in Colonial New England." *The Gettysburg Historical Journal* 3, Article 4. https://cupola.gettysburg.edu/ghj/vol3/iss1/4.

Fellerer, Karl Gustav. "Church Music and the Council of Trent." *The Musical Quarterly* 39 (1953) 576–94.

Fisher, Warren. *The Illustrated History of the Roman Empire*. Bloomington, IN: AuthorHouse, 2010.

Foley, Edward. *Foundations of Christian Music*. Nottingham, UK: Grove, 1992.

Folger, Tim, and Shanti Menon. "... Or Much Like Us?" *Discover* (January 1997). http://discovermagazine.com/1997/jan/ormuchlikeus1026.

Forbes, Bruce David, and Jeffrey H. Mahan, eds. *Religion and Popular Culture in America*. Berkeley: University of California Press, 2005.

Fortescue, Adrian. "Sanctus." In *The Catholic Encyclopedia*, vol. 13. New York: Appleton, 1912. http://www.newadvent.org/cathen/13432a.htm.

Foster, Douglas Allen, et al., eds. *The Encyclopedia of the Stone-Campbell Movement: Christian Church (Disciples of Christ), Christian Churches/Churches of Christ, Churches of Christ*. Grand Rapids: Eerdmans, 2004.

Frassetto, Michael. *Encyclopedia of Barbarian Europe: Society in Transformation*. Santa Barbara, CA: ABC-CLIO, 2003.

Galli, Mark. "A Deeper Relevance." *Christianity Today* 52.5 (May 2008) 38–41.

———. "Martin Luther's Later Years." *Christian History Magazine* 39 (1993) 1–9.

———. "Persecution in the Church: A Gallery of the Persecuting Emperors." *Christian History Magazine* 27 (1990) 1–3.

———. "Revival at Cane Ridge." *Christian History Magazine* 45 (1995) 45.

———. "Thomas Cranmer and the English Reformation: Did You Know?" *Christian History Magazine* 48 (1995) 1–2.

Garside, Charles, Jr. "Calvin's Preface to the Psalter: a Re-appraisal." *Musical Quarterly* 37 (1951) 566–77.

———. "The Origins of Calvin's Theology of Music: 1536–1543." *Transactions of the American Philosophical Society* 69 (1979) 1–36.

———. *Zwingli and the Arts*. New Haven: Yale University Press, 1966.

Gates, J. Terry. "Music Education's Professional Beginnings in America: Early Eighteenth-Century New England Singing-School Teacher Qualifications and Program Goals." *The Quarterly Journal of Music Teaching and Learning* 16.1–2 (2010) 43–48.

Ghose, Tia. "Oldest Grave Flowers Unearthed in Israel." https://www.livescience.com/37881-ancient-grave-flowers-unearthed.html.

Gilley, Gary E. "Pentecostalism." http://www.rapidnet.com/~jbeard/bdm/Psychology/char/more/pente.htm.

Girard, Chuck. "Church Girard Remembers." *Cross Rhythms* October 8, 2006. http://www.crossrhythms.co.uk/articles/music/Love_Song__Chuck_Girard_remembers_his_days_with_the_pioneers_of_Christian_rock/24251/p1.

Godfrey, W. Robert. "Calvin and the Worshp of God." *Resource Center*. April 1, 2007. https://www.wscal.edu/resource-center/calvin-and-the-worship-of-god.

———. "Contemporary Christian Music." https://banneroftruth.org/us/resources/articles/2003/contemporary-christian-music/.

———. "Reforming the Church's Singing." https://www.wscal.edu/resource-center/reforming-the-churchs-singing.

Godwin, Susan F. "Is the Contemporary Music Industry Really Dead?"https://christiancopyrightsolutions.com/blog/is-the-contemporary-christian-music-industry-really-dead/.

Gould, Nathaniel D. *Church Music in America*. Boston: Johnson, 1852.

Gradenwitz, Peter. *The Music of the Jews*. New York: Norton, 1949.

Graves, Dan. "#203: Life of Charlemagne." https://christianhistoryinstitute.org/study/module/charlemagne.

———. "Charlemagne Crowned as Holy Roman Emperor." http://www.christianity.com/church/church-history/timeline/601-900/charlemagne-crowned-as-holy-roman-emperor-11629758.html.

Grew, Eva M. "Martin Luther and Music." *Music and Letters* 19 (1938) 67–78.

Griggs, Richard I. "Musical Worship as a Pentecostal Sacrament: Toward a Soteriological Liturgy." Southeastern University Selected Honors Theses 64 (2017).

Haïk-Vantoura, Suzanne. *The Music of the Bible Revealed: The Deciphering of a Millenary Notation*. Edited by John Wheeler. Translated by Dennis Weber. 2nd rev. ed. North Richland Hills, TX: Scott, 1991.

Hammond, Susan L. "To Sing or Not to Sing: Music and the Religious Experience from 1500–1700." *International Journal of Religion & Spirituality in Society* 3 (2014) 67–76.

Haraszti, Zoltan. *The Enigma of the Psalm Book*. Chicago: University of Chicago Press, 1956.

Harder, Gary. "Congregational Singing as a Pastor Sees It." In *The Pastor-Congregation Duet*, edited by Bernie Neufeld, 107–20. Victoria, BC: Friesen, 1998.

Harmon, Kathleen. *The Mystery We Celebrate, the Song We Sing: A Theology of Liturgical Music*. Collegeville, MN: Liturgical, 2008.

Harrison, Douglas. *Then Sings My Soul: The Culture of Southern Gospel Music*. Urbana: University of Illinois Press, 2012.

———. "Why Southern Gospel Music Matters." *Religion and American Culture: A Journal of Interpretation* 18 (2008) 27–58.

Hawkins, Frank. "The Didache." In *The Study of Liturgy*, edited by Cheslyn Jones et al., 84–86. London: SPCK, 1992.

Hawn, C. Michael. "Congregational Singing from Down Under: Experiencing Hillsong's 'Shout to the Lord.'" In *The Hymn: A Journal of Congregational Song* 57 (2006) 23.

Heyrman, Christine Leigh. "The First Great Awakening." http://nationalhumanities center.org/tserve/eighteen/ekeyinfo/grawaken.htm.

Holleman, A. W. J. "The Oxyrhynchus Papyrus 1786 and the Relationship between Ancient Greek and Early Christian Music." *Vigiliae Christianae* 26 (1972) 1–17.

Hooper, William. *Church Music in Transition*. Nashville: Broadman, 1963.

———. *Worship History for Worship Leaders*. Petersburgh, VA: Alexander, 2010.

Hope, Norman V. *Isaac Watts and His Contribution to English Hymnody*. New York: Hymn Society of America, 1947.

Howard, Jay R., and John M. Streck. *Apostles of Rock: The Splintered World of Contemporary Christian Music*. Lexington: University Press of Kentucky, 1999.

Hubbard, W. L., ed. *American History and Encyclopedia of Music*. Toledo, OH: Squire, 1910.

Huebsch, Bill. "How Did Vatican II Change the Mass?" *U.S. Catholic* 68.3 (March 2003) 39.

Hunter, A. M. *Paul and His Predecessors*. London: SCM, 1940.

Hurowitz, Victor Avigdor. "YHWH's Exalted House—Aspects of the Design and Symbolism of Solomon's Temple." In *Temple and Worship in Biblical Israel*, edited by John Day, 63–110. London: T. & T. Clark, 2007.

Hurtado Larry W. *At the Origins of Christian Worship*. Grand Rapids: Eerdmans, 1999.

———. "On 'Hymns' in the New Testament: A Suggestion." https://larryhurtado. wordpress.com/2015/05/11/on-hymns-in-the-new-testament-a-suggestion/.

Huyser-Honig, Joan. "Contemporary Worship Music Matures." https://worship.calvin. edu/resources/resource-library/contemporary-worship-music-matures/.

Hylen, Susan. "Commentary on Ephesians 5:15–20." https://www.workingpreacher. org/preaching.aspx?commentary_id=376.

Idelsohn, Abraham Z. *Jewish Music in Its Historical Development*. New York: Holt, 1929.

Ingalls, Monique M. "Style Matters: Contemporary Worship Music and the Meaning of Popular Musical Borrowings." *Liturgy* 32 (2017) 7–15.

Irwin, Joyce. "The Theology of 'Regular Singing.'" *The New England Quarterly* 51 (1978) 176–92.

Jackson, George Pullen. *White and Negro Spirituals*. New York: Augustin, 1944.

Jackson, Samuel. *Huldreich Zwingli: The Reformer of German Switzerland*. London: Putnam's, 1901.

James, Jonathan D. "Hillsong Church: Postmodern Parishes, World-Wide Music and Anointed Acquisitions." In *Transnational Religious Movements: Faith's Flows*, edited by Jonathan D. James, 1–5. Thousand Oaks, CA: Sage, 2017.

Jensen, Paul. "Devotio Moderna." In *The Encyclopedia of Christian Civilization*, edited by George T. Kurian. Malden, MA: Blackwell, 2011.

Johansen, John Henry. *The Olney Hymns*. New York: Hymn Society of America, 1956.

John Paul II, Pope. *Chirograph on Sacred Music*. Rome: Congregation for Divine Worship and Discipline of the Sacraments, 2003.

Jones, Cheslyn, et al., eds. *The Study of Liturgy*. Rev. ed. London: SPCK, 1992.

Julian, John. *A Dictionary of Hymnology*. New York: Scribner's, 1892.

Kaske, Robert E., et al. *Medieval Christian Literary Imagery: A Guide to Interpretation*. Toronto: University of Toronto Press, 1988.

Keen, Karen R. "Beyond Sacred Marriage: A Proposed New Reading of 'Birth of the Beautiful and Gracious Gods' (KTU1.23)." ThM thesis, Duke University Divinity School, 2010.

Kelsey Museum. "Ancient Egyptian Instruments." http://www.umich.edu/~kelseydb/Exhibits/MIRE/Introduction/AncientEgypt/AncientEgypt.html.

Kiefer, James E. "Hildegard Bingen, Visionary." *Biographical Sketches of Memorable Christians of the Past*. Woods Hole, MA: Society of Archbishop Justus, 1999. http://justus.anglican.org/resources/bio/247.html.

Kilmer, Anne Draffkorn. "The Discovery of an Ancient Mesopotamian Theory of Music." *Proceedings of the American Philosophical Society* 115.2 (Apr. 22, 1971) 131–49.

Kilmer, Anne Draffkorn, and Miguel Civil. "Old Babylonian Musical Instructions Relating to Hymnody." *Journal of Cuneiform Studies* 38 (1986) 94–98.

———. "The Oldest Song in the World." *Archaeologia Musicalis* (February 1988) 35–36.

King, Barbara J. "Were the Neanderthals Religious?" *13.7: Cosmos and Culture*, (December 7, 2016). https://www.npr.org/sections/13.7/2016/12/07/504650215/were-neanderthals-religious.

———. "The World's First Temple! Or . . . not?" *13.7 Cosmos and Culture* (October 13, 2011). https://www.npr.org/sections/13.7/2011/10/13/141216522/the-worlds-first-temple-or-not.

Kirby, Peter. "Didache." http:www.earlychristianwritings.com/didache.html.

Klassen, Walter. "A Fire That Spread: Anabaptist Beginnings." *Christian History Magazine* 5 (1985) 4–7.

Knust, Jennifer, and Tommy Wasserman. "The Biblical Odes and the Text of the Christian Bible: A Reconsideration of the Impact of Liturgical Singing on the Transmission of the Gospel of Luke." *Journal of Biblical Literature* 133.2 (Summer 2014) 341–65.

Korpel, Marjo C. A., and Johannes C. de Moor. *Adam, Eve, and the Devil: A New Beginning*. Sheffield: Sheffield Phoenix, 2014.

Kulp, Joshua. "Arakhin, Chapter Two, Mishnah Three." http://learn.conservativeyeshiva.org/arakhinchapter-two-mishnah-three/.

———. "Rosh Hashanah, Chapter Three, Mishnah Three." http://learn.conservativeyeshiva.org/rosh-hashanah-chapter-three-mishnah-three/.

Lambert, Erin M. "'In Corde Iubilum': Music in Calvin's Institutes of the Christian Religion." *Reformation & Renaissance Review* 14 (2012) 269–87.

Lang, Paul Henry. *Music in Western Civilization*. Rev. ed. New York: Norton, 1997.

LaRue, John C., Jr. "Contemporary Worship Music Growth Slows." http://www.christianitytoday.com/yc/9y6/9y6080.htm.

———. "Worship Music Trends." http://www.christianitytoday.com/yc/2004/004/7.64.html.

Le Huray, Peter. *Music and the Reformation in England, 1549–1660*. Cambridge: Cambridge University Press, 1978.

Leonard, David C. "Davidic Worship: A Model for Renewal." https://www.laudemont.org/a-dwmfr.htm.

Levinson, Jerrold. "The Concept of Music." In *Music, Art, and Metaphysics*, edited by Jerrold Levinson, 267–78. New York: Oxford University Press, 2011.

Levy, Kenneth. "Charlemagne's Archetype of Gregorian Chant." *Journal of the American Musicological Society* 40.1 (1987) 82–102.
Lightfoot, J. B., trans. "The Didache." http://www.earlychristianwritings.com/text/didache-lightfoot.html.
Lim, Swee Hong, and Lester Ruth. *Lovin' on Jesus: A Concise History of Contemporary Worship*. Nashville: Abingdon, 2019.
Lloyd, Rebecca. "Bach: Luther's Musical Prophet?" *Current Musicology* 83 (2007) 5–32.
Loades, David. "Why Queen Mary Was Bloody." *Christian History* 14.4 (1995) 38–54.
Loewe, J. Andreas. "Why Do Lutherans Sing? Lutherans, Music, and the Gospel in the First Century of the Reformation." *Church History* 82 (2013) 69–89.
Lord, Suzanne. *Music in the Middle Ages: A Reference Guide*. Westport, CT: Greenwood, 2008.
Lovelace, Austin. "Early Sacred Folk Music in America." *The Hymn* 3 (1932) 11–14, 56–63.
Lowens, Irving, "Our Neglected Musical Heritage." *The Hymn* 3 (1932) 49–55.
MacDougall, Scott, et al. "Revising the Episcopal Church's *Book of Common Prayer* (1979): Liturgical Theologians in Dialogue." *Anglican Theological Review* 99.3 (Summer 2017) 499–518.
Mackenzie, Cameron A. "Worshiping in the 21st Century: Taking Our Cue from Martin Luther." Unpublished essay delivered to the Evangelical Theological Society, Midwest Region, March 23, 2001.
Manniche, Lise. *Music and Musicians in Ancient Egypt*. London: British Museum, 1991.
Marini, Stephen A. *Sacred Song in America*. Urbana: University of Illinois, 2003.
Martin, Ralph. "Aspects of Worship in the New Testament Church." *Vox Evangelica* 2 (1963) 6–32.
———. *Carmen Christi: Philippians 2:5–11 in Recent Interpretation and in the Setting of Early Christian Worship*. Society for Biblical Literature Monograph Series 4. Cambridge: Cambridge University Press, 1967.
———. "An Early Christian Hymn (Col. 1:15–20)." *The Evangelical Quarterly* 36 (1964) 195–205.
———. "Some Reflections on New Testament Hymns." In *Christ the Lord: Studies in Christology Presented to Donald Guthrie*, edited by Harold H. Rowdon, 37–49. Leicester, UK: InterVarsity, 1982.
———. *Worship in the Early Church*. Rev. ed. Grand Rapids: Eerdmans, 1974.
Martyr, Justin. "First Apology 67: Weekly Worship of the Christians." https://www.ccel.org/ccel/schaff/anf01.viii.ii.lxvii.html.
Mason, Paul. "The Pastoral Implications of John Paul II's Chirograph for the Centenary of the Motu Proprio 'Tra Le Sollecitudini' on Sacred Music." *Worship* 82 (2008) 386–412.
Mbzt. "Baal Cycle Tablets." *Ancient History Encyclopedia*. https://www.ancient.eu/image/9403/.
McBeth, H. Leon. *The Baptist Heritage*. Nashville: B&H, 2014.
McClaren, Rob C. "A Wesleyan Theology of Worship and Its Development in Free Methodism." DMin diss., Fuller Theological Seminary, 2003. www.clfmc.homestead.com/files/Dissertation.pdf.
McClure, M. L., and C. L. Feltoe, trans. *The Pilgrimage of Etheria*. New York: Macmillan, 1919.

McCullen, Don. "We Must Weaken the Contemporary Christian Music Industry." *The Christian Post*, March 7, 2018. https://www.christianpost.com/voice/we-must-weaken-the-contemporary-christian-music-industry.htm

McGowan, Andrew B. *Ancient Christian Worship*. Grand Rapids: Baker, 2014.

McIntyre, Dean. "Did the Wesleys Really Use Drinking Song Tunes for Their Hymns?" https://www.umcdiscipleshnip.org/resources/did-the-wesleys-really-use-drinking-song-tunes-for-their-hymns.

McKinnon, James, ed. *Music in Early Christian Literature*. Cambridge: Cambridge University Press, 1987.

Mead, G. R. S. "Hymn of Jesus." In *Music in History*, edited by Howard D. McKinney and W. R. Anderson, 76–77. New York: American Book, 1957.

Metzger, Marcel. *History of the Liturgy*. Collegeville, MN: Liturgical, 1997.

Miller, Kevin. "From the Editor—Silent String." *Christian History Magazine* 31 (1991) 3–4.

Minneapolis Institute of Fine Art. "World Myths and Legends in Fine Arts." http://www.artsmia.org/world-myths.

Monson, Craig A. "The Council of Trent Revisited." *Journal of the American Musicological Society* 55 (2002) 1–37.

Mosher, Craig. "Ecstatic Sounds: The Influence of Pentecostalism on Rock and Roll." *Popular Music and Society* 31.1 (2008) 95–112.

Murray, John. "The Calling of the Westminster Assembly." https://www.apuritansmind.com/westminster-standards/the-calling-of-the-westminster-assembly/.

Nadel, Dani. "Archaeological Views: Why People Interested in Biblical Archaeology Should Also Be Interested in the Prehistory of the Land of Israel." *Biblical Archaeology Review* 40 (2014) 24–25, 64.

National Museum of Natural History. "Ancient DNA and Neanderthals." http://humanorigins.si.edu/evidence/genetics/ancient-dna-and-neanderthals.

National Public Radio. "Christian Contemporary Music." *Talk of the Nation*, June 3, 2004. https://www.npr.org/templates/story/story.php?storyId=1921620.

Navarro, Kenneth. *The Complete Worship Leader*. Grand Rapids: Baker, 2001.

Nettl, Paul. *Luther and Music*. Translated by Frida Best and Ralph Wood. Philadelphia: Muhlenberg, 1948.

Newman, Albert H. *A Manual of Church History I*. 2 vols. Philadlphia: American Baptist Publication Society, 1904.

Newman, Paul B. *Growing Up in the Middle Ages*. Rev. ed. Jefferson, NC: McFarland, 2007.

Ngo, Robin. "The Earliest Matches." *Bible History Daily*, June 8, 2017. https://www.biblicalarchaeology.org/daily/news/ancient-fire-making-israel/.

Noll, K. L. "Canaanite Religion." *Religion Compass* 1 (2007) 61–92.

Noll, Mark. "Singing the Word of God." *Christian History* 95 (2007) 10–13.

O'Bannon, Kathleen. "Divine and Moral Songs: A Summary." Grand Rapids: Classics Ethereal Library, n.d. https://www.ccel.org/ccel/watts/divsongs.html.

O'Connor, Edward D. *The Pentecostal Movement in the Catholic Church*. Notre Dame: Ave Maria, 1971.

Oesterly, W. O. E. *The Religion and Worship of the Synagogue*. New York: Scribner's, 1907.

Olsen, Ted. "American Pentecost." *Christian History* 58 (1998) 5–10.

Olson, Roger E. "What is Pentecostalism? What Do Pentecostals Believe?" http://www.patheos.com/blogs/rogereolson/2016/10/what-is-pentecostalism-what-do-pentecostals-believe/.

Osei-Bonsu, Robert. "John Calvin's Perspective on Music and Worship." *Ilorin Journal of Religious Studies* 3 (2013) 83–101.

Owen, James. "Bone Flute is Oldest Instrument, Study Says." *National Geographic*, June 24, 2009. https://www.nationalgeographic.com/culture/2009/06/bone-flute-is-oldest-instrument—study-says/.

Packer, J. I. "Physicians of the Soul." *Christian History Magazine* 89 (2006) 10–14.

———. "The Puritan Approach to Worship." https://www.apuritansmind.com/puritan-worship/the-puritan-approach-to-worship-by-j-i-packer/.

Park, Andy, et al. *Worshiping with the Anaheim Vineyard: The Emergence of Contemporary Worship*. Grand Rapids: Eerdmans, 2017.

Parrett, Gary A. "Raising Ebenezer." *Christianity Today* 50.1 (January 2006) 62.

Payne, John B. "Zwingli and Luther: The Giant vs. Hercules." *Christian History Magazine* 4 (1985) 4–11.

Peterson, David. *Engaging with God*. Downers Grove, IL: IVP Academic, 1992.

Phillips, David. "The Oxford Movement." *CrossWay* 110 (Autumn 2008). http://archive.churchsociety.org/crossway/documents/Cway_110_TheOxford Movement.pdf.

Porter, Roger. "What Did Huldrych Zwingli Achieve for the Swiss Reformation?" https://www.biblicaltheology.com/Research/PorterR01.pdf.

Potter, John, and Neil Sorrell. *A History of Singing*. Cambridge: Cambridge University Press, 2012.

Powell, Mark Allan. "Jesus Climbs the Charts: The Business of Contemporary Christian Music." *Christian Century* (December 2002) 20–26.

Presbyterian Mission Agency. "Planning and Leadership." https://www.presbyterianmission.org/ministries/worship/faq/faq-planning/.

———. "Planning and Leading." https://www.presbyterianmission.org/ministries/worship.org/ ministries/worship/faq/faq-planning.

———. "Revised Directory for Worship." https://www.presbyterianmission.org/ministries/worship/directory-for-worship/.

———. "Who is Responsible for Planning Worship?" https://www.presbyterianmission.org/ministries/worship/faq/faq-planning/#lead.

Preus, Rolf. "Lutheran Worship Wars." National Conference on Worship, Music & the Arts, Kenosha, WI, July 21–24, 2002. www.christforus.org/Papers/Content/LutheranWorshipWars.html.

Rabey, Steve. "The Profits of Praise." *Christianity Today* 43.8 (July 1999) 32–33.

Rabinovitch, Israel. *Of Jewish Music*. Translated by A. M. Klein. Montreal: Book Center, 1952.

Reagan, Wen. "A Beautiful Noise: A History of Contemporary Worship Music in Modern America." PhD diss., Duke University, 2015.

Reed, Kevin. "Biblical Worship." http://www.swrb.com/newslett/actualNLs/BibW_cho.htm.

Reed, Luther D. *Luther and Congregational Singing*. New York: Hymn Society of America, 1947.

Reese, Gustave. *Music in the Middle Ages*. New York: Norton, 1940.

Reformed Church in America. *Directory for Worship*. Grand Rapids: Reformed Church in America, 2015.

Rein, Lisa. "Mystery of Va.'s First Slaves Is Unlocked 400 Years Later." *Washington Post*, September 3, 2006. https://www.washingtonpost.com/archive/politics/2006/09/03/mystery-of-vas-first-slaves-is-unlocked-400-years-later/7015c871-aabd-4ba2-b5ce-7c0955aa0d75/.

Reisenweaver, Anna J. "Guido of Arezzo and His Influence on Music Learning." *Musical Offering* 3.1 (2012) Article 4.

Rempel, John. "An Anabaptist Perspective on Music in Worship." In *Music in Worship: A Mennonite Perspective*, edited by Bernie Neufeld, 30–45. Scottdale, PA: Herald, 1998.

Rendu, William, et al. "Evidence Supporting an Intentional Neanderthal Burial at La Chapelle-aux-Saints." *Proceedings of the National Academy of Science* 111 (2014) 81–86.

Reynolds, William J. *A Survey of Christian Hymnody*. Carol Stream, IL: Hope, 1991.

Richardson, Cyril, trans. and ed. *Early Christian Fathers*. Louisville: Westminster John Knox, 1995.

Robeck, Cecil M. *The Azusa Street Mission and Revival: The Birth of the Global Pentecostal Movement*. Nashville: Thomas Nelson, 2017.

Roberts, Alexander, and James Donaldson, eds. *The Ante-Nicene Fathers: Translations of the Fathers Down to A.D. 325*. 10 vols. Buffalo: Christian Literature, 1885–96.

Roberts, Donald L. "John Wycliffe and the Dawn of the Reformation." *Christian History Magazine* 3 (1983) 10–13. https://www.christianitytoday.com/history/issues/issue-3/john-wycliffe-and-dawn-of-reformation.html.

Rogers, Kate. "Neanderthal Origin of Iberian Cave Art (Science)." Video, 4:40, February 22, 2018. https://www.youtube.com/watch?time_continue=142&v=oH_wFNfrMmU.

Romanowski, William. "Evangelicals and Popular Music: The Contemporary Christian Music Industry." In *Religion and Popular Culture in America*, edited by Bruce D. Forbes and Jeffrey H. Mahan, 103–12. Berkeley: University of California Press, 2005.

Ross, Allen P. *Recalling the Hope of Glory: Biblical Worship from the Garden to the New Creation*. Grand Rapids: Kregel, 2006.

Rotblum, Yehuda. "Exodus and Rock Art." http://israelrockart.com/posts/exodus.

Rothmüller, Aron Marko. *The Music of the Jews: An Historical Appreciation*. Stockport, UK: Beechwood, 1954.

Ruth, Lester. "Question: Should Worship Be Traditional, Contemporary, or Both?" https://www.umcdiscipleship.org/resources/should-worship-be-traditional-contemporary-or-both.

Sachs, Curt. *The Rise of Music in the Ancient World*. Mineola, NY: Dover, 2008.

Sacred Congregation of Rites. *Musicam Sacram: Instruction on Music in the Liturgy*. Washington, DC: United States Catholic Conference, 1968.

Scheer, Greg. *The Art of Worship*. Grand Rapids: Baker, 2006.

Scholes, Percy. *The Puritans and Music in England and New England*. London: Oxford University Press, 1934.

Schwartz, Baruch J. "What Really Happened at Mount Sinai? Four Answers to One Question." *Bible Review* 13 (1997) 20–30, 46.

Shaked, Guy. "Music in the Bible." http://www.geocities.com/Vienna/Choir/4792/bible.htm.

Shanks, Hershel. "Commemorating a Covenant." *Biblical Archaeology Review* 41 (2015) 63–65.

Sibley, Larry. "Calvin's Geneva Liturgy." http://www.calvin.edu/worship/idis/theology/reformed/Geneva_liturgy_essay.phb.

———. "The Legacy of the Geneva Liturgy." http://www.calvin.edu/worship/idis/theology/reformed/Geneva_liturgy.phb.

Smith, C. S., ed. *The Ainsworth Psalter*. Early Psalmody in America, Series 1. New York: New York Public Library, 1938.

Smith, John Arthur. *Music in Ancient Judaism and Early Christianity*. London: Routledge, 2016.

Smith, Mark S. *The Rituals and Myths of the Feast of the Goodly Gods of KTU/CAT 1.23*. Atlanta: Society of Biblical Literature, 2006.

Smith, Preserved. *The Life and Letters of Martin Luther*. Boston: Houghton Mifflin, 1911.

Smith, Chuck, and Hugh Steven. *The Reproducers*. Philadelphia: Calvary Chapel, 2011.

Stapert, Calvin R. *A New Song for an Old World*. Grand Rapids: Eerdmans, 2006.

Steinberg, David. "Ugarit and the Bible: Ugaritic Literature as an Aid to Understanding the Hebrew Bible." http://www.houseofdavid.ca/ugarit.htm.

Sternfeld, Frederick W. "Music in the Schools of the Reformation." *Musica Disciplina* 2 (1948) 99–122.

Stetzer, Ed. "Church Music Conflicts." *The Exchange* (blog), May 28, 2013. https://www.christianitytoday.com/edstetzer/2013/may/church-music-conflicts.html.

———. "Hillsong Church at a Glance." *The Exchange* (blog), June 24, 2014. https://www.christianitytoday.com/edstetzer/2014/june/closer-look-at-hillsong-church.html.

Stipp, Neil. "The Music Philosophies of Martin Luther and John Calvin." *The American Organist* 41 (2007) 68–72.

Strayer, Hope R. "From Neumes to Notes: The Evolution of Music Notation." *Musical Offerings* 4 (2013) 1–14.

Stringer, Martin. *A Sociological History of Worship*. Cambridge: Cambridge University Press, 2005.

Strunk, Oliver. *Source Readings in Music History*. New York: Norton, 1950.

Sweet, William W. *Men of Zeal: The Romance of American Methodist Beginnings*. Nashville: Abingdon, 1935.

———. *Methodism in American History*. New York: The Methodist Book Concern, 1933.

———. *Religion in the Development of American Culture, 1765–1840*. New York: Scribner's, 1952.

———. *Revivalism in America*. New York: Scribner's, 1944.

Synod of Laodicea. "The Canons of the Synod." In *Nicene and Post-Nicene Fathers, Series 2*, edited by Philip Schaff, 125–60. Volume 14. 1901. Reprint, Grand Rapids: Christian Classic Ethereal Library, 2009. https://www.ccel.org/ccel/schaff/npnf214.html.

Szalay, Jessie. "Neanderthals: Facts about Our Extinct Relatives." https://www.livescience.com/28036-neanderthals-facts-about-our-extinct-human-relatives.html.

Tait, Edwin Woodruff. "The Road Not Taken." *Christian History Magazine* 122 (2017) 12–15.

Tait, Jennifer Woodruff. "Editor's Note." *Christian History Magazine* 118 (2016) 4.
Tanton, Tim. "Ten Years Later, 'United Methodist Hymnal' Still Sings." United Methodist Church, press release, 25 May 1999. https://archive.wfn.org/1999/05/msg00165.html.
Tattersall, Ian. "Homo sapiens." In *Encyclopedia Britannica*. Chicago: Encyclopædia Britannica, 2015. https://www.britannica.com/topic/Homo-sapiens.
Taylor, W. David O. "John Calvin and Musical Instruments: A Critical Investigation." *Calvin Theological Journal* 48 (2013) 248–69.
Teicher, Jordan G. "Why Is Vatican II so Important?" National Public Radio, October 10, 2012. https://www.npr.org/2012/10/10/162573716/why-is-vatican-ii-so-important.
Terry, Richard R. "Calvin's First Psalter." *Music and Letters* 13 (1932) 1–21.
———. *Calvin's First Psalter*. London: Ernest Benn, 1932.
Tertullian. *The Apology*. Translated by William Reeve. London: Griffith, Farran, Okeden & Welsh, 1889.
———. *Apologia 39:17–19*. Translated by S. Thelwell. In *Ante-Nicene Fathers*, vol. 3, edited by Alexander Roberts and James Donaldson, 107–14. Edinburgh: T. & T. Clark, 1885.
Than, Ker. "Neanderthal Burials Confirmed as Ancient Ritual." *National Geographic*, December 16, 2013. https://www.nationalgeographic.com/news/2013/12/131216-la-chapelle-neanderthal-burials-graves/.
———. "World's Oldest Cave Art Found—Made by Neanderthals?" *National Geographic News* June 14, 2012. https://www.nationalgeographic.com/news/2012/6/120614-neanderthal-cave-paintings-spain-science-pike/.
Thompson, Bard. *Liturgies of the Western Church*. Minneapolis: Fortress, 2003.
Thompson, Helen. "Rock (Art) of Ages: Indonesian Cave Paintings Are 40,000 Years Old." *Smithsonian*, October 8, 2014. https://www.smithsonianmag.com/science-nature/rockart-ages-indonesian-cave-paintings-are-40000-years-old-180952970/.
Tomkins, Steven. "John Hus, Reformer of Bohemia" Module 302. Worcester, PA: Christian History Institute, 2019. https://christianhistoryinstitute.org/study/module/hus.
Toon, Peter. "Whatever are the Anglican Books of Homilies?" *The Prayer Book Society*. Savannah, GA: The Society for the Preservation of the Book of Common Prayer 2002.
Townsend, James. "The Golden Age of Hymns: Did You Know?" *Christian History Magazine* 31. https://christianhistoryinstitute.org/uploaded/50cf7d742803f0.93003975.pdf
Tripp, D. H. "The Letter to Pliny." In *The Study of Liturgy*, edited by Cheslyn Jones et al., 80–81. London: SPCK, 1992.
———. "Methodism." In *The Study of Liturgy*, edited by Cheslyn Jones et al., 325–27. London: SPCK, 1992.
Truron, Walterus. "The Rhythm of Metrical Psalm-Tunes." *Music and Letters* 9 (1928) 29–33.
Tufts, John. *An Introduction to the Singing of Psalm-Tunes*. Philadelphia: Dichter, 1954.
Turk, Ivan, ed. *Mousterian Bone Flute & Other Finds from Divje Babe I Cave Site in Slovenia*. Translated by Martin Cregeen. Opera Instituti Arhaelogici Sloveniae 2. Ljubljana, Slovenia: Institut za Arhaeologijo, 1997.
United Methodist Discipleship Ministries. *The Basic Pattern of Worship*. Nashville: United Methodist, 1992.

———. "CCLI Top 100." https://www.umdiscipleship.org/worship/ccli-top-100.

———. *An Order of Sunday Worship Using the Basic Pattern*. Nashville: United Methodist, 1992.

Universität Tübingen. "Paleolithic Bone Flute Discovered: Earliest Musical Tradition Documented in Southwestern Germany." *ScienceDaily*, June 25, 2009. https://www.sciencedaily.com/releases/2009/06/090624213346.htm.

Vander Laan, Ray. "Fertility Cults of Canaan." https://www.thattheworldmayknow.com/fertility-cults-of-canaan.

Van Marter, Jerry L. "Presbyterian Hymnal Producers Respond to Misinformation," *Presbyterian Mission Agency*, August 9, 2013. www.pcusa.org/news/2013/8/9/presbyterian-hymnal-producers-respond-misinformati/.

Van Unnik, W. C. "A Note on the Dance of Jesus in 'The Acts of John.'" *Vigiliae Christianae* 18 (1964) 1–5.

Vatican Council II. *Sacrosanctum Concilium: Constitution on the Sacred Liturgy* (December 1963). http://www.vatican.va/archive/hist_councils/ii_vatican_council/documents/vat-ii_const_19631204_sacrosanctum-concilium_en.html.

"Vatican Council, Second." *The Columbia Encyclopedia*, 6th ed. (June 2019). https://www.encyclopedia.com/philosophy-and-religion/christianity/roman-catholic-and-orthodox-churches-councils-and-treaties/second-vatican-council.

Vatican II. *Sacrosanctum Concilium*. London: Catholic Truth Society, 2004.

Veith, Gene. "Is Contemporary Christian Music Dead?" *Cranach* (blog), June 9, 2017. https://www.patheos.com/blogs/geneveith/2017/06/is-contemporary-christian-music-dead/.

"Vineyard Churches." http://www.religionfacts.com/ vineyard-churches.

Vineyard USA. *Core Values and Beliefs*. Stafford, TX: Vineyard Resources, 2016.

von Dehsen, Christian D. "Hymnic Forms in the New Testament." *Reformed Liturgy and Music* 18 (1984) 7–11.

Vos, Howard F. *New Illustrated Manners and Customs of the Bible*. Nashville: Thomas Nelson, 1997.

Wagner, Peter. *Introduction to the Gregorian Melodies: A Handbook of Plainsong; Part 1, Origin and Development of the Forms of the Liturgical Chant up to the End of the Middle Ages*. 2nd ed. 1901. Reprint, Boston: Da Capo, 1986.

Wagner, Thomas J. "Hearing the Hillsong Sound: Music, Marketing, Meaning, and Branded Spiritual Experience at a Transnational Megachurch." PhD diss., Royal Holloway College of the University of London, 2013.

Wainwright, Geoffrey, and Karen B. Westerfield Tucker, eds. *The Oxford History of Christian Worship*. Oxford: Oxford University Press, 2006.

Walton, John H. *The Lost World of Genesis One*. Downers Grove, IL: InterVarsity, 2009.

Watson, J. R. *The English Hymn: A Critical and Historical Study*. Oxford: Oxford University Press, 1997.

Watts, Isaac. "Preface." In *Hymns and Spiritual Songs*, edited by John Lawrence, iii–xiv. London: J. Humphreys, 1707.

Webber, Robert E. *Ancient-Future Worship: Proclaiming and Enacting God's Narrative*. Grand Rapids: Baker, 2008.

Weisberger, Bernard A. *They Gathered at the River*. Boston: Little, Brown, 1956.

What is Worship? Stafford, TX: Vineyard Resources, 2014.

Wheeler, Anne P. "The Music of the Early Nineteenth-Century Camp Meeting: Song in Service to Evangelistic Revival." *Methodist History* 48 (2009) 23–42.

Whiston, William, trans. "Letters of Pliny the Younger and the Emperor Trajan." https://www.pbs.org/wgbh/pages/frontline/shows/religion/maps/primary/pliny.html

White, James F. *Protestant Worship: Traditions in Transition.* Louisville: Westminster John Knox, 1989.

———. *Roman Catholic Worship.* Collegeville, MN: Liturgical, 2003.

Wiles, Roger N. "Style and Substance: Are Traditional, Contemporary, and Blended Legitimate Categories of Worship?" http://www.reformationtodayonline.com/Uploads/Style_and_Substance.pdf.

Williamson, H. G. M. "Temple and Worship in Isaiah 6." In *Temple and Worship in Biblical Israel,* edited by John Day, 123–44. London: T. & T. Clark, 2005.

Willis, Jonathan. *Church Music and Protestantism in Post-Reformation England.* Farnham, UK: Ashgate, 2013.

Wilsey, John D. "The Impact of the Reformation on the Fine Arts." Liberty University Faculty Publications and Presentations 175 (Spring 2006).

Wimber, John. *The Way in is the Way On: John Wimber's Teachings and Writings on Life in Christ.* Atlanta: Ampelon, 2006.

Witherington, Ben. "In the Beginning: Religion at the Dawn of Civilization." *Biblical Archaeology Review* 39 (2013) 57–60.

———. *We Have Seen His Glory.* Grand Rapids: Eerdmans, 2010.

Wohlgemuth, Paul. "Anabaptist Hymn." *Direction: A Mennonite Brethren Forum* 1 (1972) 92–97.

Womack, Edwin. "What Does 'Contemporary Worship' Really Mean?" *United Methodist News,* September 30, 2013. http://www.umc.org/news-and-media/blogs-commentaries/post/what-does-contemporary-worship-really-mean.

Wong, Kate. "Ancient Cave Paintings Clinch the Case for Neanderthal Symbols." *Scientific American Newsletter,* February 23, 2018. https://www.scientificamerican.com/article/ancient-cave-paintings-clinch-the-case-for-neandertal-symbolism1/.

Woods, Key. "Neanderthal Noisemaker." *Science News* 150.21 (November 1996) 328.

Woods, Robert, and Brian Walrath, eds. *The Message in the Music.* Nashville: Abingdon, 2007.

Worthington, Daryl. "Neandertals and Humans—What Are the Differences?" *New Historian,* February 13, 2017. https://www.newhistorian.com/2017/02/13/neanderthals-humans-differences/.

Wren, Brian A. *Praying Twice: The Music and Words of Congregational Song.* Louisville: Westminster John Knox, 2000.

Wright, N. T. "Jerusalem in the New Testament." In *Jerusalem: Past and Present in the Purposes of God,* edited by P. W. L. Walker, 53–77. Grand Rapids: Baker, 1994.

Wyatt, E. G. P. *St. Gregory and the Gregorian Music.* London: Plainsong & Mediæval Music Society, 1904.

Young, Penny. *Dura Europos: A City for Everyman.* Norfolk, UK: Twopenny, 2014.

Zaidner, Yossi. "A Series of Mousterian Occupations in a New Type of Site: The Nesher Ramla karst Depression, Israel." *Journal of Human Evolution* 66 (2014) 1–17.

Zeller, George. "A Brief History of Pentecostalism." http://www.rapidnet.com/~jbeard/bdm/Psychology/char/abrief.htm.

Zilhão, J. "Symbolic Use of Marine Shells and Mineral Pigments by Iberian Neanderthals." *Proceedings of the National Academy of Sciences* 107 (2010) 1023–28.

Zvielli, Alexander. "Why Did Moses Go Up Sinai Twice?" *The Jerusalem Post,* June 7, 2011. https://www.jpost.com/Jewish-World/Judaism/Why-did-Moses-go-up-Mount-Sinai-twice.

www.ingramcontent.com/pod-product-compliance
Lightning Source LLC
Chambersburg PA
CBHW061430300426
44114CB00014B/1618